Born to
SHOP

NEW YORK

Third Edition

Born to
SHOP

NEW YORK

Third Edition

SUZY GERSHMAN
and
JUDITH THOMAS

Introduction by
CAROLYNE ROEHM

A
BANTAM
TRADE
PAPERBACK

BANTAM BOOKS
NEW YORK • TORONTO • LONDON
SYDNEY • AUCKLAND

BORN TO SHOP: NEW YORK

A Bantam Book / September 1987
2nd printing ....March 1988
Bantam Second edition / June 1989
Bantam Third edition / November 1990

Produced by Ink Projects
Design by Lynne Arany
Maps by David Lindroth, Inc.

ISBN 0-533-34945-7

Published simultaneously in the United States and Canada

Bantam Books are published by Bantam Books, a division of Bantam
Doubleday Dell Publishing Group, Inc. Its trademark, consisting of the
words "Bantam Books" and the portrayal of a rooster, is Registered in U.S.
Patent and Trademark Office and in other countries. Marca Registrada.
Bantam Books, 666 Fifth Avenue, New York, New York 10103.

PRINTED IN THE UNITED STATES OF AMERICA

FG   10 9 8 7 6 5 4 3 2 1 0

The BORN TO SHOP Team:

reported by:
Suzy Gershman
New York correspondent: Paul Baumrind
editor: Jill Parsons
executive editor: Toni Burbank
assistant to executive editor: Linda Gross

Acknowledgments

Nothing is as much fun as revising this New York edition. There is no better excuse to run around town and go shopping. Several friends and professional spies turned us on to new neighborhoods and new shops, so we thank them with a big New York kiss: Michele Geddes Peck, Lois Gerber, and Paul Baumrind were all essential in this update. We must have lunch, guys. And thanks also to Ann O'Brien for the legwork.

Thanks also to Werner Erlich and the team at the Omni Berkshire, our base camp for doing a lot of the research, and to the team at Bantam, who love to help out with this edition.

CONTENTS

Preface

We've been part of New York for so long that we forgot there was a time when we didn't know Downtown from Midtown. Then our French friend Pascale went to New York and we found ourselves explaining to her how everything works, giving her notes on where to shop, telling her secrets, and feeding her the inside scoop. She finally pointed out that we had a book in all that knowledge—that millions of people visit New York and don't know the ins or the outs, whether they are from Paris, France, or Paris, Texas.

We've refined our "Pascale notes" and tried them out on a bevy of friends, from first-time visitors of many nationalities to American businesswomen and longtime New York mavens who thought they knew it all; all have found at least something they thought was worth the price of admission. We don't claim to have every shopping possibility in the Greater New York area in these pages, but we have spent over twenty years refining this book—and thousands and thousands of dollars.

The resources listed in these pages come directly from our personal phone books. There are stores in New York that are wonderful that did not make these pages. Although every effort was made to ensure the accuracy of prices appearing in this book, it should be kept in mind that prices will vary.

Please note that the text has been updated for this revision. It remains, as in all our books, full of essential, behind-the-scenes facts. If you're just interested in our revised and up-

dated listings, go right ahead—cheat. That's
OK. If you've just plunked down your money
for the juicy stuff, here's something to whet
your appetite: Leonard Kahn, 130 West 30th
Street—wholesale furrier *par excellence*. And
yes, fur prices are going down (before they go
up in 1991).

Satisfied?

If you crave more, stand by. We are about to
take you to the core of the Big Apple.

Suzy Gershman and Judith Thomas

Introduction

I grew up dreaming of New York. I lived in the Midwest, and my idea of New York was *Breakfast at Tiffany's.*

I could always picture myself with diamond earrings—huge diamond earrings. When I thought of New York back then, it was those earrings I thought of. New York was diamond chandeliers hanging from my ears, wearing a little black dress, and being ever-so-Holly Golightly. . . .

When I finally moved to New York I wasn't wearing diamond earrings. When you're twenty-three and just out of school you think of Harry Winston or Bulgari as pretty intimidating places. Tiffany has more of an all-American image, so you think it's OK to look there. You don't buy, you just look. When you're twenty-three, you buy antique pieces on 47th Street. I still go there.

It's still fun. I look, I shop, I compare. I have the same little places I go to. I have my silversmith who makes the little things I ask him to make—just for me. You develop these sources over the years. I've never worried about people switching stones on me or not being honest. What I was buying when I started out wasn't worth the time or trouble to switch. I just keep going back and over the years I have traded up. It's like Oscar de la Renta said to me, "Once you've had quality merchandise, you can never go back to junk."

That's the thing that's so wonderful about New York. There are two extremes here: the best of everything, from the best cashmere to caviar. Everything. I used to get up at the crack of dawn to go to Orchard Street for the bargains. I remember the arcade sales, the Tepper Gallery. That's the fun of New York, the challenge of New York—you can find anything at any price point.

I have no empathy for people who say to me, "What do you know; you can buy anything." That may be true now, but when I came here to New York to make it big I was a design assistant living on what little a design assistant makes. But you can have great-looking things, and dress yourself well, if you have taste and style and a good eye. You can have charm for very little money. You can get the look with energy and imagination. We in fashion love having things around us that please the eye. You can do it on the most modest or on the grandest scale in the world. And New York does offer you both possibilities.

So I welcome you to New York, with all its challenges and all its choices. While I love shopping around the world, I always come back to New York for the excitement of a Sunday spent in bookstores and record stores and walking along Madison Avenue; for the joy of buying old books or antiques or musical items from salespeople who teach you something as they sell you something; to a city where you can walk into a store as a consumer and come away having learned something as well. The department stores in New York are among the best in the world. There are special districts for everything from furs to flowers, and more. I love the special food shops. The shopping in New York has character.

I love New York, and I know you will too.

Carolyne Roehm

I ▼ THE BIG APPLE

New York, New York

The world is filled with fabulous cities. We know, because we've been to most of the big ones. We've seen the art, the architecture, and, yes—of course—the stores. And we love every bit of it. But we never forget that America has it all. New York, New York. It's your kind of town. Everything you seek in Europe and the Far East can be found in New York. If it's sights you seek, adventure and high times, you need not leave this country. If it's glamour you seek, and shopping thrills and bargains, well then, New York, and the surrounding metropolitan area, is the king of America. Paying homage to this king is a royal treat.

We Love New York

New York. It's in our blood. Before we knew we were born to shop, we knew we were born for New York. We've each lived here for a large portion of our lives. Whenever we return, we feel the magic.

We love the fast pace that leaves you breathless at the end of a day, but exhilarated and younger and smarter and fresher and more alive.

We love the contrast between how extraordinarily rude some strangers can be and how incredibly nice others can be.

We love that only in New York can someone walk up to you and feel the fabric of your coat or jacket and say "Nice goods" while walking by you.

We adore that you can find anything you want at any price you want in any condition you want—and, yes, in any size you want.

New York's got it all.

And we want it all.

Our Kind of Town

Indeed, New York is our kind of town. And if you don't mind being in the world's largest marketplace, if you can stand the thrill of the choice, the selection, the possibilities, the varieties of grades of merchandise and retailing outlets—then New York is your kind of town, as well. You can get anything you want in New York. If they don't have it, they'll make it up special.

You can shop the high end—the finest European designer boutiques, the kind of stores where children's shoes cost $250; where the doorman has to know your family tree to buzz you in. You can shop a bevy of the world's best department stores, deciding for yourself if Bloomingdale's is everything it's cracked up to be or if maybe it's lost its touch and has been upstaged by Macy's . . . or has Bergdorf's embarrassed them both by walking off with the cake? You can parade on Fifth Avenue, with or without your Easter bonnet; you can hop on a bus at the Port Authority and be driven to some of the world's best bargain cities—in the area, only an hour away. You can do it all.

You can shop the low end, where the merchandise is piled in bins and the size you want is hidden beneath the stack. You can find flea markets, bazaars, street peddlers, and everything in between. Or you can shop where you may not be able to afford a scarf, let alone a suit or a pair of shoes—but no one will know. In New York, there are private entrances to paradise and high-floor showrooms where you knock three times and whisper low just to be admitted. In New York, there are sales to friends of family and those in the know, ethnic neighborhoods, and warehouse outlets. In New York, there's wholesale, there's discount, there's fake, there's trust, and there's deceit. There's diamonds, and they can be rough or polished, depending on your outlook. There's a little—no, make that a lot—of everything. Some of it is easy to find; some requires help. But it's yours for the energy it takes to come and get it. It's yours for the asking, the taking, the paying, the enjoying.

New York Selection

N ew York offers great window shopping. You can have a ball just by being on the ball.

New York offers fabulous store decor; you can lose your breath merely inspecting the displays in stores, be they museumlike vases filled with flowers or room sets designed to tantalize. Come November, when Christmas decorations go up, you can tour from F.A.O. Schwarz to Lord & Taylor just to stare at the intricate creations of the best designing minds of the world. In fact, this book offers a special holiday tour designed for just that purpose. (See page 264.)

New York offers more selection than any other marketplace in the United States, probably in the world, and that includes Tokyo. (Tokyo may have more merchandise, but it won't all fit you.) Shopping in New York offers the mental challenge of all times—can you bear to see this much stuff and not buy it all? Can you possibly choose the one best thing for you at the one best price? Shopping in New York is like living a game show.

And shopping is good sport, because traffic congestion in New York can be so fierce that the best way to get around is to walk. Walking huge distances is nothing when you have the stimulation of New York windows to keep you occupied. Leave your high heels at home, or tuck them into a tote bag as New Yorkers do, and put on those sensible shoes.

If you're in the mood to buy, then shopping will have the added fitness benefit of being a little bit of weightlifting. Shopping bags need the proper balance, so be sure to load each arm and each hand with plenty of stuff. True, it may be easier and less expensive to ship your purchases home, but it wouldn't be nearly as much fun to go on a shopping spree if you couldn't wear everything that night . . . if you couldn't return to your hotel room and lay out all your purchases just to bask in the glory of your bargains while you admire each item and your cleverness.

If you think New York is dirty, think of Hong Kong.

If you think New York is crowded, think of Tokyo.

If you think New York is dangerous, think of any other large international city.

If you think New York is one of the best buys for your dollar, start lacing up those sensible shoes.

For fitness of mind and body, to say nothing of the grand opportunity to lighten your bank account, shopping in New York is better than shopping anyplace else in the United States.

And maybe in the world.

The Bronx Is Up

New York is a city of neighborhoods. If you deal with each neighborhood as a small city, you will never feel overwhelmed. Just about every ten blocks, the neighborhood seems to change. While certain neighborhoods are more residential than others, or certain areas more dangerous than others—wait ten blocks and the scene will change again. Wait six months, and the neighborhood you hated will become the neighborhood you love best. More and more parts of the city are being renovated and gentrified, more and more parts of the outer boroughs and outlying areas are becoming citified. What was once distinctly New York style is now found in Norwalk and New Jersey in ready abandon. Style is why you came to New York to shop, and style is what you're gonna get.

Almost every place has become interesting; almost every place has some great shops. Every nook and cranny of New York (well, almost) is jam-packed with just the kind of stuff you came here to buy. Tourists seem to travel in a certain few circles and like their shopping also to be in these areas; locals like to avoid the tourist crowds and prefer their shopping to be close to home, office, or public transportation. As a result, shopping always is convenient to one or another of your pursuits, and no one place is the must-see, end-all shopping district of Manhattan.

Even when you are talking about discounts, there are several enclaves of discounters that serve the same metropolitan area. So people in Manhattan can choose to go to New Jersey or Connecticut for a certain type of bargain, but they needn't go to both; nor do New Jersey residents need to drive three hours to get to bargains in Connecticut. To shop in New York is to shop for convenience as part of the equation. Many, many stores sell the same things. You can never shop it all, so there is no need to feel you must.

Look at our neighborhoods chapter (see page 60) to get a better idea of the little towns that make up our town, and plan your shopping accordingly. There's no reason to be overwhelmed if you've planned your day carefully: You can have it all by limiting yourself to a few well-chosen neighborhoods, streets, or outlet cities.

East Side, West Side

Not only should you study up on your New York neighborhoods before you pounce, but you also need a few tips that once learned will help to keep you from getting lost. Getting lost in New York is usually a lot of fun, but it does take time, and if your visit is limited, you'll want every precious minute spent spending.

Most of Manhattan was laid out on a grid system with a clearly distinguishable north, south, east, and west. Look at any map to see the basics. The East and West sides are divided by Fifth Avenue, so the location of many addresses can be rather well guessed at by the numbers and the East or West in front of them. North and south are not much used by visitors, or in directions, but locals will tell taxis to stop on the southeast corner of a certain block. If you care to learn this system, it's easy enough: Uptown is north and Downtown is south.

The use of the words "Uptown" and "Downtown" can be confusing to visitors who are used to the word "Downtown" meaning the part of

Manhattan

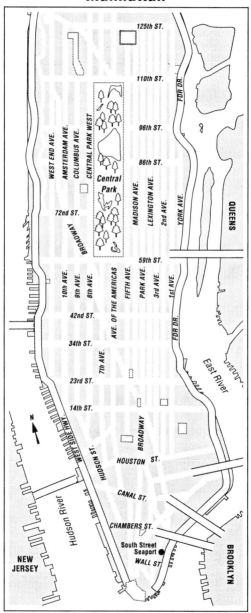

7

town where all the big buildings and department stores are. In Manhattan, Uptown and Downtown are relative to where you are going and where you are standing. The numbered streets make this easy. The higher numbers are in the Uptown direction and the lower numbers are in the Downtown direction. While street numbers in Manhattan go as high as 220th, most mavens consider that Manhattan ends at 125th Street, which is the center of Harlem. The main retailing area is centered from 59th Street to 34th Street, and this is Midtown. Greenwich Village (known to New Yorkers simply as the Village) is Downtown; SoHo is Downtown; Battery Park City is Downtown.

If you are at all concerned about where a shop or address may be, call first for directions. Ask for the "cross streets" and get the avenues and the street numbers to know exactly where in the grid of Manhattan you will be going. There are a few parts of Manhattan that do not work on a grid, but you can spot them on a map. (They're mostly Downtown at the tip of the island, but the Village can also be rather tricky.)

To figure out a cross street on your own, there is a system that really does work.

The Cross-Street System

There you are, looking at an address and trying to figure out where it is. In some cities, all the numbers are coordinated to a block; for example, in downtown Los Angeles, the buildings with 700 numbers have Seventh Street as a cross street. Pretty good deal, huh? Not New York. Nor do all the numbers line up evenly in New York; a given number on Park Avenue is not in the same latitude on Madison Avenue. But don't give up; there is a system.

A warning about the system: It looks hard, elaborate, and confusing. You will take one glance at this information, curse, and go to another page. Big mistake. The system isn't as hard as it looks.

Crosstown streets first, because they're the easiest:

From Eleventh Avenue to Tenth Avenue, addresses run from 599 to 500 West

Tenth Avenue to Ninth Avenue: 499 West–400 West

Ninth Avenue to Eighth Avenue: 399 West–300 West

Eighth Avenue to Seventh Avenue: 299 West–200 West

Seventh Avenue to Sixth Avenue (Avenue of the Americas): 199 West–100 West

Sixth Avenue (Avenue of the Americas) to Fifth Avenue: 99 West–1 West

Fifth Avenue to Madison Avenue and Park Avenue: 1 East–99 East

Park Avenue to Lexington Avenue: 100 East–140 East

Lexington Avenue to Third Avenue: 140 East–199 East

Third Avenue to Second Avenue: 200 East–299 East

Second Avenue to First Avenue: 300 East–399 East

First Avenue to York Avenue: 400 East–499 East

Above 59th Street, Eleventh Avenue becomes West End Avenue, Tenth Avenue becomes Amsterdam Avenue, Ninth Avenue becomes Columbus Avenue, and Eighth Avenue becomes Central Park West. Numbers on crosstown streets up to the top of Central Park, at 110th Street, begin with 1 West at the corner of Central Park West, and go up as you head west (addresses from 100 West begin at Columbus Avenue, from 200 West at Amsterdam Avenue, and so on).

The avenues, in an easy step-by-step process:

1. Look at the address of the building where you are going—for example, 725 Fifth Avenue, which is the Trump Tower. If you are bad at math or can't visualize numbers, write down the number on a piece of scrap paper.

2. Drop the last digit of the building's number. You are now working with the number 72.

3. Divide this number in half. That puts you at 36.

4. Using the chart below, add or subtract the number given (note that there is one ringer: In Fifth Avenue numbers between 775 and 1286 you do not divide in half; but this area is residential, anyway. Also, Central Park West and Riverside Drive do not fit into this plan at all, but they are also residential areas):

First Avenue: Add 3
Second Avenue: Add 3
Third Avenue: Add 10
Fourth Avenue: Add 8
Fifth Avenue: Up to 200, add 13
            Up to 400, add 16
            Up to 600, add 18
            Up to 775, add 20
            From 775 to 1286, do not divide by 2; subtract 18
Sixth Avenue (Avenue of the Americas): Subtract 12
Seventh Avenue: Below 110th Street, add 12
Eighth Avenue: Add 10
Ninth Avenue: Add 13
Tenth Avenue: Add 14
Amsterdam Avenue: Add 60
Broadway: Above 23rd Street, subtract 30
Columbus Avenue: Add 60
Lexington Avenue: Add 22
Madison Avenue: Add 26
Park Avenue: Add 35

The Trump Tower, our little example here, is at 56th Street by these calculations—and that's just where it is!

2 ▼ THE BUSINESS OF BARGAINS

Nontraditional Retailing

Nontraditional retailing happens to be a much older practice than traditional retailing. Money and even stores, for that matter, are relative newcomers in the age-old practice of swapping goods and services. And certainly, once there was one store with posted prices, there was a hungrier merchant who was ready to deal. The business of dealing has become a big business as more and more shoppers become interested in getting the most for their money.

New Yorkers pride themselves on being able to get around the high cost of living with a sixth sense called "street smarts." Most New Yorkers depend on various nontraditional methods of retailing to keep up their standard of living.

Department Store Secrets

Department stores always have been king of traditional retailing. Although they remain traditional, business has been so bad in the recent past that they will do anything they can think of to get people to return to the fold. The overhead of a large department store is so immense that the store cannot easily change its price structure; but it can do other things to lure customers.

Besides offering fantastic sales, look to department stores to offer promotions and cus-

tomer services you just can't find anyplace
else. A large department store once gave away
a second strand of pearls to customers who
bought one strand (a Mother's Day promotion). And so on. Department stores have
restaurants, exercise studios, makeup artists,
and free gifts when you buy certain kinds of
products.

When it comes to color, ambience, enter-
tainment, and cachet, a with-it department store
has mouth-watering appeal. For bargains, remember that department stores have to unload
merchandise just as every other retailer does.
They do this through the rather staid old
method we all love best: sales. But when the
sale merchandise isn't all sold, what happens
to it? It does not go to retail heaven. Usually it
goes back to the warehouse, to be held for the
annual department-store warehouse sale.

That's right, folks: Once a year the most
famous department stores in America clean
house by busing their customers from Midtown
stores to the outer regions of the Greater Manhattan area to partake in what can only be
described as a very serious shopping event.
We'll take a Bloomingdale's warehouse sale
over the after-Christmas Harrods affair any
day. Warehouse sales are not held at any specific time of year, so you just have to watch
the newspapers for the ads. These ads are
impossible to miss: They fill at least one page
of the paper and are complete with gigantic
letters, a few huge arrows, and usually a little
map (inset into a corner) that shows you where
the warehouse is located. A bus schedule will
be printed in the ad.

Some department stores open their warehouse for regular business during the week, or
just on weekends. These stores are usually called
clearance centers, and merchandise is reduced
at least 50% from the original ticketed price.
Some centers deliver goods; others ask you to
provide your own trucking. Even stores such
as Sears have warehouse stores (they call theirs

surplus centers) that sell leftovers, whether they are floor samples, returned merchandise, or unsold items.

Although a warehouse sale is a distinct type of bargain bonanza, the very same store may stage an annual event, on a more quiet scale, that helps clean house but that doesn't involve warehouses, buses, or even major advertising.

Some department stores have semisecret rooms where the unsold sale merchandise actually is thrown—some of it is hanging, lots of it is drooping. You'll find a good number of old items and many damages here, but sometimes you can find a worthwhile bargain. Ask store information or any salesperson.

Store Wars

Long ago, in a galaxy far, far away, there was Bloomingdale's, and it was wonderful. But that was light-years ago in the ever-changing world of retail, where whatever we write in this space can easily be outdated by the time you read it. And we're not talking science fiction, folks; this is real life.

We cannot predict what will happen in the department store wars—who will win, who will lose, or when the last volley will be fired. We can tell you that we were shopping recently in Loehmann's for a coat, and found the exact same coat for less money in Bloomie's! But don't fret. Department stores' troublesome times are your opportunity to get a break. As merchandise is cleaned out to make room for new regimes, there have got to be bargains.

As for the stores themselves, there's no certainty in any of this, but some stars look brighter than others. Saks will come out on top, no matter what, and is going ahead with planned renovations for the Fifth Avenue flagship store.

Bloomingdale's will probably also survive in much the same form that it is in now—maybe becoming more like Macy's was when Macy's was boring but still in there as a major contender and not a discounter.

Beyond these two, we hesitate to predict the future. Trump may put his store concept, Trump's, into the former Bonwit Teller flagship space, since he owns the building anyway. It's unlikely that he will actually get Nordstrom to take over at Alexander's, but he'll probably keep working at it for a while. There will be four to six Nordstroms in the nearby 'burbs in no time at all, so anything is possible.

Macy's should stay status quo. So should A&S, which seems more like a specialty store than a department store to us, because of the way it is bought; but their numbers are strong (they tell us), and the store will keep on keeping on without much trouble.

Bergdorf Goodman is a specialty store, and will only blossom and grow, ignoring the turmoil around it. The makeup department moves to the 57th Street side of the store as the new men's store opens, and they continue in their own little dream world. Bendel's is also a specialty store, with a whole new future ahead of it.

Just as B. Altman has joined Best & Co. and De Pinna in the great department store in the sky, there will be some fallout in Manhattan, but the principal players will come back stronger than ever—vowing to give us better service and selection.

Discount Stores

A new breed of department store has begun to flourish in the United States: the discount store. Although E. J. Korvette set retailing on its ear by discounting some major brands in the 1950s, Korvette's has gone out of business. Today's discount stores are fancier than Korvette's and are in strips or shopping malls all over the United States. Some of them are even owned by big department stores or by the same retailing chains that own the big department stores.

The discounter sells some branded merchandise and some private-label merchandise at a 20% to 25% discount from prices in department stores, but does so in a self-service, department store atmosphere. Target, Bradlee's, and Caldor are some of the more famous discounters. K mart is not considered a discounter; it is an off-pricer.

To give you a very simple idea, let's look at a bag of mini candy bars sold for Halloween:

▼ regular retail price: $3.29
▼ discounter price: $2.99 to $2.79
▼ off-pricer price: $2.19

An item like Halloween candy is relatively simple, but you may buy from a store thinking they offer great prices only to discover, to your chagrin, that they offer merely good prices. Discount stores are usually not as inexpensive as we want them to be or think they are.

Off-Price Shops

Off-pricers are the last word in savings. Off-price shops also sell current, seasonal merchandise, but at prices below 20% off. These stores can be smaller and less fancy than discounters, or as big as a warehouse and very nicely decorated. There are so many different types of off-pricers that it is impossible to suggest there is only one way of doing business. Off-pricers usually specialize in certain categories of merchandise, such as women's or children's ready-to-wear, appliances, beds, etc. Many off-price stores sell designer merchandise, but K mart also has to be classified as an off-price retailer, and they sell a combination of well-known brand names and private-label and no-name merchandise.

In the new American revolution, a whole bevy of ready-to-wear off-pricers has sprung up all over the country. You may have better outlets in your hometown than you will find in New York City. Mostly, these new-style off-pricers do well in suburban areas—New Jersey and Connecticut have a much better selection than Manhattan does. Some of the big off-pricers include Dress Barn, Hit or Miss, T. J. Maxx, Kids "Я" Us, Marshall's, and the most famous of all—Loehmann's.

We must warn you about yo-yo pricing. Some off-pricers will manufacture the price tag with a high price on it and then will mark it down to make you *think* you are getting a great bargain. This is called yo-yoing because it is marking up to mark down. We are real cynics, to be sure, but we always are suspicious of labels that all look alike. The kind of off-pricers we like have layers of labels on the goods so we can see all the previous markdowns and believe in them.

Seconds

Since we all make mistakes, it's easy enough to understand that when manufacturers make mistakes they end up with imperfect merchandise that cannot be sold through traditional retailing channels. Yet the manufacturer is loath to throw the baby out with the bathwater. Instead, the manufacturer collects his imperfects and sells them to a store or to a jobber who likes damaged merchandise because he's got customers who are careful shoppers and who realize that the imperfection may be insignificant but the saving is not.

In the fashion industry, this imperfect merchandise is called seconds, irregulars, imperfects, or damages. The stores that sell this merchandise fall into several categories:

▼ Some are owned by the manufacturer himself. At the Calvin Klein outlet in Secaucus, the merchandise is carefully hung in categories that are marked "irregulars," "samples," etc.

▼ Some department stores have the means to buy up this merchandise and sell it to their regular customers on an "as is" basis—Filene's of Boston is a traditional department store that uses its double basement space as one of the country's most exciting bargain basements. Although the merchandise elsewhere in the store is perfect, Filene's Basement is a treasure trove of seconds, irregulars, markdowns, write-offs, and orphaned pieces of clothing.

▼ Sometimes the damages are sold to little stores that specialize in buying up this kind of stuff—all specialize in overruns, end lots, and irregulars.

▼ Seconds or imperfects are also unloaded on small-time businesspeople who may sell through their own outlets, or on street corners, at flea markets, in subway stations, or in any other place where they can get away with it.

Depending on the brand, the imperfect merchandise may not be very imperfect. Some brands, especially high-priced designer brands, have such strict quality control that a reject is virtually perfect.

Damaged merchandise may also be fixable. Say you buy a suit at your favorite department store. In your rush to get into the outfit, you jam the zipper. You take the suit back to the store and, feigning outrage, tell them you have bought defective merchandise and want either a refund or a new suit. Any good department store will give you either. The department store then sends the suit back to the manufacturer and gets a credit for the damage. The manufacturer doesn't have time to replace the zipper and get the item back into a store before the season ends. So he will release it—probably unfixed—with all his other damages to a jobber or seconds store. You will be able to buy this perfectly wonderful skirt for a fraction of its valued price and $2.80 for a new zipper.

Whether the item became a damage in the factory or in a department store, by the time it gets to a nontraditional retailer, you must watch for these possible problems:

▼ dye lots that do not match
▼ bubbles in plastic or glass
▼ chips in enamel or finish
▼ uneven finish
▼ nonmatched pattern at seams
▼ off-register prints
▼ misstitched logo
▼ poorly inset zipper or broken zipper
▼ stitching missing in a section, or uneven stitching
▼ belt loops that do not match or that are not all present
▼ nonexistent belt (although the belt loops are perfect)
▼ broken belt
▼ broken or missing buttons or fasteners
▼ snagged, puckered, or stretched knits
▼ holes

Remember, seconds are not sale merchandise that has not sold; they are stepchildren. When you inquire after them, don't be upset if a shopkeeper gives you a less than friendly answer. Also understand that the help in seconds stores may be less than perfect—just like the merchandise they sell.

Sales

L ike all parts of the United States, New York has two big sale periods: Spring and summer merchandise are sold at rock-bottom prices from mid-June until the end of July; fall merchandise goes on sale right after Christmas or in January. You can get a good bargain at any good store, but in New York you get incredible selection during a sale time. Since many department stores carry the same merchandise, you may be able to add to your wardrobe as you continue to shop. Take the story of our friend Alana. She bought the Anne Klein T-shirt on sale at a Saks branch store and never saw the skirt that went with it. In another Saks, she discovered there was a fabulous wrap skirt that went with her T-shirt—this, too, was on sale. But Saks didn't have the skirt in her size and couldn't find a branch store that did. She began the sale prowl, and found what she was looking for—also on sale—at Lord & Taylor.

Not all sales are during the twice-a-year big-sale periods. In America, all sorts of holidays become the excuse for a sale: Columbus Day is traditionally the day for coat sales, Presidents' Day for spring suits. When retailing is slow, there are even preseason sales—for example, after Thanksgiving, when the Christmas buying season usually starts, many stores like to give pre-Christmas sales to get people into the spirit of shopping and spending.

Some stores have cyclical sale periods—they clean house every sixty to ninety days and mark down automatically, with or without big sale announcements. Or they may have private sales for charge or preferred customers.

All sales are announced in local newspapers; some special sales are written about editorially, as in *New York* magazine's "Sales and Bargains" column. Even factory outlets have sales. Some sales are privately announced, such as the Perry Ellis sale (see page 30).

The conditions of the sale are posted in the store during the sale. Some stores specify a no-return policy. If an item is not returnable, the clerk must tell you that it is not returnable, and the sales slip also must state it is not.

Factory Outlets

T the factory outlet business has become so attractive (that means profitable) that many makers are overproducing perfect merchandise to fill factory outlets newly built in parts of the country that aren't anywhere near where the factory is. This is very smart because it capitalizes on the designer's well-known name and expensive advertising campaign, which has already been paid for, and reaches a totally different segment of the market, so it doesn't compete with traditional retailers.

In some cases, especially in the housewares and home-product businesses, factory outlets are used to test-market new products. Although new products are never sold in ready-to-wear outlets, sometimes samples are. Samples are those garments that are never mass-produced. They are made to fit a fitting model and have no specific size, but are either a women's size 6 to 8 or an 8 to 10. Always try on a sample, as it could be anything.

For the most part, the person who buys at the factory outlet is not the same person who buys in a department store. This isn't totally true, since department stores are fading and outlets are thriving, but generally speaking, the off-price shopper uses factory outlets and is willing to drive a great distance to get to them, while the traditional retail customer stays close to the comforts of nearby malls and department and specialty stores.

The prices in factory outlets are usually the same as at discount stores or department store sales—retail less 20% to 25%. A dress that has a $100 price tag usually sells for $79 at a factory outlet. But it can sell for $50, and certainly will be marked down to $50 as the season draws to a close. The discount may vary on a per-item basis, since irregulars should be less expensive than overruns.

For more on specific factory outlets in the Manhattan area, see Chapter 7.

Street Merchants

What Manhattan lacks in factory outlets it makes up for in street merchants. In good weather, there's a guy at every corner selling a small selection of something—watches, sunglasses, robots, books, pearls, ties, sweaters, etc. In bad weather, there are guys selling umbrellas, gloves, mufflers. The quality of all this merchandise is suspicious, but if you take it with a grain of salt, you may find that the shoe fits. The umbrella will last long enough to get you through the storm, the pearls won't turn, and watches may work for at least a year. We've had worse luck with expensive watches.

The merchandise for sale on the streets seems to vary with the season and the year. One year everywhere you go there are fake designer watches for sale. The next year, when you decide to spend $25 for an imitation Gucci, you can't find a fake anywhere. Murphy's Law of Retailing applies with street hawkers: Just when you finally think you need it, you can't find it.

Street hawkers work for king hawkers and are paid a small percentage of what they make. Street hawking is essentially illegal, so most hawkers are on the lookout for the police and will roll the merchandise into a ball and be gone in less than thirty seconds should anyone look at them suspiciously. Depending on the police reaction at any given time, street hawkers are abundant or scarce. They try to work popular areas and to attract tourists—Fifth Avenue, in Midtown, boasts a fair number; Sixth Avenue in the Village (near Bleecker) and lower Broadway (near Astor Place) are other good places to find street merchants.

Counterfeits and Imitations

I f you're talking street merchandise, you have to be thinking of the most nontraditional retailing ploy of them all: counterfeit. Or stolen. Or merely "lost." The watches are no doubt counterfeit, while the sweaters may have just gotten lost from their original warehouse. It's so hard to keep track of all those trucks, you know.

There is some room for debate as to when an item becomes a counterfeit, a copy, or a knockoff, and at what point it's all illegal. We figure that if the intent is to defraud the true maker, the item is a counterfeit. Thus all those $25 Gucci, Rolex, Dunhill, and Cartier watches that the street merchants sell are counterfeits. It is illegal to sell them and probably illegal to buy them. Should you buy one and be caught at Customs in your home country, you may have to forfeit the item.

Other brand names that are sold on the street may indeed be frauds; look carefully at the way the signatures are made. Some Gucci fakes look like Guccis from afar, but a careful inspection reveals that those aren't even G's in the pattern. That's not a fake. Various big names go through cycles of severity in their crackdowns, so there is some rotation as to what fakes are readily available on the street.

New York does not have nearly the sophisticated counterfeits that can be found in Italy or Bangkok—most U.S. fakes scream "fake" and are just for fun.

When it comes to jewelry design, there are *faux* styles that are line-for-line copies of original pieces, made in either real or fake stones, and that sell for less money than the original. Ciro, Jolie Gabor, and Kenneth Lane are the biggest names in costume jewelry, but the jewelers on 47th Street will copy a design from a famous catalogue if you ask them.

Blatantly fake merchandise is rather easy to spot. It looks cheap, feels cheap, and may even smell cheap. Good copies take a more practiced eye. Know what the real thing looks like . . . and feels like. Check the weight of goods, the hand (texture) of the fabrics, the lining, the stitching, the make of the label, the way the trademark is made, the hardware, the suppleness of the leather. Fixings and hardware are good clues to fakes. Look at the clasp of a necklace. Check weight and, in watches, how thick the watch is. Good watches are very thin these days.

If you are purposely choosing an imitation, consider the light in which your fake will be shown. If all your friends have the real thing and you are wearing the fake, you better believe that sooner or later someone will discover your secret. However, if you are making a one-time appearance at the Oscars, or if your gemstone will be seen only by candlelight, no one will know the difference unless you tell. Do remember, however, that high-quality fakes are not cheap, and that inexpensive fakes always look fake.

Personal Shoppers

I f you hate the idea of shopping the nontraditional way in New York, but still want
some of those hard-won bargains, you probably will love one of America's most nontraditional methods of buying and selling: the
personal shopper. A personal shopper has the
connections, the "in," or the nerve to get into
a showroom and to buy the exact garment you
want, in your size, at wholesale. You pay a fee
to the shopper for this service—usually 20%.
If the wholesale price is 40% less than the
retail ticket (it may be 50% less, but 40% is
normal), you will get a 20% discount by using
the personal shopper.

It gets better. You will have saved yourself
the time and the aggravation. Best of all, you
don't have to live in New York. Most personal
shoppers have out-of-state clients, even foreign clients. You get brand-new, never-worn
merchandise, and you can have it at the beginning of the season.

Obviously, being a personal shopper is a
very special job. Designers don't want department stores to know they allow personal shoppers into the showroom, since this is biting the
hand that feeds. Personal shoppers don't like
to talk about what designers they can get you,
because this violates a trust, similar to a doctor
or lawyer blabbing about clients. Also, a shopper may be able to get into a showroom one
season and then not get in another season.
When designers have merchandise to clear out,
they are much nicer to personal shoppers. None
of the personal shoppers we know would allow us to publish her name and phone number. But we will tell you that we have seen
stories about some of the more famous personal shoppers in *Avenue* magazine. For the

most part, you need a personal reference from a friend in order to be taken as a client. It's a highly confidential business, with no entry to strangers.

If you hear of someone who has a personal shopper, ask if you can call upon her services. The best way to use a personal shopper is to know what you want and to have a professional attitude about the shopping. Know what designers you are most interested in, and ask which designers or firms are her specialty. Each shopper has her "in" at certain houses, but rarely at all. Although shoppers get to be friends, they are not in business to tell you what to wear. Go to the best department stores in your town and see the new clothes as soon as they arrive for the season. Try on for accurate fit, and write down style numbers in the secrecy of the dressing room. DO NOT pull tags off garments. If you visit New York regularly and do a good bit of business with one designer, ask your personal shopper if she can arrange for you to see the show. Write down the style numbers of the items you wish to purchase as they come down the runway. You will not get to try them on; there is some chance that a few of your selections will not be cut. If you see a style you want in a magazine, clip the ad or editorial and send it to your shopper. If the garment is featured in an ad, it probably is available. If it's in an editorial, it could be a sample and not for sale. You never know until you ask.

The term "personal shopper" can be confusing. A personal shopper is a person, male or female, who gets a showroom to do a personal order. There are consultants and department store personnel who claim to be personal shoppers. These people do shop for you, but usually not at wholesale. (See page 56 for information on shopping services.)

Some personal shoppers provide real personal service in that they take you shopping or spend an entire day with you discussing lifestyle, working with your existing wardrobe, and helping you choose clothes that will all fit together. Working with this kind of personal shopper is not a passive activity. You cannot necessarily sit back and say "Buy for me."

There are personal shoppers who can get a Bill Blass or Oscar de la Renta to make you an exclusive garment, or to make a garment that fits when you are quite unabashedly a size 22. There are shoppers who specialize in moderate clothing who cannot get you into Blass or Beene but who know absolutely everyone in other markets. Then there are personal shoppers whose specialty is shipping-room orders—they have a buddy in the shipping department who lets them into the stockroom on a Saturday, and for a strictly cash-and-carry agreement, with a little green in the pocket, the desired garment has been procured at wholesale. If you think you are interested in getting this kind of serious shopping help, here are some rules of the game:

▼ A personal shopper may want to spend an entire day with you. Call ahead to book the date. Four weeks is the average lead time. The best and fanciest personal shoppers get their clients from personal connections, social clubs, etc. You must have the right introduction to get to some of these people. Society matrons generally like society shoppers and have contacts through their silver-spoon brokers.

▼ Be prepared to spend a minimum of $1,000 to $2,000. It doesn't pay for the shopper to spend a day with you if you just walk out with a white blouse. If, for some crazy reason, you don't think you want to buy and just want to look, ask your shopper if you can pay her a day rate or minimum fee. This probably will be $300 to $500. If you are a high roller, you will automatically gravitate to a high-roller shopper—there the stakes may be $6,000 to $10,000.

▼ If you are using a personal shopper on a per-item basis and don't want a day consultation, discuss it. Many shoppers like these clients; others want to be more involved in your total look. If you want a very close relationship, you may need a consultant or a shopper service (see page 56), not a personal shopper.

▼ The personal shopper makes her money by charging 20% above the wholesale cost. There should not be any additional fee. The designer will never discuss price with the client, only with the shopper. (For some reason, shoppers do not get kickbacks, so don't worry about the bill being padded.)

▼ Pay cash. If you are working long-distance, ask your shopper up front how she wants to be paid. Some will accept your check but wait for it to clear before they ship you the merchandise. If you are having a custom order made for your own little body, a 50% deposit will be required. Sometimes the personal shopper pays it, sometimes you do. Ask your shopper privately.

▼ Expect to pay all business expenses of your personal shopper while you are together—you pick up the costs of the taxis and the lunch. If you are working through the mail, you will have no other charges save postage and insurance and the price of the garment plus the fee. You do not pay for the transportation or lunches of shoppers who are not physically with you.

▼ Be certain of your choices; there are no returns and no refunds. If you aren't sure, have someone in mind at home to whom you can give or sell the garment. You will not be able to try it on, so have a backup plan if you make a mistake.

▼ Work one on one with a personal shopper. Do not bring your mother, your sister, or your best friend along. Do, however, have a strong sense of what's right for you. Don't let a shopper talk you into something you don't like simply because she's been in the fashion business for a long time and thinks a certain look is to die for. You're the one who has to wear the outfit.

Super Shoppers

I f you need the help of someone who does more than get you a break on the goods, you might want to call on one of the Manhattan companies that specialize in helping you do all the little things in life that you don't have time to do yourself—including shopping. We found some of these services listed in the *New York Times* and have kept the list by the phone; other names on the list are our personal secrets.

ANTIQUES RESOURCE INC.: Need anything in the area of decorative arts? Whether they're searching for antiques or pieces that are merely used, this company charges you by the hour or adds a 15% commission to those items they purchase for you that cost less than $10,000 each. (Telephone: 212-769-9462)

ULTIMATE SHOPPING SERVICE: This company will do all your shopping for you, including everyday necessities like groceries and household goods, with a charge of a flat 10% over the retail price. There is a membership charge of $100. (Telephone: 212-724-2300)

SAVED BY THE BELL: That's Susan Bell, and she's the owner of this business—she'll do your shopping, your organizing, or your errands for about $50 an hour plus expenses. (Telephone: 212-874-5457)

Complaints and Returns

With all the hustle and bustle and retail excitement in Manhattan, there's more than the average share of stores that come and go. And there's more than the average opportunity for rip-offs on a small or grand scale.

One of the easiest ways to protect yourself is to buy goods with an American Express or Optima card or another bank card that offers a protection plan, so that if you cannot make a return to the store where you bought the goods originally, or if items are lost, broken, or stolen within ninety days of purchase, you can get a refund or a replacement.

If that doesn't work for you, consider the Department of Consumer Affairs, 80 Lafayette Street, New York NY 10013 (212-566-5700), which requires you to fill in an official complaint form they supply, or the Better Business Bureau, 257 Park Avenue South, New York NY 10010 (212-533-6200).

Samples Sales and Special Sales

Fashion is a very perishable commodity. Once clothes go out of style, they have little value. Furthermore, designers and manufacturers must pay for warehouse space to house their unsold merchandise, which gets pretty expensive.

Let's say that 3,000 units of one style are hanging in a warehouse. To clean house, the makers will make deals with jobbers and offpricers, such as Loehmann's. But, come the end of the season, they still may have a few hundred odd pieces hanging around—or maybe fewer than 100 pieces total—that they would just as soon realize a little cash from. They may be forced to sell these brand-new, perfectly fabulous clothes to a jobber at $1 a hanger, which will break their hearts. To avoid this, they just may have a special sale, or even a sample sale.

A few designers keep all their samples in an archive. They lend these clothes out to friends or family (many of the evening clothes you see photographed in society pages are loaners), but they do not sell them. Other designers figure any amount of cash they can bring in is worthwhile, and realize that the cost of storing decades' worth of samples can get to be exorbitant. They have samples sales, mostly for friends or family. But when it comes to buying samples, you don't have to be too friendly with the family. You have to pay cash.

Just about anyone can get in to shop a samples sale; many special sales have a day when they are open to the public.

The most famous example of all is the Perry Ellis sale. There are two sales: The first is of Portfolio pieces; the second is Collection. They are a month apart. But the time to think of all these sales is April and October—although European lines sell earlier, as in September and February.

When it gets to be time for the Perry Ellis sale, friends, employees, and family members will be told their days, and may even be issued a badge or admission ticket. The sale is not in the Perry Ellis showroom but in a different, rented, location each year. You must know the address of the sale to get there, but—good news—you can get the address merely by calling the showroom. The showroom will also tell you what day the sale is open to the public. We made a blind phone call and, *voilà!*, got the information. No problem. Expect to wait in line to get in.

At the Ellis sale, the clothes are sold at wholesale. In the last days of the sale, the leftovers are marked down even further. Perry Ellis clothes in a Manhattan Industries factory outlet are ticketed above wholesale and then reduced to wholesale on a second markdown.

Stock is sold at the Ellis sale. At a samples sale, some stock may be sold, but the samples themselves will be 30% cheaper than the stock. Stock sells for merely the wholesale price. Samples sell for 70% to 80% less than the retail price. Samples sales are posted on handwritten signs in Garment Center buildings (see page 107) or the news is spread by word of mouth. Usually they are considered precious secrets. We get into a few samples sales as friends of certain designers, yet we would not even be so bold as to ask if our sisters also could attend. These are big-deal sales that are very, very closed.

The best way to find a special sale or a samples sale is simply to ask. Call your favorite designers, especially in April and October, and ask: "Do you sell samples or extra stock to the public?" If the answer is "No," you might next ask, "Do you have a factory outlet where you sell samples or extra stock?" It never hurts to ask.

Or you can make life easier on yourself and subscribe to *The S&B Report* (it stands for Sales and Bargains). The price for a subscription goes up every year, so every year we've listed the price, we've been wrong. For information call or write: *The S&B Report*, 112 East 36th Street, 4th floor, New York NY 10016 (telephone: 212-643-0100). Last time we looked a one-year subscription was $40; two years, $65.

The monthly report lists the showroom and samples sales for that month. There are from 75 to 200 such sales each month. Some of them are advertised in *Women's Wear Daily,* but most of them are for the trade or are not advertised at all. By getting the monthly booklet, you're on top of all the information you need—sale, merchandise, hours, locations, accepted forms of payment. Please note that the manufacturers pay for their listings, so their descriptions of the merchandise for sale may be generous—but still, when the items for sale are from a big-name designer's collection, no words are needed!

Mail Order and Catalogues

Mail-order retailing can be a very simple arrangement. You see something in a store that you do not buy but later realize you cannot live without. You call the store and give them a credit-card number, and they mail it to you.

On a far more complex level, many stores go after business from shoppers who cannot get into the store either because they are too busy or because they live too far away. These people receive some sort of catalogue to help them process their orders. As catalogue shopping has blossomed in the past few years, catalogues have become very slick and sophisticated. There are now two types of catalogues:

▼ Store catalogues: The store gives you a minisampling of their wares through listings, pictures, and offerings. Everything offered is for sale in their store, but the store itself has even more.

▼ Merchandise catalogues: These have groupings of merchandise chosen for a target audience interested in a certain lifestyle or type of merchandise. There may not even be a store, although if the catalogue is a huge success a store may be created just because of the catalogue.

The latest thing with department store catalogues is what's called the "magalogue": The
really big, chic department stores publish a
stunning fashion magazine that features their
clothes but that also gives information on how
to buy them through the magazine. These
magalogues look and even feel like fashion
magazines; they may even have feature pieces
in them. Two London stores (Harrods and
Harvey Nichols) do it; now Bloomingdale's
and Neiman Marcus also do it.

Some department stores will put you on
their catalogue list automatically after a purchase, or you can pay for a catalogue (usually
$2—often redeemable toward purchase) and
get newer editions if you buy something.
Bloomingdale's is famous for its catalogue, as
is Tiffany. In the months prior to Christmas
you can make the rounds of the Midtown
retailers and put together a collection. Usually,
if you just ask nicely, you can get a free catalogue. Many women's magazines have order
forms for all the fancy catalogues—but you
must pay for these. Check out *Town & Country, Vogue,* or *Harper's Bazaar* from September
to November.

If you are in a store that catches your fancy
and you want to consider mail-order, ask. Also
get on their mailing list at the same time.
International orders are no problem for a good
mail-order house, but make sure you know the
postage charges before you order. Many houses
offer three forms of delivery: overnight courier
service; UPS blue label (two-day delivery); or
regular postage, which may be UPS or the
U.S. Postal Service. Allow five days for UPS,
seven for the U.S. Postal Service.

Corporate Discounts

T hen there are corporate discounts offered by regular, traditional retailers. Tiffany & Co. has one of the most famous corporate plans; if you qualify (you must be incorporated), you can get a very nice discount (usually 10%) on their merchandise.

Some corporate discounts are based on location. We know of a fancy jeweler on Madison Avenue who gives a discount to businesspeople who work in the neighborhood—he wants their business. A certain camera shop offers a discount to photographers who work for Time, Inc., because he likes to tell his regular customers that all the *Life* magazine photographers buy from him. And so it goes.

If you are visiting your corporate headquarters, it pays to ask a local company representative which retailers offer corporate benefits. You just may be surprised at the choice.

Auctions

A uctions service the high, mid-, and even lower midmarket for art and home furnishings. There is another type of auction business in unclaimed merchandise: Police departments and the U.S. Postal Service as well as the U.S. Treasury Department (Customs) all have auctions on confiscated and nondelivered or unclaimed merchandise. (Drugs are not sold.)

There's a post office auction about once a month; call (212) 971-5180 for details. It's held at what we call the Big Post Office, which takes up about a city block slightly west of Madison Square Garden, at 380 West 33rd Street. There are viewing days, and there is a catalogue. You bid by use of a paddle, which costs $20 (it's refundable or can be applied to the first purchase), and you must pay in cash.

For the Police Auction at One Police Plaza, New York, call (212) 406-1369. They have a catalogue and a viewing period, although you do have to tramp around to various police warehouses—not our idea of safe or fun. You can get a great buy, although we hear that the police keep the really good cars to use as unmarked vehicles for stakeouts.

The schedule for Customs auctions is released about a year ahead of time, with big auctions held twice a year at various regional offices. The Los Angeles date may be different from the New York date. You also need a paddle for this auction (the $25 fee is refundable). The items for sale are usually the things people refused to pay duty on. Items that were confiscated usually were seized for legal reasons, so they are seldom sold—this is not the place to buy the leopard coat you have been dreaming of. This is great rainy-day fun. Ask to get on their mailing list. Call (212) 466-2924 for more details.

For buying art, antiques, collectibles, or fancy junk, auctions are a good training ground. If you study catalogues, go to viewings, eavesdrop on conversations, and attend enough auctions, you will become knowledgeable not only in the art of auctioning but also in the nuances of the items you collect and of those who also collect them.

There are two types of auction houses: bigtime and fun-time. They never get the same kinds of lots.

Things go to auction for two reasons. One, a collector has decided to give up a piece or pieces of his collection, or two, a collector has died and the estate (heirs) needs to liquidate the assets. Country auctions usually are the best places to find overlooked pieces. These auctions are advertised in local papers as well as in *Antiques and the Arts Weekly,* published by Bee Publishing Company in Newtown, Connecticut. (If you're looking for something more serious to keep you up on the latest of auctions, get a subscription to *Art & Auction,* a glossy magazine dedicated to those who care.)

Previews (also called viewings or exhibitions) are very important and occur the week before the auction. During the auction there is no time to think or change your mind. You must know ahead of time if you are going to bid on a piece. It is also important to know what your limit will be. We have found ourselves so caught up in the competition of bidding that the price became unimportant . . . until later. It is better to leave your competitive spirit at home. Auctions are business, and you will be bidding against dealers who have little emotion about the pieces being auctioned. Of course, if you really *love* something and *must* have it, you can outbid the dealers every time. If you are willing to overpay, they will not compete. During previews it is important to look for the following:

▼ Are there provenance papers on the item? All quality pieces of furniture and art will have them.

▼ What is the condition of the item? How many repairs have been done to the legs? Can you tell if anything has been replaced? Has the piece been refinished recently, and if so, by whom? Can you ask the owner for details? Usually the answer is "No." In this case you might consider hiring a consultant to look at the piece for you.

▼ Can you guarantee authenticity? Provenance helps, of course. We need not tell you about all the fakes that have gone through the auction houses. Quality houses will authenticate as best they can, but even they get fooled sometimes. Authentications will be found in the catalogue listing. If nothing is listed, ask why. Very often the auction house cannot risk giving a guarantee unless there is no question as to the origin of the item. We once attended an auction where the auctioneer asked the artist to stand up and authenticate her work of art in person.

▼ Once you leave the preview, take the catalogue home and read the fine print. Everything you need to know about how the auction will be run and what the house is responsible for handling is in the front or back of the catalogue.

▼ Check to see if the piece you will be bidding on is "subject to reserve." Reserve is the minimum price for which the piece will be sold. It is a confidential price known only to the auction house and owner. However, it is important for you to know if you will be bidding against this price. Sometimes the piece will be taken off the block if the reserve is not met. Sometimes the house will bid on behalf of the consignee to meet the reserve.

▼ Tucked into the catalogue, or on the final pages of the book, will be a list of prices for the lot numbers that show what a similar item went for at a previous date, or what the house estimates the sale price to be. This means nothing, but it can give you an idea of where to expect the bidding to fall. One of the reasons auctions are so much fun is that you never know what really will happen—it could go either way.

Once you have done your homework and decided to attend the auction to bid on one or more "lots," there are a few more details:

▼ You may be asked to register when you arrive at the auction house. If the auction involves high-stakes items and you are going to be bidding above $10,000, bring credit references with you. Once you have registered you will be given a "paddle" with your bidding number on it. This number corresponds to your registration. During the auction, names are never used. Lots are assigned to the highest bidder's number.

▼ Don't be shy when bidding. If the auctioneer can't see your paddle, you will lose out on the bidding. Everything you've heard about sneezes, flicks of the wrist, or eyebrows arching is nonsense. While some people bid in a subtle motion, everyone does know what's going on—even if paddles aren't being used.

▼ If you can't be present at the auction, you can name a representative to bid for you, or be on the phone with a member of the auction-house staff. It is also possible to bid by mail. Absentee bid forms are published in the auction catalogue, or can be obtained from the auction house by mail.

▼ When figuring price, don't forget to add in the auction-house commission and the tax. Ask ahead of time what the auction house will be taking as its cut. If you thought the price you bid was the price paid, welcome to the cruel world. The auction house gets from 10% to 20% of the sale price. If you are bidding on a large item, figure in the cost of delivery also. The auction houses all have services to help you. . . . But they are not free.

▼ Payment will be asked for at the time of the sale, unless you have an account with the house or have arranged ahead of time to be invoiced. All large auction houses preregister bidders and check references.

▼ Payment for goods will be asked for in American dollars. Although you will see prices being quoted on the currency board in many foreign currencies as the bidding is taking place, it is merely for the convenience of the foreign clientele to compare the price in dollars with their currency. On small items you often can pay with American Express, Visa, or Master-Card.

▼ If you are planning on shipping your purchase out of the country, be sure to obtain an export permit. As in European countries, some items may not be exportable. Check with a Customs expert in this area.

▼ You will be expected to take possession of your purchase within three working days. After that time you will be charged a storage fee.

▼ You need to read *The New York Times* Thursday Home section for listings of weekly events. Also check ads in the Friday *Times* and perhaps the Saturday *Times*.

▼ If you want to keep up with country auctions, the company that publishes *The S&B Report* (see page 31) also publishes a separate auction report.

If you are observing in the big time but aren't planning to buy, you may be a tad nervous. Relax. You're welcome here, even if you don't bid. Dress like you own a bank, and you'll be fine. Admission to a big-time event is always by catalogue (the catalogue admits two) —you may pay for the catalogue at the front desk before the preview or right before the actual auction. Catalogue prices range from $2 to $25. Half a catalogue does not admit one. Many big-time auctions are star-studded events and may be black-tie. A collection of important jewels, by the way, does have a viewing, but the bidding is done with slides on a screen, as if it were home-movie night. Remember to keep your cool when the really big rocks are screened. Previews are far more casual than auctions; you may even attend in blue jeans, if you are wearing Gucci loafers with them. It is better to have been to the preview, but it's not imperative if you are not planning on buying.

You will see the items much better at the preview, and can touch many of them. This is a no-no during the auction. Should you be planning on buying for the first time in the big time, you may want to walk through it all at an auction that is not yours, just to get the lay of the land. There's no reason to be intimidated or unduly nervous when you will have enough on your mind spending your trust fund on a piece of canvas and oil paint.

CHRISTIE'S: Christie's is in hot contention with Sotheby's to be number one. We can't tell you that one house is better than the other or that we know what all the competition is about. Christie's is a British firm; Sotheby's is U.S.-based.

People who shop big-time auctions do not prefer one house to the other; they merely choose the auction they are interested in. The difference between the two houses is probably inside, behind closed doors, and is possibly in how they woo potential customers and their estates. Both houses will treat you and your money with equal charm or disdain, depending on your money . . . and your manners.

CHRISTIE'S, 502 Park Avenue, at 59th Street
CHRISTIE'S EAST, 219 East 67th Street

▼

PHILLIPS FINE ART AUCTIONEERS: Phillips is an international auction house of the same caliber as Christie's and Sotheby's. With offices around the world, they are able to acquire lots of good quality items, some with incredible pedigrees representing centuries of ostentatious buying or conservative wealth poured discreetly into fabulous collections. It is also possible to participate in their European auctions without going abroad.

PHILLIPS FINE ART AUCTIONEERS, 406 East 79th Street

SOTHEBY'S: We hate to admit to being partial, but we've been going to auctions at Sotheby Parke Bernet (pronounce the "t" at the end of Bernet; do not eliminate the "t" as if this were a French name) for over twenty years.

Sotheby's publishes a catalogue for all sales, national and international. You can subscribe to the catalogues that deal only with your collecting mania (painting, pre-Columbian, furniture, etc.), which is a wonderful way to keep up with the international market in your area.

Sotheby's experts are available for consultation to both buyers and sellers. (Other auction houses also provide this service.) If you have a piece of art that you think is worthy of being put up for auction, you can make an appointment to bring it in or have an expert visit you. Sotheby's people make periodic trips to major cities around the country. Their visits are advertised in the local newspapers the week before they arrive; they also have representatives in most of the major cities in the United States.

Sotheby's Arcade Auctions are for the yuppies who love to buy but can't yet afford an old master. These sales are well within the affordable range and often involve surprise packages. Lots are sold in groups. You might be bidding on a spectacular gold bracelet and also end up with some earrings and a pin.

SOTHEBY'S, 1334 York Avenue, at 72nd Street

▼

WILLIAM DOYLE GALLERIES: A very popular auction house with the successful Wall Street crowd, Doyle's has prices that are usually affordable although not "cheap." They seem to acquire some unusual items not seen in the other houses, and are not quite as intimidating to us as the big-timers. They certainly are more tony than others listed in this category. Doyle's has important auctions and must get your equal attention if you are a serious shopper; but snobs will tell you it just isn't Christie's.

WILLIAM DOYLE GALLERIES, 175 East 87th Street

▼

LUBIN GALLERIES: Fun, fun, fun, and a far cry from Sotheby's rarefied air. Even Doyle's seems rarefied when considered with Lubin. Lubin has an auction every Saturday at 11 A.M., and just about everything is affordable. Thursday is the regular viewing day—you can get the catalogue then. They use the paddle method here—you plunk down a refundable $25.

LUBIN GALLERIES, 30 West 26th Street

▼

MANHATTAN GALLERIES: Not nearly as fancy as Doyle but fun because they sometimes empty out the leftovers in Manhattan Storage, which have become antiques while waiting for their owners to pick them up. They also have summer clearance sales, words other auction houses may not use. Their viewings are called "exhibitions," by the way. If you want a good time without the pressure of the big time, this is your place.

MANHATTAN GALLERIES, 1415 Third Avenue, at 81st Street

▼

EDELMAN GALLERIES: Watch the auction ads—they just may have something that interests you. Not at all intimidating; we caught a good quilt auction here once. People come here to buy and have fun. Some dealers.

EDELMAN GALLERIES, 523 East 73rd Street

Used Merchandise

In New York, many people give their unwanteds to charity to get a tax deduction for the donation. But often they put perfectly good pieces of furniture out on the street for garbage collectors to haul away. Now it is a bit complex if you are wandering down the street, see a table you want, and have to hail a truck to haul it away for you. But New Yorkers are very resourceful. Naturally, if you're looking at garbage, you want to do so in only the best neighborhoods.

If you are looking instead for goods that were donated, scads of thrift shops and charity-related stores sell previously worn merchandise. We happen to like the Posh Sale (see page 44) because of the high quality of the designer merchandise, but many good items end up at other good charity stores.

People who prefer to get cash for their used clothes take them to consignment shops, where they get a percentage of the selling price. We have patronized a few shops on a sporadic basis but have never found what we were looking for—except at the Posh Sale. Good luck.

ENCORE: This store got our attention about fifteen years ago when it was rumored that Jacqueline Kennedy Onassis was turning in her used clothes here. Much of the selection is in very fancy, sequined and beaded, dressy outfits. A lot of people swear by this resource.

ENCORE, 1132 Madison Avenue, at 92nd Street, Room 2F

▼

MICHAEL RESALE: This store is close enough to Encore that you can hit both in the same trip. Michael is supposed to be very chichi and is *de rigueur* if you need an evening gown. Strange hours; call first. We've never bought here but have been impressed by the labels.

MICHAEL RESALE, 1041 Madison Avenue, at 77th Street, Room 2F

Special-Event Retailing

A n event just wouldn't be special if you couldn't buy anything, would it? Museums have gift shops, circuses have vendors, and New York City has all sorts of special events that revolve around the selling of something or other. Many of these events are food-related—the Ninth Avenue Association has an annual block party that allows you to roam through throngs of people as you explore a variety of ethnic food stands. There are similar festivals in Little Italy; there's Chinese New Year in Chinatown. Check with your hotel concierge or *Where* magazine to find out if such events will be held when you are in town. The Visitors Bureau also sends out a quarterly list of all special events in Manhattan. Little street festivals often are ideal for those who collect antique clothes and small bric-a-brac.

Also investigate charity events; many of them are related to retailing. For antiques and furniture, we like the twice-a-year sale at the Armory on Park Avenue at 67th Street (the Seventh Regiment Armory Antiques Show). For clothes, our favorite is the Posh Sale, and it is held as a benefit for the Lighthouse for the Blind, at the Lighthouse, 111 East 59th Street.

Twice a year the great ladies of New York society clean out their closets (designers do this, as well) and send their tired, their poor, their wretched excesses to the Posh Sale, where we are yearning for them to be free but will pay $30 to $50 for them. The Posh Sale has become quite an event—usually we plan a trip to Manhattan to coincide with the proper dates. Call the Lighthouse for the Blind or check magazine listings—there's a spring and a fall sale. They're worth lining up for.

There happens to be some great shopping at charity dinners; many of them have auctions at which merchandise is sold for incredibly low prices. And we mean fancy merchandise donated (for a tax break) by the city's finest retailers. You can also buy unusual services at these events—such as dinner at a celebrity's home or a flight and picnic on a hot-air balloon. All you need to shop these galas is the ticket, which can cost from $35 to $350 or more. Higher-priced events include dinner and dancing and are black-tie. Your purchases at the gala may be tax-deductible. *Avenue* magazine has a monthly listing in which they publish the city's social calendar. This includes charity events; most often if there is a retail event tied to the evening it will be mentioned. There also is a contact for tickets. Just about anyone, with the price of admission and proper telephone manners, can be invited to one of these galas—but the night can cost $500 or more a couple. Part of this is tax-deductible, of course.

Special Visitors

For a clothes encounter of the bargain kind, also check for listings about special visitors from foreign retailing establishments. The British are particularly adept at flying to New York for a week, taking a suite in a Midtown hotel, and visiting with private customers, to whom they sell at wholesale or rock-bottom British prices.

To become a private customer one needs only sharp eyes—ads usually run in newspapers or selected magazines such as *New York* or *Avenue*. Tailors often employ this method, but so do manufacturers and even entire department stores. A representative from Harrods comes over to sell from the store catalogue on a regular basis. Chinacraft comes to all major U.S. cities and takes hotel space for a few days. The hotels get a good bit of this business, so we've gotten into the habit of asking the concierge if any sales in the meeting rooms are open to the public.

Trade Show Shopping

Inveterate shoppers usually shun the standard shopping services and go on the prowl themselves. Trade shows are one of their favorite haunts. Manhattan hosts almost 1,000 conventions a year. Not all of these will interest you. But events such as the Gift Show, the Stationery Show, and the Linens Show are not only fun to attend (you get a sneak preview of next season's wares) but also fun to shop—on the final day of the show, the representatives of the company often will sell the samples right out of the booths rather than pay to truck the merchandise home. You will pay wholesale, sometimes less. You also may get a lot of small-time freebies.

To shop a trade show:

▼ Get a list of the week's trade shows from your concierge, from a magazine, or from the Visitors Bureau.

▼ Find out the last day of the show and the hours.

▼ At about 11 A.M. on the final day, go to the convention hall and fill out the papers for accreditation. Attendance at a trade fair may be free, or there may be a charge ($10–$25); either way, you must have some business credentials. This is what business cards are for.

▼ Your business card should be related to the business of the trade fair whenever possible; it should have some kind of company name rather than anything too cute. Your name should also be on the card.

▼ Be prepared to answer a few innocent questions about your business, such as what you do. Having a gift-buying service or being in the party-planning business are two good entrées to just about anything.

▼ When you see something that interests you, introduce yourself—with your professional demeanor and company name—and ask if samples are being sold. If the answer is "yes," pay in cash. No one wants your check. No one will change a traveler's check. No one has American money for lire. Cash and carry. Our friend Dale even brings her own heavy-duty shopping bags.

Every now and then, before the last day of the show, you can get a maker to run a personal for you—but you still must meet a minimum order. Sometimes this is only $100. Shipping will be extra. If you are prepared to do your Christmas shopping in July, your Halloween shopping in May, and your kiddie birthday shopping by the dozen, you can get some great bargains—and save a lot of time in future months when all your friends will be frantic and you'll be cool as can be. Trade show shopping takes organization, storage space, and extra cash resources, but it's the best way to save money and time and still give fabulous gifts.

Javits Center Shopping

T rade shows at the Jacob Javits Convention Center (655 West 34th Street) have so excited the public that now there are public sales in this building. Mostly they are one-day events, but some may stretch three or four days, and are advertised in all of the newspapers. We can't vouch for the quality of everything sold here, since the sales are usually a method of dumping a lot of merchandise. We certainly would not buy a fur coat here; but it's fun to look.

3 ▾ DETAILS

Hours

O ne of the most marvelous things about New York is that the town rarely sleeps. There is good shopping every day of the week. Many goods and services are available before and after work hours—some on a 24-hour basis. Meet a town that has 24-hour hairstylists, delis, and tailors.

Business hours do have something to do with the neighborhood where the business is located. Neighborhoods made up predominantly of businesses have stores that open before and after work. Stores on the Lower East Side are closed on Saturday due to religious, not business, reasons. (The Lower East Side is bustling on Sunday.) Stores on the Lower East Side are also closed for all Jewish holidays.

Sunday retailing is hot. Department stores are usually open on Sunday from noon to 5 P.M. Fancy shops in tony neighborhoods are rarely open on Sunday, except between Thanksgiving and Christmas, when almost every store in New York has extended hours and is open seven days a week. Certain specific neighborhoods have become famous for their Sunday promenade and shop routines— SoHo is usually bustling, as is upper Madison Avenue.

Traditional business hours are Monday through Saturday, 10 A.M. to 5:30 or 6 P.M. But service businesses that provide for the needs of the working community open at 7:30 or 8 A.M. and close at 7 P.M. By service businesses we mean shoe-repair shops, copy-machine stores, office-supply stores, etc.

About the only store that closes for lunch in

New York is Gucci, which is closed from 1 to 2 P.M. every day.

Lunch hour is usually a high traffic time for stores because working people use it for their own shopping and errands.

Many nontraditional retailers open at off hours. On the Lower East Side, many shops open at 9 A.M.; most are open by 9:30. They close at 4 P.M. on Friday in the winter. On the Upper West Side and in SoHo, most shops don't open until 11 A.M. but stay open until 8 P.M. Some bookstores, especially the big ones on Fifth Avenue, are open until 10 P.M. or even midnight.

If you have some question about whether a store will be open, call first. If you are looking to fill the hour from 9 to 10 A.M. in a shop, give some thought to the neighborhood where you will be. Many bookstores in Midtown open between 8:30 and 9 A.M.; many showrooms in the Garment Center open at 9 A.M. Stores in the Wall Street area open at 9 A.M. or earlier. Department stores never open before 9:30 A.M.; most open at 10. If you are planning on doing some museum retailing, make sure the museum is open that day—some museums are closed on Monday. Museums and department stores have at least one late night a week, during which they are usually open until 9 P.M. The night may vary with the museum, but department stores in the metropolitan area use Thursday as their one late night and may also honor Monday night.

Summer and Christmas-season hours often are unusual—many smaller boutiques (as well as Tiffany) close on Saturday between Memorial Day and Labor Day (the last weekend in May and the first weekend in September). In the pre-Christmas season, stores may stay open until 9 or 10 P.M. every night; others may be open until midnight or on a 24-hour basis on Christmas Eve.

Getting Around

Public transportation in New York is not as civilized as in Tokyo or Paris, but there is a good network of subways and buses. Buses usually are safe and relatively clean. Subway travel can be marvelous or horrendous.

You can ask for a free subway map at the token booth of any subway station. Train routes change temporarily depending on repairs on the line. If you ask for directions to a specific shop (perhaps one that is out of Manhattan), ask if several trains go there.

Many out-of-the-way shopping areas have their own means of transportation. Most of the big out-of-state factory outlets have buses from the Port Authority terminal in Manhattan.

Subways are not to be avoided at all costs, no matter what you hear. You just have to use them wisely. We recommend the "F" train even at late hours. But no matter what train you take, use the same common sense you would use in riding the rails, be it in Paris or Rio. When you are on a subway, turn your ring into your palm and keep your necklaces inside your blouse—or wear no jewelry. Do not wear a fur coat on the subway. Keep your handbag across your body rather than just over your arm. Keep shopping bags between your feet or on your lap.

Buses are easy to use and may feel much safer than the subway. They cost the same as the subway and can be paid for with coins (exact change) or subway tokens. You can get a free transfer. Bus routes are clearly marked on signposts, but always ask the driver to confirm that you are headed the right way. Buses can be very crowded during rush hours and

are particularly slow at this time of the day
due to traffic congestion.

If you want to get someplace in a hurry, do
what all locals do: Walk.

If you just can't hack the walk, try a taxi.
Taxis in New York can be flagged with a rise
of the hand and a flick of the wrist. If the
yellow light on the top of the cab is lit, the cab
is available. Get into the taxi and shut the
door before you give your destination. This
avoids the hassle of the driver telling you he
doesn't want to go where you want to go.
Naturally, it's impossible to get a taxi in the
rain, and usually impossible during rush hour;
other than under those two conditions, it is
not that hard to hop a cab. Murphy's Law
applies to all: When you most need a cab, you
can't get one; when you don't need one, there
are scads of them. Go figure. Taxi drivers
expect a 15% to 20% tip.

Booking New York / I

When you decide to visit New York,
take time out to do something you
probably think is very hokey: Write
or call the New York Convention
and Visitors Bureau, Inc., 2 Columbus Circle,
New York NY 10019 (telephone: 212-397-8200).
Ask them to send you their complete kit on
the Big Apple. You will receive about ten
pounds' worth of papergoods, including bro-
chures about tours, good deals, hotel packages, discounts, restaurants, and everything else
important to life. You'll get a nice free map
and a lot of stuff you think you don't want but
really should have. (You can also save it for
your child's next social studies project.) If you
spend twenty minutes looking through all this

material, you will learn a lot—and maybe save some time and money.

Booking New York / 2

I f you are tempted to buy a plethora of guidebooks about the city—don't. The free package from the Convention and Visitors Bureau will start you off just fine. When you get to New York, if you need more guides, you can buy them in any bookstore. There's no lack of guidebooks to the area.

Check out *Where* magazine, which is distributed free in your hotel (if you aren't staying in a hotel, you can go in and still get a free copy). Besides listing the expected tourist information, *Where* posts the big fashion shows and public sales and auctions. Sometimes there are coupons for discounts in *Where*.

Your hotel concierge also may know of sales or trade shows that may interest you. The Convention and Visitors Bureau can tell you what trade shows are currently booked into the big convention centers of the city—you just may want to do your shopping at a trade fair. (See page 46; also see page 44 for special-event shopping.)

If you are intent on dissecting a particular neighborhood and find that our coverage is insufficient, you may want to buy one of the Raw Books and Graphics neighborhood maps, which cost $1.25 and are limited to the area in the title. *Warning:* These books do solicit listings (we don't) from stores and restaurants; but the foldout maps are detailed and well marked. Any good city map is essential for the person who is really on the prowl.

There are two city magazines we suggest:

▼ *New York* magazine: This has listings in the back for theaters, television, etc.; a regular column called "Sales and Bargains" (don't miss it!); restaurant information; and fast-paced, with-it editorials that will make you feel very plugged in.

▾ *Avenue* magazine: Our single favorite magazine in the world, *Avenue* caters to the high rollers in the world of posh New York and the retail world of upper Madison Avenue. Your hotel may have it as a freebie, but it's not given away with the same abandon as *Where*. *Avenue* is available on newsstands.

New York Hotel Deals

I t's not hard to find a hotel in New York, but to get a good deal is an art. We often come in for a few days of shopping, and have learned a few tricks. Professionals coming for conventions (even Garment Center buyers) should be aware of special rates offered by certain hotels that cater to conventions or to visitors on market weeks. Weekend visitors should check the Sunday Travel section of *The New York Times* for the various weekend rates—note that some are per room and some are per person! Don't be misled by headlines; read the fine print. If you're just on board for personal shopping and a good time, try our regulars. We rate these hotels as: Expensive = over $150 per night; moderate = $101–$150 per night; and inexpensive = $100 a night and less.

THE REGENCY: The Regency is a very fancy New York hotel with top-of-the-line prices. It's also got one of the best locations in New York for businesspeople and shoppers, and is far enough off the beaten path (it's on Park

Avenue) that you avoid the convention and tourist traffic. The hotel is located about a mile (easy walking distance) from Grand Central Station, so you can get in and out of town easily. You're two blocks from Fifth Avenue and two blocks from Bloomingdale's. Don't miss the power breakfast scene—the hot ticket in New York. Expensive. Reservations: (212) 759-4100.

THE REGENCY, 540 Park Avenue, at 61st Street

▼

THE GRAND HYATT: Rising directly above Grand Central Station, the Grand Hyatt is the hotel we use when we bring our children, our families, or our friends to New York. They have excellent promotional rates; the executive floor has a free breakfast, and the location couldn't be better. You are on top of the train station and also have public transportation at your fingertips. Or footsteps. Moderate to expensive; excellent weekend packages. Reservations: (212) 883-1234.

THE GRAND HYATT, Park Avenue at Grand Central Station (42nd Street)

▼

OMNI BERKSHIRE: This is where Bantam puts us on book business and where we put ourselves frequently: we're right smack in the middle of Midtown shopping. The summer promotional rates are particularly attractive. There's a great coffee shop across the street for cheap breakfasts or feeding the kids, if you don't go in for fancy hotel stuff. One of the best things about this hotel is that kids stay for free. Very elegant in the small, intimate hotel manner; a sensational Midtown location for shoppers. Moderate. Reservations: (800) THE-OMNI.

OMNI BERKSHIRE, 21 East 52nd Street

In-Store Shopping Services

Special Shoppers

If you like the idea of getting special help but want something more dependable than a once-a-year encounter, you should know that all the department stores offer special shoppers and shopper services.

A special shopper will work the entire store with you, helping to coordinate your outfits or put together table settings for a dinner party or plan your wedding—although most stores have special wedding consultants for the bride-and-groom part. Or a special shopper will put together clothes for you and then invite you into the store to try them on. She can even bring them to your home, if you don't like to go to stores or have time constraints.

A special shopper is available with a store translator if communications are your problem. Make an appointment and specify what language you will be speaking.

You should not pay extra for the services of a shopper, since she is an employee of the department store, but the shopper does not use outside resources for your buying, nor does she tell you where to get bargains or discounts. She may give you fashion tips and point you toward a good buy, but her job is to sell the store's merchandise. Men as well as women often use special shoppers. Expect to buy a seasonal wardrobe (fall or spring) and to spend at least $1,000.

Charge and Send

If you are on a mad shopping spree, check with the concierge of your hotel about having someone pick up your purchases for you. Department stores will deliver for you, but they charge UPS rates and it takes a few days. Your concierge can get you a messenger to pick up and deliver your packages on the same day. The charges are computed by distance.

All department stores honor a variety of international charge cards as well as their own. A few stores have reciprocal arrangements with other stores in the chain. All major department stores are prepared to ship overseas; many specialty stores provide this service as well.

Interstate Shipping

Stores will happily send a package to any address for you—they probably will pull out a zone chart and bill you a flat fee for the packing, wrapping, and mailing. Insurance is probably not included; ask specifically.

Technically, mail costs should be charged by weight and distance—but many stores guess at the weight and charge you a flat fee for the whole works. Snap at it. Any time we have insisted on weighing, we have lost money.

Interstate shipping is also a good way to avoid sales tax, although New Jersey and Connecticut residents who shop in New York must pay a users' tax.

We have not found that trucking major appliances across the country from a discount source in the New York area pays. A discounter near you will offer you a better deal. You may, however, want to truck antiques or furniture.

Courier and Delivery Services

Although the U.S. Postal Service is excellent, many people think it's just not as good as it used to be. More and more people rely on private mail services and one- or two-day delivery services. The U.S. Postal Service offers such a service, called Express Mail, which promises next-day or second-day delivery.

We use Federal Express, a private courier company, because they have worldwide delivery. Although Federal Express is not the least expensive method for getting things across the United States, their European prices are comparatively moderate. You can send a two-pound package from New York to Paris for about $30. That's door-to-door delivery within two days. Not bad.

If you are transporting something so valuable that it needs personal attention, there are international couriers who will fly your item right through. Usually this is done with art, jewels, and some kinds of business papers.

If you need any overnight, delivery, or courier services, check with your hotel concierge. The hotel will have a relationship with certain firms, and you will be guided toward the right service for your need. Your hotel may well have a Federal Express drop right there.

Translation, Please

If you do not speak English, don't worry. You can still go shopping. All major department stores have staff that speak other languages.

If you are really in a bind, walk into a store in the Midtown area that has a name that sounds like it might be related to you. Someone at Rizzoli Bookstore will speak Italian; someone at Charles Jourdan may speak French. Many stores have signs in the windows noting what languages are spoken; on the Lower East Side, the retailers list as many as ten different languages spoken in their shops. The concierge in any leading hotel also speaks several languages or can get someone for you who will help you.

You can, of course, hire a translator (your hotel may have one on hand). We think this need arises more on the business level than the shopping level. As long as you can say "How much?" we think you're gonna do just great. Welcome to America.

VAT and Sales Tax

New York does not at this time have a value-added tax or an export-tax program (Louisiana does!). Visitors from foreign countries are required to pay the state sales tax and cannot get a refund on this money when they leave the country. Sales tax does vary from state to state. Some states have no tax on clothes.

Final Calculating Thoughts

▼ Use a calculator, whether you are used to foreign currency or U.S. dollars—you will still find this little invention a godsend. It's also good in discount stores, where prices may be in percentages. ("Take 20% off our already low ticketed price.")

▼ Never travel without your checkbook and proper ID. Most stores require a major credit card and driver's license, or other photo ID.

▼ Know where an American Express office is if you run out of money; have your bank PIN number handy so you can use a bank machine.

▼ Deak Perera specializes in currency exchange and transactions that are multicurrency-oriented. They also will buy back your dollars if you want to get rid of them. Their rates aren't the best in town, but they do provide a lot of useful services and have personnel who speak many different languages (as do banks).

4 ▾ NEIGHBORHOODS

New York Neighborhoods

New York is a city of neighborhoods. Like most international cities, it can brag of a host of ethnic groups, diverse architecture, and a chameleonlike nature that enables it to change its personality as frequently as every ten blocks. Neighborhoods are best used to plan your time in the city, since it's very difficult to get from Uptown to Downtown and back again in any short period of time. Manhattan is not as large as Tokyo, but Tokyo has one of the world's best subway systems. New York doesn't. You'll enjoy your shopping expeditions best if you organize them by adjacent neighborhoods.

Neighborhood Map

As you can tell from our neighborhood map, the various districts of New York serve as unofficial *arrondissements*. Each has its own personality; the addresses often label shops and residences in an instant, and possibly unfair, niche. New Yorkers, like Parisians, are fond of summing up a person or a shop by his, her, or its address, without ever getting to know more information.

When you plan your shopping, try to work in a circle or a straight line, so that you move from one neighborhood to another, skipping over the ones that don't interest you and saving time and energy for those that do. No one

Manhattan Neighborhoods

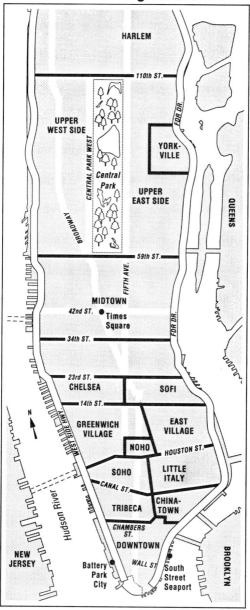

HARLEM

110th ST.

UPPER WEST SIDE

CENTRAL PARK WEST

Central Park

YORK-VILLE

UPPER EAST SIDE

BROADWAY

QUEENS

59th ST.

FIFTH AVE.

MIDTOWN

42nd ST. • Times Square

FDR DR.

34th ST.

23rd ST.
CHELSEA

SOFI

14th ST.

WEST SIDE HWY.

GREENWICH VILLAGE

EAST VILLAGE

NOHO

HOUSTON ST.

SOHO

LITTLE ITALY

CANAL ST.

CHINA-TOWN

TRIBECA

CHAMBERS ST.

DOWNTOWN

Hudson River

NEW JERSEY

Battery Park City

WALL ST.

South Street Seaport

BROOKLYN

N

can possibly see all of New York in a week; no one can possibly shop all of New York in a month. We think our tours (see page 257) give you a really good look at most of New York, but a few minutes of map-studying will stand you well when you plan your own visits. You will exhaust yourself, physically and mentally, if you have to crisscross the town regularly. A battle plan is what you need. And a good sense of humor, if you're taking public transportation.

Fifth Avenue/Midtown

The main shopping area of Manhattan also is in the main business area—between 57th Street and 34th Street. This is known as Midtown; Fifth Avenue is not a neighborhood, it is a street. It's a very long street that neatly bisects most of the island of Manhattan and is the main drag of Midtown. It once owned a reputation as the swankiest address in town, possibly in the United States. Don't look now, but Midtown Fifth Avenue just isn't the same anymore. For retailing, anyway. It's a fine residential address, for sure. It's great for office buildings, banks, and airlines. But just as the Champs-Élysées has changed for shoppers, so has upper Fifth Avenue. This part of the street no longer is the be-all and end-all of chic shopping.

Begin your tour at Fifth Avenue and 63rd Street, on the residential side of the street. Take in the beauties of Central Park and some of America's most famous names. Pass the Sherry Netherland Hotel. Peer into the recesses of **A LA VIEILLE RUSSIE**, an antiques shop that specializes in tsarist treasures, and note the difference among the three blocks as the neighborhood changes from homes to hotels to now, at 59th Street, the General Motors Building—home of many corporations and **F.A.O. SCHWARZ**. Walk down Fifth Avenue all the way to 34th Street, noting the changes in the crowds, the types of stores, the way the people are dressed, and the very feel of the air. No matter who you are, or how long you've been shopping in New York, or what kind of a tour you are interested in, there are some bright spots to sparkle up your day. Try not to miss:

BERGDORF GOODMAN: If you're just thinking about Fifth Avenue and the essence of New York style, think no further. The men's store is the newest addition.

BERGDORF GOODMAN, 754 Fifth Avenue, at 58th Street

MEN'S STORE, 745 Fifth Avenue, at 58th Street

▼

TIFFANY & CO.: Contrary to popular thought, Tiffany is not that expensive. Or, put more properly in perspective, Tiffany has many items you can afford.

TIFFANY & CO., 727 Fifth Avenue, at 57th Street

▼

TRUMP TOWER: It's an apartment house with a four-story shopping arcade of expensive and tony shops, the likes of which you have never seen before and will want to tell your grandchildren about. Beware the slippery marble floors on wet days; note the Christmas lights in the trees on the roof from outside. There are some fifty shops. It's all here in abundance.

TRUMP TOWER, 725 Fifth Avenue, at 56th Street

FENDI: It's so European that you have to browse . . . if only for ambience.

FENDI, 720 Fifth Avenue, at 56th Street

▼

HENRI BENDEL: Welcome to the new Fifth Avenue! When Bendel's was bought by The Limited, it suffered tremendously at the hands of the New York press, and New York shoppers slowly abandoned it. This move to Fifth Avenue should convince everyone that although, sadly, the old Bendel's just doesn't exist anymore, retailing under the name Henri Bendel is not dead. In fact, Bendel's has a store in Chicago and is slowly and carefully expanding. The new Bendel's is five stories of gorgeous town house space joined together into a mini department store of creative chic. Because it's impossible to know what you'll find at Bendel's, it's worth shopping by just to take a peek. Opens Spring 1991.

HENRI BENDEL, 721 Fifth Avenue, at 56th Street

▼

BULGARI: A key part of the new Fifth Avenue and the Europeanization of Fifth is the Bulgari showroom taking up much of the space once inhabited by I. Miller, the shoe landmark. From boots to baubles. Most of Bulgari's sales are in jewelry, but they do offer watches and very exclusive silverware as well. The store is much like other Bulgari shops around the world, sumptuously decked out in pink and beige marble from, of course, Italy. And yes, you can afford to shop in Bulgari. You can buy a pair of cuff links for $70.

BULGARI, 730 Fifth Avenue, at 57th Street

▼

CARTIER: Don't be afraid of the big-time spenders who shop here—there're several different departments, and nooks and crannies for all kinds of merchandise.

CARTIER, 653 Fifth Avenue, at 52nd Street

▼

SAKS FIFTH AVENUE: Saks Fifth Avenue has managed to make itself indispensable to us. It has a large selection of everything (except furniture), so it serves as that one-stop shopping spot we all crave—especially when we're busy.

SAKS FIFTH AVENUE, 611 Fifth Avenue, at 50th Street

▼

ALFRED DUNHILL: If you want the total New York experience, you must stop by Alfred Dunhill. Check out the humidors, the cigars, the silk dressing robes, and the plush cashmeres. You get what you pay for, and this is one of the finest men's shops in the world.

ALFRED DUNHILL, 620 Fifth Avenue, at 50th Street

▼

LORD & TAYLOR: This is a classic American department store that caters to the all-American look.

LORD & TAYLOR, 424 Fifth Avenue, at 38th Street

West 34th Street

T he West 34th Street neighborhood is actually a zigzag stretch from Penn Station
to Fifth Avenue by way of a lot of shopping real estate—much of it new. You
can take a bus from Fifth Avenue to Penn
Station and then walk back, or just prowl on
your own. Don't miss **A&S PLAZA, MACY'S,
THE GAP OUTLET** (which doesn't have the great
bargains you are hoping for), **THE GAP** itself,
KIDDIE CITY, the several branches of **CONWAY**
(including a Bed & Bath Conway's, a Kids'
Conway's, etc.), and a really terrific branch of
EXPRESS.

57th Street

M ore a state of mind than a neighborhood, 57th Street is a high-ticket address for residential and retailing real
estate, especially where it bisects Fifth
Avenue. Although the street does stretch across
the island, we consider it to end in the west at
the Russian Tea Room (at 150 West 57th Street)
and begin in the east at Park Avenue. In these
three or four blocks you'll find a lot of expensive antiques shops (many are upstairs), art
galleries, a few design firms, many clothing
shops, and an air of European superiority en-
veloping those who walk the street. There're
rarely any bargains here, but this is the commercial area that you want to soak up and
enjoy. Don't miss:

MARTHA: You have to go one block north of 57th Street, but for a certain shopper it's worth the detour. Martha and her daughter run the fanciest store in New York, possibly in the world, where the ladies who lunch sit down on brocade loveseats, sip tea, and shop. All major designers like Bill Blass, Galanos, Carolina Herrera, and others are sold. Martha International sells a younger, kickier look from up-and-coming and established designers.

MARTHA, 475 Park Avenue, at 58th Street
MARTHA INTERNATIONAL, 473 Park Avenue, at 58th Street

▼

LILLY RUBIN: There are Lilly Rubin branches in other cities, but this one has the best selection of glitz and Joan Collins tea dresses. They will make to measure and copy the latest styles from Paris.

LILLY RUBIN, 22 West 57th Street

▼

ANN TAYLOR: Even if you have an Ann Taylor in your hometown, you will enjoy stopping in here to see the large selection stuffed into a narrow, multifloor space.

ANN TAYLOR, 3 East 57th Street

▼

DEMPSEY & CARROLL: This doesn't look like much from the outside, but it is one of the most elegant suppliers of stationery to debs and their moms. They will keep your die for you.

DEMPSEY & CARROLL, 110 East 57th Street

▼

LAURA ASHLEY: This is a small Ashley boutique, like the branches in smaller or foreign cities, and it carries most everything in the ready-to-wear line. There are several other branches throughout Manhattan.

LAURA ASHLEY, 21 East 57th Street

▼

N. PEAL: Peal is about the most expensive cashmere store in London, so the New York prices may make you wince. However, Peal has always had the best selection of high fashion in cashmere—this is not where you go for a turtleneck! Men's socks come in a million shades.

N. PEAL, 118 East 57th Street

Lower Fifth Avenue/SoFi

For those who want to be on top of it, Fifth Avenue is indeed the place to be and to see—but it's lower Fifth Avenue we're talking about! So come on down, as they say on a game show: SoFi means South of Flatiron. Get off the Fifth Avenue downtown bus at 23rd Street, right where Fifth Avenue veers to the right, and right at the famous triangular Flatiron Building.

The gentrification of this area began a few years back when some publishing companies took advantage of the low rentals in the gorgeous big buildings on Lower Fifth. With publishing types in the neighborhood, fine eateries quickly followed. It didn't take long for retail to perk up. There's a **BARNES & NOBLE** bookstore (105 Fifth Avenue, at 18th Street)—a longtime tenant, not a new trendie. **BARNEYS** is not far away (106 7th Avenue, at 17th Street), and if you walk one block north you get to the sporting-goods store **PARAGON** (867 Broadway, at 18th Street) and the Greenmarket at Union Square. But stay right on Fifth to experience one of New York's hottest neighborhoods.

PAUL SMITH: Smith is a London designer known for his inventive ways with quality clothes that appear to be traditional but have a tiny twist to them—like unusual colors or fabrics. While he makes menswear, many items in the store are for either sex. Prices are high, to match the quality.

PAUL SMITH, 108 Fifth Avenue, at 16th Street

▼

ALAIN MIKLI: Francophiles already know Mikli's name—he's famous in Paris for innovative (and sometimes outrageous) eyeglass frames. Prices are a little higher than run-of-the-mill frames, but you get what you pay for. Large celebrity clientele, and the fashion-conscious bunch. Frames begin at $100. Well worth the trip downtown if you need spectacular specs.

ALAIN MIKLI, 100 Fifth Avenue, at 15th Street

▼

DAFFY'S: This is one of New York's best bargain basements—35,000 square feet on two levels, jammed with bargains for men, women, and children. Stock varies tremendously—a lot of it comes from big-name department stores after they've taken it off the floor.

DAFFY'S, 111 Fifth Avenue, at 18th Street

▼

EMPORIO ARMANI: Where Giorgio Armani goes, we follow. This huge shop (10,000 square feet) is like the Rome branch of Emporio, where hipsters with money can buy something from the master in an easygoing fabric (often denim) at a somewhat affordable price. There's a line of bath salts and other luxury items if you find the jeans too *cher*.

EMPORIO ARMANI, 110 Fifth Avenue, at 18th Street

DOT ZERO: Dot Zero is a fun store. The look is kind of high-tech and trendy while still very New York and smart. A lot of the stuff is Japanese. Tabletop and giftables are sold here, as well as home furnishings and decorative objects, but this is more like the kind of store where you happen to wander in and then find a million things you need for yourself.

DOT ZERO, 165 Fifth Avenue, at 22nd Street

BOY OH BOY: Maybe because we have sons, maybe because we shopped at a similar store in L.A., or maybe just because the time has come—whatever the maybe, we're happy to have a store just for boys that goes all the way up to size 20 when many stores stop short at the size 14s. While there are some toys and accessories here, and a few gift items, this is really a one-stop minimart for dressing your son from head to toe. And the store is open seven days a week.

BOY OH BOY, 18 East 17th Street

KENNETH COLE: Cole has made as much of a name for himself in advertising and char-

ity work (he is very involved with AIDS aware-
ness and donations programs) as he has for his
shoe designs and stores. Trendy to the max,
Cole has a few stores around town, including
this newer one on Fifth.

KENNETH COLE, 95 Fifth Avenue, at 17th
Street

▼

MATSUDA: The building may be a hundred
years old, but the clothes sold at Matsuda are a
hundred years ahead of their time. Matsuda is a
Japanese designer who does elegant and expensive
sportswear in classic shapes with a flair appropriate for those on the cutting edge of fashion
or rock and roll. Prices begin around $100 but fall
more frequently into the $300–$400 range.

MATSUDA, 156 Fifth Avenue, at 21st Street

Madison Avenue

Welcome to the U.S. version of European
shopping, where every big-name designer has a boutique on Madison
Avenue. When we speak of Madison
Avenue we mean three different parts of the
long street that runs parallel to Fifth Avenue.
From 59th Street to 79th Street is where the
fancy European boutiques congregate; the Midtown area is still blossoming but hosts some
nice boutiques and branches of famous stores;
and the area just north of 42nd Street is chock-
ablock with men's clothiers. At its Downtown
end, Madison Avenue has several wholesale
gift buildings; at its upper end there are homes
over the storefronts and art galleries.

The area we call Middle Mad is coming into

its own in the low 50s, and Upper Madison is hot in the Carnegie Hill area. (See page 77.)

So you walk along a street that has the feel of Europe, the ambience of old New York, the smell of money. The most interesting thing about the shops along upper Madison Avenue—aside from the shops themselves—is that only a few of them are money-makers. The big names feel compelled to be here for prestige purposes. The recognition that comes from having a shop here helps propel them into the big leagues. Also, most of the designers themselves do not own those shops. There is another interesting aspect to Madison Avenue: Many very successful middle-of-the-road designers are now opening their own shops on upper Madison. We're talking the kind of designers who sell to every major department store, who are worth millions, but who are not ranking members of the Great American Designer Club like Calvin Klein or Ralph Lauren. Tahari has such a shop; so does Nicole Miller. These stores offer a wonderful environment, a great selection of these designer clothes, and the opportunity to find something moderately priced in a high-priced area where you might otherwise feel uncomfortable.

Madison Avenue makes a very simple tour of itself: You simply walk up one side of the street and down the other. Our favorite way to tour: Walk crosstown from Fifth Avenue on 57th Street one block to Madison Avenue. Walk Uptown on Madison Avenue until 90th Street, taking the east side of the street. Cross the street at 90th and walk back Downtown, now on the west side.

Depending on our mood, or the bulk in our wallets, we take in a few or all of the shops. You may just want to do galleries; perhaps you prefer antiques. We love ready-to-wear and always try to visit the big names (see pages 114–132) and these boutiques:

FURLA: Great handbags in the moderate to upper price range, but so different and sophisticated that they give off the unspoken message that you are a woman of style. Note the hot-colored leathers and the unique styles. There is a Furla boutique on the first floor of Saks. There also are accessories, although earrings can be expensive.

FURLA, 705 Madison Avenue, at 63rd Street

▼

THE GAZEBO: Americana-type home fashions and dresses; a total-concept kind of place. Most things are new, but they feel old-fashioned. Quilts; patchworks; wonderful at Christmas; cute baby clothes and Laura Ashley–look dresses for grown-ups.

THE GAZEBO, 660 Madison Avenue, at 61st Street

▼

THE LS COLLECTION: Lazy Susan, get your elbows off the table . . . and into this shop owned by the owners of the Lazy Susan shops in Japan. The space is so sensational to look at that you may not care if you buy anything or not. It's large (about 4,000 square feet), and was created by the firm Patino/Wolf. The decor is plain old drop-dead elegant. Tabletop is the name of the game, with a lot of gifts—perfect house presents for perfect snobs come from this store. While a lot of the merchandise is in the $500 category, don't panic—there are affordable things here.

THE LS COLLECTION, 765 Madison Avenue, at 62nd Street

▼

STEWART ROSS: Handknit sweaters from England; fun, imaginative clothes for everyone. Expensive, but oh, so hip.

STEWART ROSS, 754 Madison Avenue, at 65th Street

▼

LA LINGERIE: If you thought Victoria's Secret was something, wait till you get here. Don't be put off by how fancy and expensive it is; this is something to work toward. Whoever the women are who can afford this stuff, we want to be one of them.

LA LINGERIE, 792 Madison Avenue, at 67th Street

▼

TAHARI: A smallish but chic store for the woman who needs office clothes and who loves this line. This is a beautiful store with gorgeous clothes in the not overly expensive tradition.

TAHARI, 802 Madison Avenue, at 68th Street

▼

MABEL'S: We're suckers for Americana and for pussycats. This is the most professionally cute shop we've ever been in. Ask about the medals with the pet pictures ... one of the most imaginative gifts you'll get for anyone.

MABEL'S, 849 Madison Avenue, at 70th Street

▼

RALPH LAUREN/POLO: Of course, the highlight of Madison Avenue is the Polo shop, no doubt about it. This place is nothing if not incredible. The dense crowds and the hunting pictures and the little rooms filled with wood paneling and so much merchandise can be overwhelming. Don't miss the home shop.

RALPH LAUREN/POLO, 867 Madison Avenue, at 72nd Street

Middle Mad

The Midtown Madison Avenue corridor has been hanging in the "what if" department for decades. At one time the area was considered very hot, when YSL's men's shop opened at Madison and 54th Street. But the store went out of business, and retailers' high hopes were dashed. In the last year or so, the Itokin Plaza and the handful of upscale shops in the two-block area around 53rd and 54th have come back into focus now that **TALBOTS** has opened across the street. With places like **ROBIN IMPORTERS** (see page 236), **LAMSTON, HALLMARK CARD SHOP,** and **CONCORD CHEMISTS,** as well as the flashier choices, this area has something to offer the out-of-town shopper as well as those who work nearby or those in transit from Saks to Uptown. Whether it ever competes with Uptown Madison is another story; but there is plenty to like right here in Midtown.

ITOKIN PLAZA: The Japanese invasion of New York is apparent in this chain of specialty stores that carry mostly the wares of both no-name and big-name Japanese designers. If you are a shoe freak, look no further than Tokio, one of our favorite shoemakers. There's also a Courrèges here.

ITOKIN PLAZA, 520 Madison Avenue, at 54th Street

▼

CAROLL: One of the best resources for moderately priced ($50 to $100) fashion knits in New York. You'll get your sweater basics in the fall and pull-on cotton knit play clothes in summer. They have 132 shops around the world, and several in Manhattan.

CAROLL, 520 Madison Avenue, at 53rd Street

▼

COSMETICS PLUS: This small chain of stores has branches in many Manhattan business areas; they cater to the women who work in the office buildings who may need mascara or a pair of panty hose. They offer a 10% to 20% discount on many major American and European brands, and sell fragrance as well as health and beauty aids. Always a great place to roam and explore.

COSMETICS PLUS
515 Madison Avenue, at 53rd Street
666 Fifth Avenue, at 53rd Street

▼

FOGAL: Fogal tights cost from $15 to $178 a pair, and they never seem to run. We've worn the same pair for years and can't get over it. If your $4 jobs are a joke, you might want to get serious. There's a Fogal boutique in Saks. Prices are slightly less expensive in Europe.

FOGAL
510 Madison Avenue, at 53rd Street
680 Madison Avenue, at 62nd Street

▼

TALBOTS: The second Talbots shop in Manhattan is one of the first to brighten up the high-traffic area of the new Madison Avenue. The store is in a charming redbrick town house. Talbots' clothes are for those who want the Ralph Lauren look at less than the Ralph Lauren price, and this store delivers on all of its three floors. Unfortunately, the children's line was not included in the original plan, and you'll have to continue to count on the catalogue.

TALBOTS, 525 Madison Avenue, at 53rd Street

Carnegie Hill

S o there it was, the basic Carnegie (as in Andrew Carnegie) mansion, which has since been converted to the Cooper-Hewitt Museum, a branch of the Smithsonian. The Carnegie name still influences this neighborhood on upper Madison Avenue, which, over the last two years, has been slowly developing into a hot retail area.

A residential area of grace and refinement, Carnegie Hill, in the low 90s, has a few select shops clustered on Madison Avenue (sometimes called Upper Mad). Some are branches of European stores (**JACADI, BONPOINT, BALLOON**); some are original retailers. **PENNY WHISTLE,** the innovative kiddie store, began here in the neighborhood where the owners live. **J. McLAUGHLIN** has one of their shops here, and because the owners are also neighborhood residents, it's one of their prize stores. Several of the businesses are child-related, because this is an upscale residential neighborhood, but all the stores have a nice, homey feel to them. The large number of new restaurants that have come on board makes this the perfect place for lunch and a quick browse.

SWEET NELLIE: One of those adorable stores where you want to buy everything, Sweet Nellie is an Upper Madison must for shoppers in the know. You'll find the country look here in gifts and table items. Some things are very affordable, but we thought others a bit expensive for what they were.

SWEET NELLIE, 1262 Madison Avenue, at 90th Street

▼

ANN CRABTREE: One of the small boutiques in the Upper Mad area, Ann Crabtree thrives because she carefully buys just the right look for her clients—combining Calvin Klein, Charlotte Neuville, and a few special, but lesser-known, designers who provide the rich sportive look for city chic.

ANN CRABTREE, 1310 Madison Avenue, at 92nd Street

▼

ADRIEN LINFORD: Michele's favorite store in the area: She shops for coffees and teas, tabletop, gifts, unusual pieces of china, etc. It's kind of the lean Italian look meets the Queen Victoria look.

ADRIEN LINFORD, 1320 Madison Avenue, at 93rd Street

JANET RUSSO: Quite the hit of Nantucket, Russo fits into the neighborhoody atmosphere with her trendy clothes for the tweens and twenties set—she's got everything from headbands that are splashier than plain black velvet to strapless sundresses. Not cheap, but very with-it and popular, in an almost statusy way.

JANET RUSSO, 1270 Madison Avenue, at 90th Street

Upper West Side

We came of age on the Upper West Side; the Upper West Side came of age long after we moved out. Now it is the kind of neighborhood that, if you remember what it used to be, actually has to be seen to be believed. We don't know one person who knows the old Upper West Side who can begin to comprehend what has happened here without seeing and experiencing it. This is a real family neighborhood, and the streets are thick with young moms pushing baby carriages and lined with the kinds of stores that cater to their needs. Shopping on the Upper West Side is concentrated on the avenues: Broadway, Amsterdam, and Columbus. It stretches from Lincoln Center, at 66th Street, up into the 90s. Each avenue has its own distinctive shopping personality. There is a pretty quick turnover in stores and restaurants, with new ones popping up constantly. If you like markets, I.S. (Intermediate School) 44, at 77th Street and Columbus Avenue, is one of the best (see page 209).

Broadway

Upper Broadway is full of high-rise condos and trendy restaurants these days, but still has many of the old staples clustered from the high 60s to the mid 80s. There's an **ANN TAYLOR** (No. 2017), with a good selection of Joan & David footwear. Choose from two of the many **GAP** stores that abound in this area (No. 2109 and No. 2373). There's also a **GAP KIDS** (No. 2373). Check out the **BODY SHOP** (No. 2195) for environmentally sound body treats. **BOL-TON'S** (No. 2251) offers discount designer women's wear. There's a branch of **UNITS** (No. 2250) for quick and easy dressing, and a **BA-NANA REPUBLIC** (No. 2376) for your safari gear. For the home there's a good-sized **CON-RAN'S HABITAT** (No. 2248). There are also a few special finds:

THE NEW YORK LOOK: These five modern, high-tech shops showcase clothing from moderately priced designers like Tahari and Basco, with some more expensive pieces from Perry Ellis and the like mixed in. There is a shop exclusively for shoes, and the other four stores all carry accessories and jewelry. If you want a sophisticated city look in one stop, this is the place to find it all.

THE NEW YORK LOOK
2030 Broadway, at 69th Street
1411 Sixth Avenue, at 57th Street
570 Seventh Avenue, at 41st Street
30 Lincoln Center, Broadway at 62nd Street
(two shops, one is shoes only)

▼

ZABAR'S: An institution on the Upper West Side, it takes up two floors on nearly a whole block. The crowded first floor is a supermarket of gourmet goodies: cheeses, smoked fish, imported specialties, and prepared foods. The second floor is stocked with cookware and kitchen utensils. You can find toasters, espresso machines, microwaves, and smaller electric gadgets from the top names. Open until midnight on Saturday, should you have a late-night craving.

ZABAR'S, 2245 Broadway, at 80th Street

Amsterdam Avenue

Amsterdam Avenue is a surprise. Don't walk along the whole avenue; you may think you're in the wrong neighborhood to do any shopping at all. Instead, head straight to the blocks in the high 70s through the 80s, where there are some antiques shops and a few other gems that make the whole trip worthwhile:

BATH ISLAND: Back in the 1970s there was a store called the California Body Shop; it specialized in bath goods and cosmetics that were biodegradable and made from all-natural ingredients. Sound familiar? An English company called the Body Shop bought up the stores, and the rest is history. Bath Island is run by one of the owners of the California Body Shop, and it offers hair and bath products, creams, cleansers, lotions, and essential perfume oils in a bright and airy setting.

BATH ISLAND, 469 Amsterdam Avenue, at 83rd Street

▼

ALLAN & SUZI, INC.: If you're looking for an eye-popping ensemble at a real bargain price, look no further. Grab a cab and head for this store with an international reputation in "retro fashion." Don't stop to stare at the silver glitter eight-inch platform shoes in the window, but dash right in and start trying on "gently worn" items from designers such as Fabrice, Patrick Kelly, Gianfranco Ferré, Bob Mackie, Christian Lacroix, or Azzedine Alaïa. The clothing comes from designers, socialites, and celebrities. Some of the merchandise is too funky for us, but with prices that run from $10 to $8,000 there's guaranteed to be something here for everyone's taste. If only we could figure out where to wear the rainbow sequin dress Mark Bauer created for Whitney Houston. . . .

ALLAN & SUZI, INC., 416 Amsterdam Avenue, at 79th Street

▼

A SHOW OF HANDS: A "Contemporary Craft Cooperative," this is a good resource for one-of-a-kind gifts. There are quilts, sculpture, handblown glass ornaments, silk-screen and batik fabrics, and jewelry (pull out the second and third drawers of the display cases to see more choices).

A SHOW OF HANDS, 531 Amsterdam Avenue, at 86th Street

▼

GALLERY 532: Two floors of furniture from the Arts and Crafts movement, as well as some old books, pottery, china, photographs, and Tiffany lamps. Many signed pieces.

GALLERY 532, 532 Amsterdam Avenue, at 86th Street

▼

THE CAT STORE: We've said it before— we're crazy for cats. And this store has them to spare: cats on clothing, on jewelry, on key chains, on kitchenware. There are stuffed cats, and even a line of cat mystery books by

Lillian Jackson Braun. A must for any feline fancier.

THE CAT STORE, 562 Amsterdam Avenue, at 87th Street

Columbus Avenue

Welcome to the mall. There's no single area in all of Manhattan with a greater concentration of the stores you're familiar with from any suburban shopping mall. The unique stores that are retailing gems are still around. It's just that you have to look past all the big chains to find them. But since all the shopping giants are so handy, why not check out: **FURLA** (No. 159A) for Italian handbags; **BANANA REPUBLIC** (No. 215); another **GAP KIDS** (No. 215); **DAPY** (No. 232) for wild and wacky gifts and toys for all ages; **SHU UEMURA** (No. 241), a veritable supermarket of the Japanese makeup we love; **THE WILD PAIR** (No. 280), with a wide selection of inexpensive footwear; **THE LIMITED EXPRESS** (No. 321), three floors of inexpensive separates and accessories for women and men; **TOMMY HILFIGER** (No. 284), for men's and women's preppy outfits; **BASIC ELEMENTS** (No. 302)—you've probably seen these casual men's, women's, and children's separates in major department stores, now see them in a store of their own; **FRENCH CONNECTION** (No. 304), specializing in inexpensive casual and office separates; **OAKTREE** (No. 306–308), for casual and dressier menswear at reasonable prices—sort of The Limited for men; **AU COTON** (No. 312), offering casual cotton sweats and separates; **ACA JOE** (No. 313) for colorful athletic and sports wear; **COTTON GINNY** (No. 311) for more casual cotton wear; **CRABTREE & EVELYN** (No. 322) for bath goodies and other luxurious toiletries; **YLANG YLANG** (No. 324) for ritzy, glitzy costume jewelry; **PUTUMAYO** (No. 339), the home of Guatemalan and eth-

nic chic; **LAURA ASHLEY** (No. 398) for flowers
and pretty prints; **ANDREW MARC LEATHER**
(No. 404), a large shop with racks and racks of
stylish leather clothing for men and women;
BEAU BRUMMEL (No. 410) for men's casual
wear as well as some big-name designers; and
DESCAMPS (No. 454) for linens and home
accessories.

As you're browsing your way past these retail chains we all know and love, keep your
eyes peeled for the following shops that offer
something a little (or a lot) more unusual:

BETSEY JOHNSON: As wild and wacky as
ever, and in twice as much space. Betsey's got
stores throughout Manhattan, and continues
to make waves in all of them. She's always the
first in the neighborhood with something
new—if slightly bizarre.

BETSEY JOHNSON, 248 Columbus Avenue, at
72nd Street

▼

COUNTRY ON COLUMBUS: A tiny shop
stuffed full of folk art, country collectibles, a
few large handpainted pine pieces, baskets,
quilts, lace, and everything you need to bring a
little of the American country look into your
home.

COUNTRY ON COLUMBUS, 281A Columbus
Avenue, at 73rd Street

▼

CHARIVARI: A longtime and strong presence
on the West Side, Charivari has several boutiques in the neighborhood. The Workshop
has more avant-garde fashion, and showcases
Japanese and English designers such as Matsuda,

Katharine Hamnett, and Jean-Paul Gaultier. Sales are legendary.

CHARIVARI 57, 18 East 57th Street

CHARIVARI 72, 257 Columbus Avenue, at 72nd Street

CHARIVARI WORKSHOP, 441 Columbus Avenue, at 81st Street

CHARIVARI WOMEN, 2307 Broadway, at 85th Street

CHARIVARI MEN, 2339 Broadway, at 86th Street

CHARIVARI SPORT, 201 West 79th Street

▼

PARACHUTE: This spare, high-tech store showcases clothes with a Euro-Japanese look rendered in natural fibers that hang with a loose drape and translate to all-American ease. You'll be elegant and comfortable at the same time. Check out the downstairs. You don't have to buy anything here, but you certainly owe it to yourself to come in and look around. There is also a Parachute in SoHo.

PARACHUTE, 309 Columbus Avenue, at 75th Street

▼

MYTHOLOGY: This shop selling adult versions of childhood wonder brings out the kid in all of us. Mythology stocks everything from baseball cards to Marilyn Monroe pictures. Dragons and kites hang from the ceiling; there're toys, books, airplanes, plastic alligators, calendars, and gifts everywhere. The more mystical nature of the store is reflected in their selection of Frida Kahlo items, Day of the Dead carvings from Mexico, and tarot cards.

MYTHOLOGY, 370 Columbus Avenue, at 78th Street

▼

ALICE UNDERGROUND: A good selection of vintage clothes, especially party dresses. Rhinestone jewelry, evening gloves, glamorous hats. Also men's and casual clothing, leather and suede jackets and overcoats, at good prices.

ALICE UNDERGROUND, 380 Columbus Avenue, at 78th Street

▼

ONLY HEARTS: They call themselves a "shop for the shameless romantic"; we think they're the perfect stop for Valentine's Day presents, romantic gestures, or self-indulgent lacy lingerie. As you might guess, most of the merchandise has a heart theme; but some of it's simply romantic.

ONLY HEARTS, 386 Columbus Avenue, at 78th Street

▼

FRANK STELLA LTD.: Moderately priced, conservative, but very nice fashions for men and women. An excellent resource for traditional business clothing and personal service.

FRANK STELLA LTD., 440 Columbus Avenue, at 81st Street

▼

MAXILLA & MANDIBLE LTD.: For the Georgia O'Keeffe freak who always wanted a few bleached skulls around the house, or for the scientific, or the merely curious, this is the ultimate shop for specimens of butterflies and rocks, bones, and other curiosities. Utterly fabulous for kids and grown-ups alike; include it with a trip to the Museum of Natural History, which is right around the corner. We're especially fascinated with the genuine mummy's head in the red velvet–lined display case.

MAXILLA & MANDIBLE LTD., 451 Columbus Avenue, at 81st Street

▼

OBJECTS OF BRIGHT PRIDE: This small shop features masks and other wood sculpture in classical Pacific Northwest Coastal Indian and Eskimo styles. Some jewelry. The shop is closed Monday.

OBJECTS OF BRIGHT PRIDE, 455A Columbus Avenue, at 81st Street

▼

HANDBLOCK: This small, home-style shop is actually a branch of a Canadian chain. There's another store on the East Side at 860 Lexington Avenue at 65th Street. Both shops feature merchandise that offers the country look we love, but does it with many fabrics from India. Remember those paisley and madras spreads from the 1960s? Now the prints (which look surprisingly like some from Pierre Deux) have been pieced together and sewn into bedspreads and quilts. There're also jewelry and some nighties, and a lot of accessories for the home. Refreshing and unpretentious.

HANDBLOCK, 487 Columbus Avenue, at 83rd Street

▼

THE DOWN QUILT SHOP: Not only do they carry 100% cotton sheets and duvet covers, but they have a large selection of handmade quilts. If there's nothing here that catches your fancy, you can design your own. A custom-made quilt will take four to six months. Quilts range from a high of $1,200 to a more affordable $179, depending on pattern, size, and sales.

THE DOWN QUILT SHOP, 518 Columbus Avenue, at 85th Street

East Village

The area that we call the East Village extends east of Broadway from 14th Street down to Houston. Independent designers and artists take advantage of the relatively lower rents to open storefront shops and galleries; there are a number of wonderful and unusual choices for the adventurous shopper. But shopping in the East Village is not for the faint of heart. You'll have to push past bikers in leather, kids with brightly colored hair and safety pins in their noses, a crush of students from nearby NYU, and panhandlers who compete for sidewalk space with vendors. But if you can brave the crowds, you're in for an unique shopping experience. If you're out with teenagers, a trip down St. Mark's Place (East 8th Street) will immediately establish you as the coolest grown-up around and give you a taste of the East Village. If you like what you see, take off on your own and wander and explore the other streets between Third Avenue and Avenue A.

Begin your tour at St. Mark's and Third Avenue, the corner of the busiest block in the East Village. There is an eclectic mix of stores and restaurants crammed onto this short block. You'll find record stores, bookshops, and clothing shops advertising "Rock Star Clothing"; check out **ST. MARKS COMICS** for a huge selection in comic books and T-shirts. If skintight leather jeans, microminis, or vinyl clothing are your teen's style—or yours—don't miss **TRASH AND VAUDEVILLE** for the best in punk gear. If you need to stock up on inexpensive goodies you'll pass street vendors selling scarves, sunglasses, earrings, socks, etc., at cheap prices. When you hit Second Avenue, check out **THE GAP** and **GAP KIDS** at the corner. (Gentrification comes to the East Village.) As you cross Second Avenue and continue east, the crush of shops gives way to residences, hipper-than-thou cafés, and cutting-edge boutiques. If you're tired of shopping, check out the schedule at Theater 80 St. Mark's, which offers oldies and cult classics in the most intimate and pleasant setting in the city. If you're looking for the trendsetting work of hot young designers, press on to the corner of St. Mark's and Avenue A. There, in a row of green-trimmed, pale wood shops that look more like a Madison Avenue offering you'll find **109,** with their selection of European and American designers. **AGI BROOKS** offers retro-inspired classic separates, and will custom-make pieces in different fabrics. **EMPIRIAL HOUSE** and **ALESSANDRA IMAGES** are two other trendy shops in this storefront complex. Heading back toward Second Avenue on St. Mark's, don't miss **LOLA MILLINERY** (No. 102) for fanciful, carefully crafted hats, each handmade by store owner (Lola Ehrlich), or **CLODAGH ROSS & WILLIAMS** (No. 122), where you'll find the absolute latest in fantastic and functional art objects for your home.

West Village

A lso known as Greenwich Village, this is the area west of Fifth Avenue from 14th Street to Houston Street. But our West Village is the tiny neighborhood west of Greenwich Avenue, the maze of streets with names like Bank, Perry, Charles, Christopher, West 10th, and West 11th streets. This is one of the most tranquil neighborhoods in all of New York City. Perfectly kept brownstones on calm tree-lined blocks are companions to an eclectic assortment of well-appointed shops selling everything from antiques to clothing to crafts. There are any number of cute little restaurants and cafés, should you need a break from shopping. This is a wonderful neighborhood for wandering, getting lost, and discovering your own special places. If you're not familiar with the neighborhood, or have limited time, a short walk down Bleecker Street provides a microcosm of West Village shopping. Begin where Sixth Avenue intersects Bleecker Street. Turn right off Sixth onto Bleecker and begin walking. You'll begin in a very commercial area, but once you cross Seventh Avenue, you'll be in strolling and shopping heaven. One of your first stops should be **LAURA HANDBAGS** (No. 249) for well-made leather bags that will remind you of certain high-quality, big-name classic designs but cost considerably less. **CHAMELEON** (No. 270) offers secondhand clothing of good quality, and **SECOND CHILDHOOD** (No. 283) is a must for anyone who collects antique toys. Once you cross Seventh Avenue, the neighborhood becomes more residential, but you can still make a big haul at **VILLAGE ARMY NAVY** (No. 328), where neighborhood residents stock up on Levis, Keds, Lee, and other brand-name sportswear. The **T-SHIRT MUSEUM** (No. 333) offers a great selection of witty tops. If you're looking for new specs, stop in at **JOEL NAME** (No. 353) for attention-attracting frames. The **PIERRE DEUX** (No. 381) and **PIERRE DEUX ANTIQUES** (No. 369) shops are just down the block. **L'UOMO** (No. 383) offers sleek Italian men's clothing. **SUSAN PARRISH** (No. 390) is famous for American antiques, especially quilts and linens. Finish up by staring in the windows of **BIRD JUNGLE,** at the corner of 11th Street—but exercise control lest you end up taking a toucan home!

SoHo

oHo stands for South of Houston (say
House-ton)—it's a neighborhood that has
seen tremendous excitement but is now
past its zenith. New blood is still moving
into the empty storefronts, so the area is not
at all dead, but it is no longer the most "in"
place in New York. Never mind. You can still
have fun here.

Of all the many New York neighborhoods,
SoHo is one of the most individual, most complete, most wonderful for shopping, and certainly one of the best neighborhoods for
out-of-towners who want to see something a
little bit different. SoHo imitations are springing up in communities all over the country.
But nobody does it like SoHo, where the elements of high style, punk art, and European
ambience combine in a totally American way.

Feel free to take our SoHo tour (see page
263) or to get out at any number of subway
stops in the area and just prowl around. Stores
may open late in the morning (many don't
open until noon; many are closed on Monday), but usually they stay open a little later at
night; most are open on Sunday. There're tons
of restaurants. All members of your family will
like it here. Just a few tips: If you don't know
what to wear, wear black. If you feel fright-
ened, don't be. Although the neighborhood is
built up from warehouses, it's perfectly safe.

SoHo is essentially a reclaimed area. In the
1970s you might have gone there on a bad bet.
Although you probably would have survived
to tell the tale, it would have taken you a week
to stop shaking. In the 1980s it was chic to
consider a venture to SoHo. High rentals in
New York, and the big schlepp Uptown, made
it a neighborhood whose time came. As artists

SoHo / TriBeCa

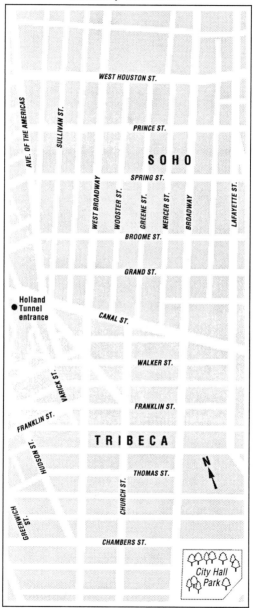

WEST HOUSTON ST.

AVE. OF THE AMERICAS

SULLIVAN ST.

PRINCE ST.

SOHO

SPRING ST.

WEST BROADWAY

WOOSTER ST.

GREENE ST.

MERCER ST.

BROADWAY

LAFAYETTE ST.

BROOME ST.

GRAND ST.

● Holland
Tunnel
entrance

CANAL ST.

WALKER ST.

VARICK ST.

FRANKLIN ST.

FRANKLIN ST.

HUDSON ST.

TRIBECA

N

THOMAS ST.

CHURCH ST.

GREENWICH ST.

CHAMBERS ST.

City Hall
Park

moved into the area and began converting the lofts into living space, they also needed retail outlets and restaurants. In no time at all it was hip to say you knew someone who lived down there, or, even more incredible—that you knew your way around the area, with streets named West Broadway, Spring, Prince, Greene, and Mercer. Nowadays, the living space has become almost middle-class; the retail shops usually are gorgeous, well-designed, and expensively planned. The old cast-iron buildings that the neighborhood is famous for serve as the basis of the architectural style, but space inside often has been gutted to make room for high-tech wonders. Art galleries take up about one third of the retail space; there are even a few museums (the Museum of Holography has a gift shop). About half of the stores for ready-to-wear are chains of successful boutiques that have Uptown addresses. Often the space in which they are housed in SoHo is more outrageously decorated than the Uptown space.

The neighborhood is inventive, bright, clever, neat, and fun. Just because a retailer has chosen this location, however, does not mean he offers bargain prices.

We think the only way to do SoHo is just to go there (preferably not on a Monday, and perhaps for lunch, then an afternoon) and do it. Remember that Sunday afternoon is primo shopping time. There're also a lot of street vendors out then. Don't forget the side streets.

Believe it or not, SoHo is still developing. While all that's chic and trendy for shoppers with tons of both money and style glitters in the designer shops around West Broadway, you might want to find the not-so-expensively-priced but still state-of-the-art, stylish shops on Thompson Street right before Prince Street. Many specialize in antique clothing; several showcase old wedding gowns. There are also several shoe shops here, and an antique furniture shop or two. It's funky and fun now, but this part of town is sure to blossom and give way to women with Vuitton tote bags in no time at all. Before they arrive, head for Thompson Street and seek out **LIZA'S PLACE** (No. 132), **OPAL WHITE** (No. 131), and the famous **BETSEY JOHNSON** (No. 130); **KIMONO HOUSE** (No. 120); **PETER FOX** (No. 105) for shoes for the bride; and then **BEBE THOMPSON** (No. 98) for yuppie kids with money and good taste. **FDR DRIVE** (No. 109) has quite the rep for hot new designers and clothes that are fresh and free-thinking.

ART WEAR: Jewelry that is one-of-a-kind; most pieces can indeed be considered works of art. Robert Lee Morris, who designs the Donna Karan accessories, sells his own work here. Art Wear is one of the SoHo pioneers. Prices are *cher,* but this is serious art. And we predict it will become a collectible.

ART WEAR, 456 West Broadway
ROBERT LEE MORRIS, 409 West Broadway

▼

DAPY: Crazy gifts, such as the plastic flamingo straws you can't live without; toys, stationery, plastic goods, clocks, etc.

DAPY, 431 West Broadway

▼

THE IRISH SECRET: Last trip to Ireland we decided we would open a shop in New York that sold Irish wool clothing, sweaters, hats, and such. Someone beat us to it, because this store is everything we dreamed of. There are wool jackets for men and women and lots of items from Avoca Handweavers; the store kind of feels like an Irish Laura Ashley.

THE IRISH SECRET, 155 Spring Street

HARRIET LOVE: Chic vintage clothing from one of the premier dealers in used or worn; don't miss it. Prices are not inexpensive.

HARRIET LOVE, 412 West Broadway

▼

ZONA: Arts and crafts and handhewn goodies. The most beautiful garden tools, fireplace equipment, plates, dishes, dried flowers, etc. All with a Southwest American touch to it.

ZONA, 97 Greene Street

▼

WOLFMAN-GOLD & GOOD CO.: The table settings make you want to snap Polaroids so you can go home and do it yourself. Class, style, and inspiration, all in one shop. Prices are not low. Don't miss the downstairs alcove.

WOLFMAN-GOLD & GOOD CO., 116 Greene Street

▼

VICTORIA FALLS: Antique and repro clothing that is more sophisticated than Ralph Lauren but still avoids being too costumey. We saw a deb trying on one of the taffeta bouffant dresses that would have made Scarlett O'Hara green with envy. Jeweler Joan Michlin sells her antique gold lace jewelry in a little niche to the side. Very different and unusual; for Victorian types.

VICTORIA FALLS, 451 West Broadway

▼

LA RUE DES REVES: The large space is filled with men's, women's, and accessories—leathers, blazers, stockings, jewelry, belts. Prices are no higher than in normal stores; $200 buys you a stunning wool blazer that is right-on chic. Many artisans sell here, as well as makers of hot ready-to-wear. You just have to see this place to believe it. The men's store is called Mano à Mano.

LA RUE DES REVES, 139 Spring Street
MANO À MANO, 580 Broadway

▼

SURA KAYLA: Every once in a while you walk into a store that is so special, so unique, so creative, and so wonderful that you remember that good retailing is good theater and there's no reason to pay $50 for a Broadway ticket. All you need to do is seek out West Broadway in SoHo and then get yourself to Sura Kayla, a florist of sorts selling dramatic dried arrangements, gifts, robin's eggs (wood, $1 each), nests, and wreaths. Prices are high (a basket costs $125), but there's no charge for dreaming.

SURA KAYLA, 484 Broome Street

▼

SALLY HAWKINS: You came to SoHo to be dazzled, to see what you'll never see anywhere else? Step this way. The outside of this shop is silhouetted with the bodies of people who continue their shadowy march through the store in the floor tiles. The designer is from London, and she certainly knows how to put on a show as she displays costume jewelry that might be called art. Lots of it is rather glitzy, but there are more subtle styles as well. See them all displayed in cases, aquariums, or on black velvet. This is a museum to good taste and talent.

SALLY HAWKINS, 448 West Broadway

▼

HEAD DRESS: Not as dramatic as some of our other SoHo finds, but just as fabulous and just as important—Head Dress is top drawer. They sell wholesale, they're opening more shops, they're outfitting the world Princess Diana–style . . . and more. The basic genre is hats (felt hats from around $100 each), but there is some jewelry and a lot of hair accessories, including things like mink headbands. The shop is small and crammed with merchandise and mirrors for trying things on. This is not just a great place to buy but also a great place to go for ideas and notes on hot looks.

HEAD DRESS, 366 West Broadway

NoHo

We admit to being over forty and we admit to being afraid of anything too new and too weird, but we also have to admit that we're in love with NoHo and have even talked about buying an apartment here. NoHo is the area of town between the East Village (which we loathe), NYU (which we love), and Houston Street—thus NoHo, meaning North of Houston. This area has many record shops, flea markets, and young-look shops like **UNIQUE CLOTHING WAREHOUSE** (726 Broadway), **THE ANTIQUE BOUTIQUE** (712 Broadway), and **SCREAMING MIMI'S,** formerly a Columbus Avenue favorite, now at 22 East 4th Street, that cater to the university crowd and the hip hangers-on. But there's a change afoot. Just above Houston on Broadway you can find **POTTERY BARN** and several kitchenware shops, while up at Astor Place **CONRAN'S** has been in place for several years, ready to serve coming-of-age yuppies. Watch this space.

South Street Seaport

We're not sure if South Street Seaport is a neighborhood, a shopping center, or an act of God, but it is something to behold. On a clear day, you can shop forever.

South Street Seaport is built around the old Fulton Street fish market, and is wedged between Wall Street and the water. If you ever want to believe in urban renewal, take a look here at what money and talent can do.

There is a maritime museum here, and it's very interesting, especially for your kids (make this a family trip). There are also three buildings full of shops—many are branches of famous stores, such as **LAURA ASHLEY, ANN TAYLOR, ACA JOE, BANANA REPUBLIC, THE LIMITED EXPRESS, THE SHARPER IMAGE,** and **BROOKSTONE. ABERCROMBIE & FITCH** is here, as well as lots of restaurants and food stands. The Wall Streeters are particularly dense during lunchtime; tourists can take over on weekends. The singles scene is fabulous after work hours.

Wall Street

Although we're not crazy about a lot of subway rides in Manhattan, one of our favorites is to hop on the number 4 or 5 from Grand Central Station and exit some seven minutes (or so) later at Wall Street, where all the excitement of Manhattan's financial and Downtown districts converge in a neighborhood with some surprising shopping highlights.

It's not gorgeous down here. The interesting architecture is reserved for the big new sky-scrapers and housing developments, not the stores, but there are branches of many Up-town stores and of some big national chains as well. **BROOKS BROTHERS** has long held forth (1 Liberty Plaza) in a smallish store as you step from the subway station. But now **ALFRED DUNHILL** has joined up (60 Wall). **ALAN FLUS-SER,** the menswear maven, has kept his Up-town penthouse open but has moved himself and his headquarters down to 50 Trinity Place. Choose from bespoke, made-to-measure, or off-the-rack. And, of course, there's **SYMS** down the block (42 Trinity Place), for the well-dressed man who's into discount.

Women will also find clothes at Syms, and men, women, and children may go gaga as they wander into **CENTURY 21** (12 Cortlandt Street), the discount department store that sells not only ready-to-wear for everyone but also bed linens and other domestic items, perfumes, cosmetics and toiletries, jewelry, watches, shoes, handbags, and some gift items at discounts that range from slight to significant. You never know what you'll find at Century 21; it can be disappointing, but when you hit gold you'll remember it for years. Besides, if you take the express train and get here in seven minutes, what's to lose? Century 21 has a larger store in Brooklyn (at 438 84th Street, between Fourth and Fifth avenues, in Bay Ridge). If you're a Century fanatic it's worth a visit, since selec-tion is much more extensive.

Walk away from Century 21, which is just north of the World Trade Center, go toward the water, check out the Vista International Hotel, and take its bridge into the World Fi-nancial Center, to see architecture meet shop-ping with a great big bang. There are some sixty shops in the World Trade Center build-ings, but the most dazzling ones are in the World Financial Center. If you've spent all your money and seen all the sights, you're conveniently situated to head off to Ellis Island, where you can remember all our forefathers who arrived here penniless!

World Financial Center

What can you say about a place that advertises itself as offering "goods, services, and shops, shops, shops"? Sound grand? You bet. It also possesses one of the city's few double whammies: about seventy shops surrounded by the amazing architecture of these buildings and the Winter Garden space. It's worth a trip Downtown just to gawk. This is one of the most special places in New York!

The World Financial Center is actually a series of buildings (One and Two and then some with names and numbers) that are a part of Battery Park City, an entire new village unto itself in New York. Built at the edge of the city, overlooking the water and the Statue of Liberty, it contains apartment houses, a new school (which looks like a page from *Achitectural Digest*), and all those office towers with spiffy shops inside. Many of the shops are branches of already famous stores, but maybe half of them are faces fresh to New York or at least to the Downtown area. For old faithfuls, look for **CASWELL-MASSEY,** the country's oldest drugstore; **BARNEYS,** in a small shop geared to the businessman who suddenly needs something (probably for a quick trip out of town); **ANN TAYLOR,** full of dress-for-success clothes at affordable prices; and **MARK CROSS** with its array of the world's most handsome briefcases, paper folios, handbags, and photo albums. **IL PAPIRO,** which does have other stores in Manhattan but is not a household name, has opened a shop to sell their made-in-Italy swirled-ink papers.

Other familiar friends include **BALLY OF SWIT-ZERLAND,** which carries well-made, traditional-style shoes to wear with your suits; **CIGNAL,** European-style menswear; **RIZZOLI,** with its selection of special coffee-table and art books; **TAHARI,** a Downtown boutique for stylish wear for the working woman; and **UNITS,** the J. C. Penney–owned store for mix-and-match cotton pull-ons that's taking the country by storm. Some of our other favorites include:

IMMAGA: Created in the image of an Italian *profumeria,* this shop is really a fancy drugstore catering to all the working women in the complex. It carries everything from the most expensive makeup and perfume brands to the necessities of life as a working woman (nail-polish remover, feminine supplies). Beautifully arranged and built with a lot of dash (and marble).

IMMAGA, Winter Garden, World Financial Center

▼

STATE OF THE ART: What will all those fancy executives put on their desktops in the offices upstairs? Italian lights and fancy ashtrays and sculpted In/Out boxes, as well **as** expensive clocks and other assorted elegant and/or high-tech designer gadgets that the yuppie on the move must have.

STATE OF THE ART, Building Four, World Financial Center

▼

GALLERY OF HISTORY: Perhaps you were looking for a genuine letter from General Grant to General Lee? Well, Malcolm Forbes beat you to it. But you can get similarly impressive arts from the Gallery of History, a store selling nostalgia in various forms—everything from the expensive kind of baseball cards (Honus Wagner, anyone?) and movie-star memorabilia to investment-grade autographs and ephemera.

GALLERY OF HISTORY, Winter Garden, World Financial Center

Lower East Side

G randma Jessie and Fanny Brice grew up on the Lower East Side. Neither introduced us to the area. We heard of it as legend, as lore; shopping sagas of incredible buys were whispered in our ears in those first years of New York independent shopping—in the days when $100 went a long way and we discovered that Delancey Street was not too far to go to make the money go further. Downtown (a polite euphemism for the Lower East Side) isn't fancy, but the prices are glorious. This neighborhood originally housed Jewish immigrants who left Russia and Eastern Europe in the mid to late 1800s. By 1910 there were almost one million Jews in New York City, and 600,000 of them lived on the Lower East Side.

The neighborhood has changed, and there is now a large Puerto Rican and Chinese population in the rows of tenements. In recent years, the neighborhood has even been rebuilt, so it's not quite so seedy anymore. Jewish retailers still maintain most of the fashion haunts, and they march to the rules of the Sabbath. They close at sundown on Friday—which may be 3 P.M. in winter—and are closed all day Saturday. Sunday is a full working day. (You can wake up and go shopping!) All Jewish holidays are scrupulously observed. This is the place to do a big haul—to buy all the kids' summer and camp clothes, to get your fall wardrobe, for your man to pick out several suits. This is the place where if you shop properly, you will save more than you spend.

A tip: Come here early in your visit to New York, so if you don't find what you want you will still have lots of other places to try in other parts of Manhattan . . . and Brooklyn and Connecticut. The Lower East Side is a concentrated area of bargain shopping, but you won't find everything here, and you may find cheaper prices on some goods elsewhere.

A second tip: At the beginning of the season, new fashion items may be discounted only 20%. At the end of the season, look for a 50% reduction on the discounted price!

One last tip: Sunday can be mobbed. This is a great Sunday adventure, but if you tend to get claustrophobic, or hate crowd scenes, you may prefer the middle of the week. On Sunday Orchard Street is completely closed to traffic and becomes a pedestrian mall. If you've ever complained that a city was closed up on Sunday morning (most are), come down to the Lower East Side, where stores open by 10 A.M. Since SoHo is nearby, you can walk or taxi from one neighborhood to the next.

The main fashion street on the Lower East Side is Orchard Street, which stretches some five blocks north and five blocks south of Delancey Street. To see it all best, walk up one side of the street and down the other, and simply cross Delancey at the lights. Grand Street, where the home textiles and linen dealers are, is two blocks over, on the south side—this is all in easy walking distance. Good restaurants are everywhere. Although there are several ways to get to the Lower East Side, we suggest you take the "F" train to Delancey Street.

Feel free to browse the whole area and go to any of the shops that appeal to you, although you may find this a slightly overwhelming task. In the past few years, we've noticed a big change in the area: New, clean, modern shops are being built, and the salespeople are actually nice. However, you still can go to one or two places where the help will crankily say, "So are you buyin' or not?" But the sons and daughters of these old-liners, and the new blood that has moved in for the lower rents and the steady flow of customers, are very plugged into the shopping scene. They try to provide you with many Uptown services.

Stores open between 9 A.M. and 10 A.M. and close at sunset, or about 6 P.M. in the summer. We do not know of one store in the area that is open on Saturday. A few Lower East Side treats:

BREAKAWAY: There are two Breakaway stores down here, and they also own Vida Vica, a furrier at 41 West 57th Street where we were traded up to a $6,000 mink coat the minute we walked in the door. (We didn't even nibble.) We don't go here for furs, which are downstairs; we go for name-brand sportswear, and we always find it. Be at the doors at 9 A.M., when they open. You'll see an assortment of merchandise you've never heard of, plus old-time regulars such as Calvin Klein, Yves Saint Laurent accessories, and Spitalnik.

BREAKAWAY, 125 Orchard Street

▼

FINE & KLEIN: Listed in leathergoods (see page 179) because this is such a famous place, Fine & Klein gives a simple 20% discount on expensive handbags. They will order something for you; the walls are plastered with ads from magazines and newspapers showing bags for sale in this small but well-stocked outlet. There's a jewelry nook and a shoe store called Sole of Italy upstairs. Although many will rave to you in a knowing way when mentioning

Fine & Klein and testing your appreciation of the Lower East Side, we happen to think this store is just another good resource—not the last word in handbags.

FINE & KLEIN, 119 Orchard Street

▼

FORMAN'S: This is one of the single best bargain basements in New York, possibly in the United States. This family of four stores is reason enough alone to take the subway ride. Smart shoppers, beware: On new merchandise, the discounts may be only 20%. The stores are of the clean, air-conditioned, modern variety, and the sales help is friendly and helpful. There are nice dressing rooms; there's a lot of stock. If you need something and don't want to pay Uptown prices, try the specialty store that fits your size range. Forman's famous bargain "Annex" has closed, but big markdowns on the already discounted merchandise can now be found on special "sale" racks in the main store. This merchandise can be hit-or-miss, but at these prices it's worth a careful look.

FORMAN'S MISSY, 82 Orchard Street
FORMAN'S COATS/PLUS SIZES, 78 Orchard Street
FORMAN'S PETITES
  94 Orchard Street
  59 John Street

▼

KLEIN'S OF MONTICELLO: Originally a children's store, Klein's now sells some adult sizes without a full range of stock. Their specialty is European looks, so if you want a Fila snowsuit for your toddler, you can find it here at something of a discount. We just don't like to pay $100 for a snowsuit. There are Ts for kids and adults, sweatshirts that are trendy, and Esprit-type looks for kids and all, but we think the prices are high. We sent a children's store buyer here and she came away enthusiastic.

KLEIN'S OF MONTICELLO, 105 Orchard Street

▼

LACE-UP: Lace-up carries major name brands including Jourdan. Whatever sizes they have in stock are what you get to choose from. The availability is marked on the back of the sample shoes that are out for viewing. You have to get lucky. Don't forget downstairs.

LACE-UP, 110 Orchard Street

▼

PAN AM MENSWEAR: Gentlemen, step this way. It isn't chic—in fact, it's just like a big double closet—but Pan Am Menswear is a great place to buy a good suit at a discount. You get a simple 20% off on the big names, but the selection is very good. That's not to say this is Barneys, with its 50,000 suits and its air of status. But if you choose the Lower East Side for a bargain prowl, you've picked a winner here. Don't miss the special sale rack in the center with the 60% reductions.

PAN AM MENSWEAR, 50 Orchard Street

▼

GOLDMAN & COHEN: It doesn't look flashy, but the store is clean, large (by Lower East Side standards), and organized. They carry lingerie, loungewear, bras, and girdles, and have all national brands. This is where you buy those flannel granny gowns you need each winter, robes, bathing suit cover-ups, and dozens of undies so you no longer have to look for the sales at your local department store. Go prepared with a shopping list and you'll be happier. This is a very bread-and-butter kind of place, where you go in and order a dozen pairs of undies and half a dozen brassieres and walk out in five minutes, having saved yourself 25% off retail and an hour of your time.

GOLDMAN & COHEN, 55 Orchard Street

▼

FISHKIN: It looks like just another store from the outside, but inside you'll find a very well organized collection of your favorite designers. The store is deep, so go toward the back for Calvin and Carole Little, etc. Small shoe department toward the front. This is an excellent resource, even if it's a little off Orchard Street; you'll find it worth the walk. Great for young women just getting going in New York, and college kids; also good for the carpool set.

FISHKIN, 314 Grand Street

Wholesale Neighborhoods

Although the city is filled with various wholesale neighborhoods for every business, we frankly don't know where to send you for bargain car parts or aluminum siding. But we do know all about buying clothes directly from the source.

The Garment Center

The Garment Center is the name of a neighborhood on the West Side of Manhattan where most, but not all, of the needle trades have

their showrooms, offices, and sometimes cutting rooms. Although the different kinds of
garments are clustered in different parts of the
Garment Center, the main area where you see
the racks whizzing by with their dozens of
brand-new fashions is on Seventh Avenue
around 40th Street. Broadway bisects Sixth
Avenue at 34th Street, so this part of Broadway,
which is very close to Seventh Avenue, also
houses much of the trade. Many buildings have
entrances (and sometimes two different addresses) on Broadway and on Seventh Avenue.

Seventh Avenue, in the Garment Center, was
officially renamed Fashion Avenue in 1972,
and signs to that effect have been duly posted,
although we don't know anyone who calls this
Fashion Avenue.

The best thing about the Garment Center is
that it is different things to different people:
Some salivate; others shudder. For the person
who has *schmatte* in the blood, the Garment
Center is one of the most exciting places on
earth—the hustle and bustle of the pipe racks,
the screaming and swearing of the workers,
the unglamorous workrooms contrasted with
glamorous showrooms, the part-Yiddish way
of speaking—all send shivers of ecstasy up the
spine. To others, these very same conditions
are cause for severe headache, stomachache,
nausea, and bad nerves.

Some people like to wander around the Garment Center buildings on a Saturday to see
what vibes (and bargains) they can pick up.
The big Broadway buildings (1407 and 1411)
are totally locked up; the smaller buildings
have one elevator man on duty, who will take
you to a specific floor for an appointment.
The elevator men usually have worked these
jobs for years and aren't stupid. They can spot
a tourist a mile away. Don't try to fool them.
Simply ask if any of the showrooms does a
Saturday business. Many samples sales are posted
on the elevator or building doors in the lobby;
doormen and elevator men know everything.

▼ Never venture forth before 11 A.M.; noon is better.

▼ Have cash on hand.

▼ Try Saturday in November (pre-Christmas), before Mother's Day or big gift-giving holidays, or at the end of the shipping seasons, when makers want to move out extra stock.

The less fancy the designer name, the more likely they have Saturday sales—although many big names do open on Saturday. Some places do a special business to those who are in the know. A few places are just happy to see your smiling face and your wallet. And, on top of it all, some places actually solicit business. Someone may be standing on a street corner in the Garment Center on a Saturday handing out photocopies of ads, business cards, or little notices. If you want some positive feedback from the experience, begin your Saturday prowl at 499 Seventh Avenue and merely try a few showrooms, or follow some other people who seem to know what they are doing. Saturday shopping in the Garment Center, especially in the fall months, is *de rigueur* for the intrepid bargain hunter. The neighborhood:

▼ Seventh Avenue (Fashion Avenue) from 42nd Street to 36th Street—women's ready-to-wear, all price ranges

▼ West 37th Street and West 38th Street—coats

▼ West 34th Street and West 35th Street between Eighth and Ninth avenues—zippers and trimmings

▼ Seventh Avenue and 36th Street—bridal (499 Seventh Avenue, 1385 Broadway)

The men's fashion business is not in the Garment Center, but is centered at 1290 Sixth Avenue for higher-end business and at 350 Fifth Avenue (the Empire State Building) for mass producers. Accessories businesses surround the Garment Center: Handbags, gloves, shoes, hats, trimmings, and lingerie are shown in nearby showrooms. Some business is moving out to Brooklyn, but not enough for you to consider it a rival to the Garment Center. After all, there can be only one Seventh Avenue.

The wholesale fur business adjoins the Garment Center and stretches along Seventh Avenue for just a few blocks, from 29th Street to 33rd Street, and along a few of the side streets, such as West 30th Street.

Ethnic Neighborhoods

Manhattan is dotted with various ethnic communities. Some are obviously different from the rest of mainstream Manhattan; others are hard to spot because they are so homogenized. Some neighborhoods, such as Little Italy, are shrinking. Others are expanding. Chinatown is actually moving in on parts of Little Italy. Some are barely known to tourists, locals, or anyone outside the old country—such as the Ukrainian neighborhood in the East Village. Most of these neighborhoods have traditional retailing outlets—cleaners, markets, greengrocers, butchers, even a florist. They are most famous for their restaurants and prepared foods. But every now and then you wander across a retail shop or two that is selling you the real McCoy, such as a shop where the Scandinavian fishermen's sweaters really come from Scandinavia. Unless you have a specific need for something from back home, or are on an eating binge of nostalgic proportions, only one ethnic neighborhood is really worth the trouble of getting there—the Lower East Side. But don't ignore other neighborhoods.

Chinatown

Chinatown is popular for tourists and locals who want a good meal. New York has one of the best Chinatowns in the United States—competing with San Francisco's. Despite the number of visitors to the area, the community is socially closed to outsiders. But tourism is big business, and Chinatown is full of smart businesspeople. They've put pagodas on top of the phone booths, and colorful silks dance in the windows of the shops. There are stores, restaurants, tea gardens, and even enough parking lots (a parking space in New York is a hot commodity) to make everyone happy. Don't forget the Chinese New Year celebration, which usually falls in the first week or so of February. For shoppers, there are old-fashioned Chinese grocery stores as well as open-air markets (on Canal Street) and specialty markets. And what would Chinatown be without its shops full of silk bedroom slippers, T-shirts, teacups, and kung fu posters?

Yorkville

The area we label Yorkville stretches along the Upper East Side from 79th to 86th streets and actually includes several different neighborhoods—one Czechoslovakian, one Hungarian, and the other German. This is a residential area that has come of age with the arrival of the yuppies. The old-fashioned stores and resources are mixed with the brand-new ones, and the overwhelming feel of the neighborhood is not ethnic at all. Unless you call Upward Mobility a new nationality.

Walk along First Avenue from 70th to 76th streets, then switch to Second Avenue and walk uptown to 86th Street. You'll pass several restaurants, delis, bakeries, and beer houses, and you'll also pass a **PAPRIKA-WEISS** at 1546

Second Avenue, in a Hungarian part of York-ville. Gourmets the world over use this shop as a resource for cooking supplies, but we like to restock our Herend china at more reason-able prices than Downtown.

Little Italy

Mostly, we go to Little Italy to eat, not shop. We love the big festival days and like to take the kids. Mulberry Street is the main drag, and bakeries, delis, and restaurants are the main fare. There are a few kitchen-supply shops and some antique and furniture dealers. But then, it's so hard to shop when you have *gelato* in your hand. Don't forget the big festivals, both major-league eating affairs. (The San Gennaro Festival is in September, the Saint Anthony Festival in spring ... actual dates vary but will be listed in *New York* magazine, *Where,* etc.)

Ninth Avenue

Although mostly Italian, the shops here are also Greek. They offer Mediterranean food specialties—and spices galore—gathered in a stretch of Ninth Avenue from 37th to 52nd streets. There is a once-a-year springtime event —a block party. Many of the stores in this stretch have been here since the turn of the century and maintain the same old-fashioned, Old World flavor. Goods are in gigantic bur-lap bags; cheeses and sausages may hang from the ceilings. Prices are often much lower than in fancy gourmet-food stores around town; cooks who care will find the expedition worth-while. Most stores ship and provide mail-order services, lest you worry about walking all over town carrying the extra virgin hand-pressed olive oil.

Ukrainian New York

There are Russian neighborhoods around Manhattan, but this district is Ukrainian. Nestled into the East Village, on just a few blocks, is the Old World that got out before Lenin got in. You can go to the fabulous church, buy cabbage-rose babushkas (made of polyester, no less), or do the only sensible thing this side of the Russian Tea Room: Stop by Surma, at 11 East 7th Street, one of the best stores in New York. At Surma you'll find the incredible handpainted Easter eggs (they have some wooden ones) and the famous embroidered blouses. We even love the little turquoise and gold gift boxes. If you loved *Dr. Zhivago,* this is for you. There's also a marvelous Ukrainian crafts museum devoted to preserving the art and folkways of the Old World. The costumes and embroidered works are marvels for anyone who appreciates fabric, and should be shown to all children who have ever wondered what there was to do when not watching television.

5 ▼ THE CORE OF THE APPLE

European and Japanese Big Names

AZZEDINE ALAÏA: One of many designers to take to Downtown, Alaïa has a typical SoHo shop in a spacious high-tech loft (designed by artist Julian Schnabel's wife Jacqueline) that is the perfect setting for the sensuous and clingy clothes the Tunisian-French designer is famous for.

AZZEDINE ALAÏA, 131 Mercer Street

▼

ALMA: Gruppo Alma is the name of a Milan-based design group that owns several retail outlets all over the world to sell the clothes they create. Their main lines are Alma, a house label; Spazio, for younger, kicky clothes; and Junko Koshino, one of the designing Koshino sisters from Tokyo. All three lines are rather pricey, but they are elegant, well-made, and drop-dead chic, with a very international flavor. Expect to pay $300 for your basic selection here, more for the whole look. You may well find it worthwhile. If you love Alma but don't have a shop in your area, remember that the line is sold to some independents, such as the famous Chez Catherine in Toronto.

ALMA, 827 Madison Avenue, at 69th Street

▼

GIORGIO ARMANI: Armani's unconstructed men's jacket revolutionized fashion back in the 1970s. Since then he has branched into women's wear and the big-name license game. Have you seen the underwear line? It is incredible! Most Armani shops look alike, following the going tradition among designers and franchises these days to keep everything as similar as possible. The New York Armani shop is in beige and black in a style that's known as soft-tech. It's part Italian modern and part softened Japanese.

The Emporio line, now in its own new shop, is the least expensive of the licensed items, and is sold mostly in Europe. There are two regular ready-to-wear lines, black label and white label; the higher-priced black label is made by Armani himself, the lower-priced line licensed through GruppoGFT. Saks has a nice women's Armani GFT department on the 2nd floor; Barneys also sells Armani for men and women in different parts of the store.

GIORGIO ARMANI, 815 Madison Avenue, at 68th Street

EMPORIO, 110 Fifth Avenue, at 18th Street

▼

LAURA ASHLEY: The original Madison Avenue shop at 64th Street is now just for home furnishings; the 57th Street shop has the clothes. There also are more green and typically Ashley boutiques in neighboring cities and towns and in other high-traffic tourist and business areas of New York, such as Columbus Avenue at 79th Street and South Street Seaport. Don't forget to check out the closeout bin for wallpapers. If you think you're a bit sick of the sweet little flowers and sometimes cloying nature of an Ashley print, the line also includes nonfloral patterns.

LAURA ASHLEY
714 Madison Avenue, at 64th Street
21 East 57th Street
398 Columbus Avenue
South Street Seaport, 4 Fulton Street

BENETTON: Benetton is restructuring to strengthen itself: There are now fewer little shops and several big, bonanza stores. They offer over 2,000 designs a year. No joke. Prices are basically the same as in Europe, but New York sales can be magnificent. Expect to check your shopping bags or briefcase with a guard at the door. Benetton has been moving away from the miniboutiques and into giant stores with the entire product line, which now includes even perfume. A few of the Manhattan shops are listed below.

BENETTON
666 Fifth Avenue, at 53rd Street
1310 Madison Avenue, at 93rd Street
452 West Broadway

▼

BOTTEGA VENETA: When your own initials are enough, you are smart enough to hold out for the twice-a-year Bottega sales, where prices can be below the European prices on some of the most fabulous high-status handbags and leathergoods in the world. If you think Bottega is beyond you, think again. On sale, you can get a nice bag for $250; shoes for $100. The Madison Avenue shop is large and complete; it's much bigger than many of the European shops, and lots more fun. This is the kind of store you want to visit in New York even if you don't buy, because it spells elegance and money. The scarves also are nice, and the shoes are a cross between sensible and drop-dead chic.

BOTTEGA VENETA, 635 Madison Avenue, at 60th Street

▼

ISABEL CANOVAS: This is a small shop very similar to the designer's shop in Paris: a dark sort of sanctuary where her accessories are displayed as if in a museum. Since we think Isabel Canovas's work belongs in a museum, this seems appropriate enough. Her belts, gloves, handbags, and jewelry items are original, fresh, and, *mais oui*, very expensive. The perfume is fabulous—they'll give you a free spritz when you walk in.

ISABEL CANOVAS, 743 Madison Avenue, at 64th Street

▼

CHANEL: The New York shop has the same look as almost all of the newly redone Chanel boutiques internationally—it's beige and cream with a few hints of black lacquer. Upstairs for serious clothing. A two-piece wool suit will cost you well over $2,000. If you are a true devotee, check out the Chanel in Bergdorf's and in Barneys. Chanel makeup is sold in almost every department store; there are few discounts on it anywhere in the United States.

CHANEL, 5 East 57th Street

▼

PIERRE DEUX: There are indeed two Pierres, and they own the U.S. distribution rights to a French firm called Souleiado, which re-creates traditional Provençal prints. There's a shop in Greenwich Village with antiques; the Madison Avenue shop is larger and has some big pieces of furniture, but is mostly linens and accessories. You must see the Christmas wreaths. Prices are lower in Bermuda (the Irish Linen Shop) and in Europe. But you may find yourself close to tears from wanting it all. In that case, splurge. You only live once. There is a trade discount on fabrics to qualified buyers; the Pierre Deux line of furniture has just been introduced and is available through your interior designer.

PIERRE DEUX, 870 Madison Avenue, at 71st
Street
PIERRE DEUX ANTIQUES, 369 Bleecker Street
PIERRE DEUX FABRICS, 381 Bleecker Street

▼

SALVATORE FERRAGAMO: Most of us think of Ferragamo as a shoe resource, especially those of us with the size 10½ foot who count on the world's chicest shoes coming in big sizes. But the Ferragamo family has been watching the rebirth of the Chanel business and has decided that they want a piece of the pie. They are expanding their accessories business with more leathergoods, true, but also scarves and jewelry (see the charm bracelet with the shoes on it), and are continuing to push men's and women's ready-to-wear, especially those fabulous Italian pull-on knits for women. A very classy uniform.

SALVATORE FERRAGAMO (Men's), 730 Fifth
Avenue, at 56th Street
SALVATORE FERRAGAMO (Women's), 717 Fifth
Avenue, at 56th Street

▼

JEAN-PAUL GAULTIER: Gaultier made his name in French fashion for being wild and New Wave and absolutely *fou*—in a fashionable way, of course. Since his blast into the business, his clothes have become wearable and his Russian group has inspired an entire subculture of clothing design. He is not *haute* like the big-name European designers; in fact, he lives in Pigalle in Paris and is backed by the Japanese firm Kashimaya. He has his own boutique in Bergdorf Goodman.

JEAN-PAUL GAULTIER, Bergdorf Goodman,
754 Fifth Avenue, at 58th Street

GUCCI: Fifth Avenue has almost as many Guccis as it does Benettons. Pretty soon they may build a tunnel to connect the whole thing. But yes, Gucci has found New York and you shouldn't have trouble finding it. But there are also Gucci factory outlet stores near Manhattan, so see page 243 before you pounce.

The Gucci stores on Fifth Avenue close for lunch.

GUCCI, 683 Fifth Avenue, at 54th Street

▼

PAOLO GUCCI: We mention this shop just to help you sort out your crazy feelings. Mr. Gucci is related to the Gucci family, and has won the right to use his own name on luggage and leathergoods. His shop sells his designs, which have nothing to do with the Gucci of Italy or Gucci USA designs with the interlocking G's we have come to consider status symbols. Paolo Gucci is hoping you will see the merit of his own work and elevate him to the level of status maker. The store also has gift items and fashions.

PAOLO GUCCI, 625 Madison Avenue, at 63rd Street

▼

HERMÈS: The shop is small but beautifully turned out and smelling just like fine old woodwork, horses, and money. The new fashion zip that Hermès has put into its things has made them even more fun to shop and wear. The dowdiness of the ready-to-wear has been replaced with silk sweatshirts and all sorts of cute things you never thought you'd splurge on. Go ahead. Do it. You're worth it. If you've ever dreamed of one of those Paris-style sales in New York, they do have them—you must watch for the ads in the newspaper. Each sale lasts about three days, and people do line up for them.

HERMÈS, 11 East 57th Street

▼

KRIZIA: If you shop for Krizia at Bergdorf Goodman you'll note that the store calls its department "Mariuccia Mandelli for Krizia" because it wants shoppers to know that this is the couture Krizia line. With Krizia licenses going in so many directions, there has been some confusion in past years. The Madison Avenue boutique remains a temple to the stylish, extravagant, and very expensive designs from the creative genius Mariuccia Mandelli.

KRIZIA, 805 Madison Avenue, at 67th Street

▼

LLADRÓ: Lladró is one of the biggest names in Spain—known the world over for their small porcelain figurines. At last, Lladró has opened a shop in New York to sell these collectibles and to introduce a brand-new aspect of the company: Lladró leathergoods. Small accessories and leathergoods from handbags to briefcases, large purses, and even some smaller pieces of luggage are sold upstairs in this shop. The work is so distinctive that while it doesn't have initials all over it, anyone with a good eye will quickly recognize the collection.

LLADRÓ, 43 West 57th Street

▼

MARIMEKKO: Off Fifth Avenue but worth tracking down if you have kids, this shop is a riot of color and excitement and ideas and good cheer. The new pizzazz of recent years makes this a great resource for kids' rooms (furniture, fabrics, accessories) and an excellent place to get some ideas about the use of space and color.

MARIMEKKO, 7 West 56th Street

▼

MISSONI: Although this is a tiny store, you have to see it for the architectural delights it offers. The clothes are incredibly expensive. All black and high-tech, highlighted by the splashy colors of the clothes. This is worthy of a museum.

MISSONI, 836 Madison Avenue, at 69th Street

▼

ISSEY MIYAKE: Issey Miyake recently opened his first freestanding shop in the United States— on Madison Avenue, of course. But suitably far from Bergdorf's, where his clothes are still sold. Miyake clothes are expensive, and aren't for every type of figure, but you've got to wander into this shop if only to enjoy the store's decor—or lack of it. It's a very spare look, with the clothes hung from a swinging chain (or two) that goes lengthwise across the space. Blue comes up out of the floor and you feel as if you are in a museum. It's invigorating and exciting. The lower-priced Miyake line, Plantation, is not sold in this store.

ISSEY MIYAKE, 992 Madison Avenue, at 77th Street

▼

PRADA: This leathergoods shop has all our attention. They'd have all our money, too, if we didn't know how much can be saved by buying in Italy or even in Paris. They also make great nylon tote bags. Their logo is their name punched out in little circles on a strip of leather. Watch for it everywhere. Shoes, $160 to $580; handbags, $200 to $3,000.

PRADA, 45 East 57th Street

▼

RODIER: We travel in knits from Rodier, the famous French mill, and we swear by them. Our little secret is that we always wait for the sales, which offer 30% to 50% savings. Since there are numerous Rodier shops in the New York area, we can always match up all the pieces we need. In Manhattan, we're quick to hit two sources, both in regular shopping paths. The best Rodier shop in the city is the Madison Avenue store (it's upstairs), but there are others. The knits wear well and stay in style forever. Besides their wool knits, Rodier makes several wonderful polyester blouses that look and feel like silk. These, too, are ideal for travelers because you can rinse them out in your hotel room. Now you know all our secrets! A factory outlet shop has recently opened in Woodbury Common (see page 247).

RODIER
1125 Madison Avenue, at 84th Street
575 Fifth Avenue, at 47th Street
South Street Seaport, 16 Fulton Street

▼

SONIA RYKIEL: Sonia's devotees are devoted, but some of them may have to take to robbing banks if the prices keep going up. The velours are affordable, but again—prices can be cheaper in France and Italy. To walk into Rykiel is to part with serious money. The marvelous thing about Sonia's clothes is that they are so timeless. She follows no fads—she is not influenced by bustles or bows or whatever the couture says. She is one of the first and most important *créatrices* and presents style and color in a unique manner that only makes you feel special. There are kids' clothes, too. The sales are great.

SONIA RYKIEL, 792 Madison Avenue, at 67th Street

▼

YVES SAINT LAURENT: There is not so much YSL merchandise in New York as there is in some other cities, so luckily in New York you see only the good stuff. The Rive Gauche shop is large and well stocked; the sales are big events. See if you can get on the private mailing list. Bergdorf's also has a good YSL selection, as well as a YSL jewelry boutique on the 1st floor.

YVES SAINT LAURENT, 855 Madison Avenue, at 70th Street

▼

JOSEPH TRICOT: One of our favorite London designers has become the cult hero in New York. Joseph's look is so *au courant* that he attracts fans from very different social sets, and dresses everyone with panache. Knits are the house specialty. Elastic waists and much comfort; it also travels well. Prices on summer knits begin at about $30.

JOSEPH TRICOT, 804 Madison Avenue, at 67th Street

▼

SHU UEMURA: Have we ever steered you wrong? When we say we've got a fabulous store for you, we mean it. So don't just sit there—it's time to test makeup at Shu Uemura on the West Side. Uemura is a big-name makeup artist from Japan who has stores in Paris and L.A., and who is sold at the cosmetic counters at Bloomingdale's. But part of the fun of shopping at Uemura is seeing the over 600 colors on display. The makeup is not cheap but is priced competitively with other top-of-the-line American brands and is less expensive than Chanel. You can also get makeovers and manicures from in-house experts.

SHU UEMURA, 241 Columbus Avenue, at 71st Street

▼

EMANUEL UNGARO: We once fell in love with an $1,800 scarf here, but there are less expensive items in the shop. Somewhere. This is where big-time money shops, and frankly, my dear, we ain't got it. There is some Ungaro in Saks, on the second floor in the GFT area. This is more affordable than the couture. Luckily for all, Ungaro heard our pleas and has introduced several less expensive lines. We're saving our pennies.

EMANUEL UNGARO, 801 Madison Avenue, at 67th Street

▼

VALENTINO: There are many price ranges for Valentino: Miss V, Studio V, and Valentino Garavani (yes, that's his whole name), as well as the couture line. Some department stores may have some of the lines. If you can't afford the clothes, look at the jewelry, which is in the $100 price range but will make any old outfit look rich.

VALENTINO, 823 Madison Avenue, at 68th Street

▼

WATERFORD/WEDGWOOD: Wedgwood owns Waterford, lest you wonder what these two luxury items are doing mingling in the same store. But then, fine china and fine crystal were made for each other, anyway. This new shop has two levels, with the more expensive and unusual items placed upstairs. On the street level you'll find your basic awe-inspiring Waterford chandeliers casting light on Wedgwood table settings. Toward the back of the rather deep shop there are promotional items and sales by the place settings on certain patterns. Bridal registry? But of course.

WATERFORD/WEDGWOOD, 713 Madison Avenue, at 63rd Street

▼

ZARA: One of the big names in Spain when it comes to young, disposable fashion, Zara has opened a shop in Manhattan that is a tad jazzier than even the nicest shop in Madrid, and offers a better look at the line than you will get in any Spanish city. The two-level, high-tech store, directly across the street from Bloomingdale's, has lots of air and attitude on the street level, but far more merchandise downstairs. The clothes are young and kicky, priced incredibly low (wool skirt: $45), and cost exactly the same in New York as they do in Spain. New clothes come from Spain every week; stock is changed twice a month. If you crave fashion but must live on a budget, this should be your first stop.

ZARA, 750 Lexington Avenue, at 59th Street

▼

ERMENEGILDO ZEGNA: No, we've never been able to pronounce his first name without stumbling, but who cares—Zegna says it all. This old Italian family has owned the finest wool mills in the hills of Biella for over a century. Plush fabrics are the name of the game; the look is conservative in the Europreppy manner. Next door to Bergdorf's new

men's store, but not inside it—as we suspect
Bergdorf's no doubt would have preferred.

ERMENEGILDO ZEGNA, 743 Fifth Avenue, at
57th Street

American Big Names

T he American big names mostly sell through
department stores, but many have opened
their own stores. Many big American designers have "couture" lines that are really expensive ready-to-wear, and boutique lines
that are less expensive. Some big-name American designers are sold in designer departments
of department stores; others are sold as designer sportswear—on a different floor.

ADOLFO: Adolfo Sardina is a Cuban designer (with a Swedish mother) who came to
the United States as a milliner in 1954, after a
stint in Paris with Balenciaga. In New York he
quickly reigned as Adolfo of Emme, the world's
leading hatmaker. His hat clients included all
the big names in Ladies Who Lunch, including
the Duchess of Windsor. Well, one day Betsy
Bloomingdale asked him to make her some
clothes. Then she introduced him to her buddy
Nancy Reagan. His ready-to-wear looks were a
bit wild and creative (embroidered antique
shawls sewn into dresses, see-through leg-o'-
mutton blouses in silk taffeta) before he latched
on to the suit that made Chanel famous. You'll
pay $1,000 and up.

ADOLFO, 36 East 57th Street

▼

GEOFFREY BEENE: Raised in Haynesville, Louisiana, Geoffrey Beene quit medical school after one year, went to Paris, apprenticed for Molyneux, and returned to Seventh Avenue, where no one wanted to make him rich or famous until he went into business with Teal Traina in 1959. In 1963 he went out on his own and made his name first as a strict traditionalist, and now as a creator of sophisticated looks that are soft, comfortable, and irresistible. He was the first American to show in Europe (1976), and he sells the popular Beene Bag line as well as his couture line.

GEOFFREY BEENE
   department stores
   Martha, 475 Park Avenue, at 57th Street
GEOFFREY BEENE BOUTIQUE, Sherry Netherland Hotel, Fifth Avenue at 59th Street

▼

BILL BLASS: The king of American fashion, Blass is known for his personal wit, charm, and style. He's also cut quite a few ball gowns in his day. Check out the couture floor of any of the big department stores, or visit Martha—the specialty shop that specializes in meeting the needs of rich ladies who require privacy and attention. We got a good buy on a suit on a second markdown at Saks once. The mass-produced sportswear is called Blassport.

BILL BLASS
   department stores
   Martha, 475 Park Avenue, at 57th Street

▼

OSCAR DE LA RENTA: Party clothes, evening clothes, and other special-occasion togs are Oscar de la Renta's fame, but he does make day clothes and has a good reputation for his suit line and the less expensive Miss O collection. Born in the Dominican Republic, de la Renta went to Spain to study painting but ended up selling sketches to Balenciaga. De la Renta worked for Lanvin-Castillo in Paris, then came to the United States at the behest of Elizabeth Arden. He bought into Jane Derby in 1965 and dropped her name when she retired in 1967. Although he has designed clothes for Barbie dolls and the Boy Scouts of America, 75% of the de la Renta line is evening gowns. Your college education cost less.

OSCAR DE LA RENTA
  department stores
  Martha, 475 Park Avenue, at 57th Street

▼

PERRY ELLIS: The Perry Ellis name continues to be a big one, despite Ellis's death several years ago. The clothes are designed by Marc Jacobs, who coincidentally looks somewhat like Mr. Ellis. Jacobs was considered an up-and-coming star on his own, and has brought the right pizzazz to the line—his forte is sportswear looks that feel like serious clothes, a credo Mr. Ellis lived by.

PERRY ELLIS, department stores

▼

JAMES GALANOS: Galanos is a California designer, said to be the only American couturier. One look inside one of his creations and you'll know why. Galanos shows in New York rather than in California, and is famous for his creations for big-name ladies, including Nancy Reagan. He sells his samples at Remin's (see page 230).

GALANOS, Martha, 475 Park Avenue, at 57th Street

▼

CAROLINA HERRERA: We list Ms. Herrera as a New York designer since she shows here, but she is from Venezuela. She comes from the Jacqueline de Ribes school of design in that she was a grand lady who wore grand clothes and then decided she could do it herself. She was right. She was chosen by Caroline Kennedy to design her wedding gown. The windows at Martha often are bright with the fabulous evening clothes that float and glitter and glide.

CAROLINA HERRERA
Martha, 475 Park Avenue, at 57th Street
Sara Fredericks, 508 Park Avenue, at 59th Street

▼

DONNA KARAN: What a talent! She took over the Anne Klein line when she was twenty-four years old and now, barely forty, has her own line of everything. Most department stores sell the separates in special boutiques; Bergdorf and Saks have the accessories on the 1st floor. This is high-concept dressing—Karan invented the bodysuit craze. Gorgeous knits, cashmeres, wonderful drape and fit for working women who want to look totally in control and very chic. Not for the timid. Her less expensive sportswear and accessories line is called DKNY.

DONNA KARAN, department stores

▼

ANNE KLEIN: Louis dell'Olio carries on for Mrs. Klein, who died well over a dozen years ago. Lush, plush sportswear that we buy on sale or at the outlet in Flemington. The Anne Klein II line—we buy scads of it in Hong Kong—is affordable and fabulous. There also is a petite line.

ANNE KLEIN, department stores

CALVIN KLEIN: Some call it a uniform; we just call it Calvin Klein—a way of life to us. In 1968, Klein borrowed $10,000 from his friend Barry Schwartz (who is now his partner) and started a line with six coats and three dresses. He personally wheeled his rack of designs along the streets of New York to an appointment at Bonwit Teller, where he was "discovered." His spare, chic line offers elegance and simplicity without a lot of doodads. We buy Calvin anywhere and everywhere—the Bloomie's boutique is a good one; so is the one at Saks. We drive to the factory outlet in Secaucus and to the jeans factory outlet (totally different) in Flemington. We find yet other treasures on the Lower East Side. We live in Calvin Klein.

CALVIN KLEIN, department stores

▼

RALPH LAUREN: Perhaps you came all the way to New York just to see the Ralph Lauren shop. We wouldn't blame you at all. It's in a landmark building (the Rhinelander mansion); has been refurbished with dignity ($10 million); and is part monument, part mini department store—selling only Ralph-designed goodies. Other outlets (department stores) still sell Lauren, so don't panic, but this is a must-see—even if you don't buy anything. Ralph always loved the preppy look, even when he was a kid in the Bronx, and always dressed the way he dresses now. He worked in a men's store, then became a tie designer with his own Polo line for Beau Brummel. He decided that to properly launch the wide ties he was selling, he needed jackets and suits with lapels that were wider—so he designed his own menswear. Women's clothes, kids' clothes, and everything else followed. Now a complete home furnishings line is also available.

RALPH LAUREN
867 Madison Avenue, at 72nd Street
department stores

BOB MACKIE: Bob Mackie has gone from being known as the man who dressed (or undressed) Cher's belly button to being one of the most glamorous designers in New York. In only a few years of doing ready-to-wear, he has ranked himself with the big names. His specialty remains the dress-up, spangly movie-star clothes he is famous for; but his wedding gowns are sublime. He also has a knit line and a sportswear line with prices at retail in the $100–$600 range.

BOB MACKIE, department stores

▼

ISAAC MIZRAHI: People are talking about Isaac Mizrahi the same way they were talking about Halston all those years ago. The hot New York designer is into cut and comfort—his clothes have the high-fashion look of good clothes but fit like a breeze and drape or shift and shimmy with ease.

ISAAC MIZRAHI, department stores

▼

CHARLOTTE NEUVILLE: She's not even forty yet, has been in business four or five years, and has just the right combination of sophistication and wit to make her the talk of those who require precisely tailored clothes of impeccable taste.

CHARLOTTE NEUVILLE, department stores

▼

CAROLYNE ROEHM: When we are reincarnated, we want to come back as Carolyne Roehm. She's gorgeous, she's married to Henry Kravis, the tycoon, she used to work for Oscar de la Renta but now has her own label, and she gives incredible dinner parties. (We read about them and see the pictures in all the magazines.) We think Ms. Roehm gives these sensational parties so people will have an excuse to buy her clothes—which are mostly glitzy evening gowns in the de la Renta vein. We wish she would open a rental business on Madison Avenue—instead of yet another designer shop where you weep because you can't afford a thing; why not a shop where you can rent one of these masterpieces for an evening? Wear one of her designs out to dinner and you'll never be the same.

CAROLYNE ROEHM, department stores

New York Style
(Moderately Priced Big Names)

LINDA ALLARD: Linda Allard has her name on the Ellen Tracy label, probably because she turned the company around and sent it into the big time. Certainly the line has changed dramatically, from a sensible, also-ran, middle-of-the-road line to something as special as any designer collection.

LINDA ALLARD FOR ELLEN TRACY, department stores
ELLEN TRACY FACTORY OUTLET STORE, 165 Polito Avenue, Lyndhurst, New Jersey

▼

DANA BUCHMAN: Dana Buchman used to design for Liz Claiborne. Now she does the same thing but under different circumstances. The line of sportswear that bears her name is owned by Liz, but does not have the Claiborne label. (However, the Claiborne factory outlets do carry the Buchman line.) The clothes are simple, smart, and good for the working woman. We've bought several pieces and find them suitable for everything and moderately priced.

DANA BUCHMAN, department stores

▼

LIZ CLAIBORNE: Yes, folks, it's true: Liz Claiborne has her own stores and they carry pieces to put together a total look. Some are Liz designs, some are other labels. The look is casual and inexpensive, and ranges from work to play. But that won't affect the department stores that carry her clothes, so not to worry. Liz has already conquered the world with her do-everything clothes—she's equally adept with polka-dot stripe knits and with Chanel suits.

LIZ CLAIBORNE, department stores

▼

NICOLE MILLER: Nicole Miller has broken away from her department-store image by opening her own shop on Madison Avenue, where you can see the whole line. Naturally, each department store has pieces. The Limited also carries a good bit of Nicole Miller and her sensible silk dresses, smart suits, and very wearable fashions.

NICOLE MILLER, 780 Madison Avenue, at 66th Street

▼

MAURICE SASSON FOR KIKIT: The name to remember is Kikit—a kicky knit line with one of those fabric hooks on the back of each sweater. Inspired by the Japanese look of big tops with skinny knit skirts, Sasson has one hot line here.

MAURICE SASSON FOR KIKIT, department stores

JOAN VASS USA: We first found Joan Vass when she was making $400 handknit sweaters (with a lot of helpers) for Bendel and Dorso. Her clothes were special but too costly, so she eventually modified them and created the Joan Vass USA line, which uses knit fabrics in hot styles but at moderate prices.

JOAN VASS USA, department stores

ADRIENNE VITTADINI: We always pictured Adrienne Vittadini as a dark-haired Italian beauty, so we were shocked when she started appearing in her own ads and we found out she looks like one of the blond-haired, blue-eyed Ralph Lauren models. But what really matters is not what she looks like but what we look like in her clothes—fabulous. She came into the business via sweaters, brought about the sweater dress, and has expanded to a full line as well as licenses. Freestanding stores are opening in major U.S. cities; there's also a factory outlet store in Woodbury Common (see page 247).

ADRIENNE VITTADINI, department stores

▼

J. CREW: J. Crew isn't a person. It's a catalogue. But like any successful catalogue, this one has decided to go for the gold: a series of stores. There is one located in South Street Seaport that sells a preppy look very compatible with the clothes sold at Abercrombie & Fitch nearby. We're talking cotton knit sweaters, corduroy jeans and skirts, turtlenecks and Top-Siders, and all those practical things so needed for a weekend in the country or a life beyond Manhattan. Prices are low to moderate, which is why the line has been such a hit.

J. CREW, South Street Seaport, 203 Front Street

Department Stores

New York department stores open at 10
A.M. and close at 6 P.M. They have one
late night a week, Thursday, when they
usually are open until 8 P.M. Note that
Bloomingdale's has two late nights a week:
Monday and Thursday. All stores have delivery service, but you will be charged for it. Few
stores have private delivery service anymore;
usually they use UPS, except for large pieces
of furniture. All stores will provide free, simple gift wrap. Elaborate wrapping costs extra.
Usually you can get a free shopping bag with
handles by asking at a customer desk or wrap
desk, although stores also have machines that
sell outsize shopping bags. All stores have
buying services, personal shoppers, and translators ... as well as clean bathrooms. Many
have checkrooms for your coats and packages.

A & S: A & S is a monster, large department
store in Brooklyn and a mini-mart department
store in Manhattan where it sits across from
Macy's in the old Gimbel's space. As anchor of
A & S PLAZA, the store deserves a round of
applause. As a department store alone, it's a bit
of a bore: very small and very blue collar-pink
collar.

A & S, A & S PLAZA, Sixth Avenue at 33rd
   Street

▼

ALEXANDER'S: If we knew the whole story
with Alexander's, we'd tell you. In fact, if the
people who owned Alexander's knew the whole
story, they'd probably tell everyone. What it
seems to come down to is that Alexander's as a

small chain of department stores is not dead. In fact, they've recently opened a new store in the Bronx—their first new store in ten years. They are also considering opening another store in New Jersey.

Meanwhile, the store we all care the most about, Bloomingdale's neighbor, is still caught in a power struggle in which the real estate and air rights are worth more than the current store ... which Donald Trump owns a hunk of. Trump has said he'll go for his own department store, called Trump's, but he's also said he wants Nordstrom to use the space, and that he wants to build a residential tower in the space. It's unlikely that the Alexander's we know now will survive at the Third Avenue location. What's coming remains to be seen ... and shopped. In the meantime Alexander's remains a good source for inexpensive officewear, shoes, and menswear. It's not fancy, but it's a good source for careful shoppers. At least it is at the moment. ... Stayed tuned.

ALEXANDER'S, 731 Lexington Avenue, at 58th Street

▼

BARNEYS: First and foremost, the most comprehensive men's department store in America. Second, one of the most exciting women's stores in America. What class. What style. What a way to go broke. Barneys began about sixty years ago as a men's store—with a large selection and slightly discounted prices. Over the years, it became known to those in the trade and to wise men everywhere as simply the best men's store in America. The stock was immense (some 50,000 suits), the size range was incredible—hard-to-fit men flocked to the store's doors and got a good fit; alterations are free. But even as recently as five years ago, the downtown location was considered a deterrent. No longer. Now Barneys is the new Henri Bendel. It is the place to see and be seen. And some rather interesting things have happened: Other stores have moved into the area to capitalize on the traffic that Barneys is bringing, and the area has become hot.

The store is run by the original Barneys family, and they are all nuts for quality. They have developed a fine private label (Basco); they go to the best dealers and makers and get just a few of something specially made; and they aren't afraid to go with something that's special. Barneys is a family venture, and every item in that store has been handpicked for you by someone who cares deeply. To see the women's store, take the elevator up to Six and walk down the stairs. Don't miss the gift department (Chelsea Passage), antique jewelry section, and children's department. There are restaurants nearby, if you want to make a day or a half day of the neighborhood. There is an information person in the men's part of the store. *Most important tip*: Barneys has twice-a-year warehouse sales that are unbelievable . . . get on the mailing list for a postcard announcement. People line up on the sidewalk at dawn . . . and it's worth it. Barneys is open seven days a week, and until 9 P.M. Monday through Saturday. The new store at the World Financial Center is smaller and does not have as wide a range of merchandise; other small branch stores are opening out of town, but none compares to the original.

BARNEYS
106 Seventh Avenue, at 17th Street
Building 2, World Financial Center

▼

HENRI BENDEL: Now in new digs, Henri Bendel is part of the rebirth of Fifth Avenue. The store concept is changing somewhat now that The Limited owns it. But Bendel's remains good.

One of the shocking things about Bendel's is that it is not necessarily expensive. Each piece is carefully chosen for a certain New

York look, regardless of price. Some dresses are $100; some are $1,000. This is also the place for the perfect house gift; the stationery department and the panty hose department are legendary. Bendel's is still a good resource for big-name designers, as well as for many avant-garde or otherwise undiscovered designers.

Hours: Monday through Saturday, 10 A.M.–6 P.M. Open Thursday evening until 8 P.M.; no Sunday hours.

HENRI BENDEL, 521 Fifth Avenue, at 56th Street

▼

BERGDORF GOODMAN: Bergdorf's is technically a specialty store, not a department store. But it still gets our vote for the best department store in New York. Sorry, Bloomie's. Sorry, Macy's. If we could make only one stop in New York, be it to shop or just to take in the atmosphere, this just might be it. Many designers who have their own Madison Avenue boutiques, as well as those who do not, have nestled into Bergdorf's. Don't miss the gift floor if you are looking for that certain something. There's a selection of English antiques, tabletop, bridal registry, and needlepoint.

Hours: Monday through Saturday, 10 A.M.–6 P.M. Open Thursday evening until 8 P.M.; no Sunday hours.

BERGDORF GOODMAN
754 Fifth Avenue, at 58th Street
THE MEN'S STORE
745 Fifth Avenue, at 58th Street

▼

BLOOMINGDALE'S: We hate what they've done to the cosmetics area, and even though we've had years to adjust to it, we never will. We love the gourmet-food section. The designer floors are neat, but Bloomingdale's can give you a headache. If that sounds un-American, we're sorry. But we're always honest. A trip to Bloomie's is a trip to the moon on gossamer wings: You start off filled with energy and excitement and love everything you see, but as you wear out, you wear down, and suddenly you realize you're lost, the store is difficult to shop, and you can't remember all the departments. You must know the territory or go with someone who does if you like to shop efficiently. Otherwise, just take small doses, always remembering that no one does it like Bloomingdale's and that's why the store has become a legend in its own time. The designer boutiques are excellent; second markdowns can make you very happy. Good petite department. The YSL boutique here is *bonne;* so is the Calvin. The kids' floor is superb, even though boys' has been moved downstairs to the basement, with men's.

Because the store takes up an entire city block, you very much have the feeling of being in two different stores—as in Macy's. The front and back of the same floor can be very different. Explore all parts. You need a scorecard to know who's on first in this place, and entire sections of the store are often rearranged, but there is an information booth between the escalators on the first floor.

Some tips: The store has many entrances. You can enter on Lexington Avenue, even though the official street address is Third Avenue. Also, there is a subway under Bloomie's, so you can coordinate your shopping tours properly. This is the subway line you use to go to Aaron's in Brooklyn (see page 223), and the two stores work very nicely together. Go to Bloomie's to see what you want; then go buy it at Aaron's at a discount; then, if you still have to have something at Bloomie's, when you come back you can run upstairs from the subway station. If your hotel has a minibar, you may want to buy delicacies from Bloomie's for a picnic in your room or for the journey home.

Airline food being what it is, we almost always stock up at Bloomie's or Zabar's. Tell them to pack the food for a plane trip.

Hours: Monday through Saturday, 10 A.M.– 6:30 P.M.; Sunday hours: noon to 6 P.M.; open Monday and Thursday evening until 9 P.M.

BLOOMINGDALE'S, 1000 Third Avenue, at 59th Street

▼

KIDDIE CITY: This is a toy department store, so we think it's just as important as Saks. Toys "Я" Us is coming to Manhattan, but now we can rejoice at Kiddie City. With its bright orange and white canopied entrance, its plastic mural of hopping kangaroos (its logo), and its upstairs crammed with toys . . . it's heaven. F.A.O. Schwarz has only one floor model of the Nintendo unit for the kids to play with; Kiddie City has three Nintendos and one Sega! There's an entire wall of Barbie. Every imaginable toy is sold here, and at an acceptable discount, making these the best toy stores in the city for selection and price.

Hours: Monday through Saturday, 9:30 A.M. to 9:30 P.M.; Sunday, 10 A.M. to 8 P.M. Credit cards accepted.

KIDDIE CITY
  35 West 34th Street
  Union Square, at 14th Street

▼

LORD & TAYLOR: New York regulars who have serious shopping to do often come to Lord & Taylor. The store is most famous for its belief in American designers and its patronage of American sportswear. There's a good, solid children's department of the traditional type and a wide selection of all the designer big names. The store isn't flashy, but many regulars depend on it. Those who know aren't surprised at the quality of the furniture and antiques department; the famous shoe department may be the only place in town you need to go for shoes, especially if you have narrow feet. One of the best things about this store is that it's rarely crowded. It's not as hot and chic and with-it as many Uptown department stores, but if you want to do bread-and-butter shopping and get something done with your time, consider this choice. It's not nearly as large as Macy's; you won't be overwhelmed. Two lunchrooms for a quick pick-me-up while shopping. All store services are available, including store shoppers and translators. Business must be good, since the store has recently expanded to encompass the whole Fifth Avenue frontage.

Hours: Monday through Saturday, 10 A.M.–6 P.M. Thursday night until 8 P.M. No Sunday hours.

LORD & TAYLOR, 424 Fifth Avenue, at 38th Street

▼

MACY'S: Nowadays, Macy's is one of the hottest stores in town. Many prefer it to Bloomingdale's. We think you should check them both out, since they are different. Macy's is two stores joined together (an older and a newer wing), so you will have the definite feel of a front and a back to the store, and they don't necessarily feel related. This is the largest retail store in America and one of the largest in the world. The designer floor is pretty good; the kids' floor is great, and the choice in terms of selection of anything, from petites to juniors to cute but inexpensive clothes, is vast. For kids, you'll be relieved to know that Macy's has low prices and the largest Esprit selection in New York. Don't miss the Cellar, the downstairs housewares and gourmet-food section—

there's Macy's Cellar Grill down here for a burger lunch. Go early. A Kenneth's hair salon for youngsters is on the kiddie floor. The cosmetics department is excellent; so is hosiery. Check out the mezzanine shops, which you would pass by if you didn't know they were there—the Metropolitan Museum of Art actually has its own little gift shop up there.

Macy's is one of the few big-time department stores open on Sunday, from 10 A.M. to 6 P.M. Otherwise the hours are also unusual. Monday, Thursday, and Friday, 9:45 A.M.–8:30 P.M. Tuesday, Wednesday, and Saturday, 9:45 A.M.–6:45 P.M.

MACY'S, Herald Square, Broadway at 34th Street

▼

NORDSTROM: No, there isn't a Nordstrom in Manhattan yet, although there is talk that the Seattle-based retail kings will take over the building occupied by Alexander's. Several suburban branch stores have already opened near Manhattan, yet Nordstroms is taking its time about committing to a Manhattan address.

NORDSTROM, coming soon

▼

SAKS FIFTH AVENUE: Even though there may be a Saks in your hometown, try to visit the Saks in New York—the selection is huge. We get dizzy going around the designer circle of sportswear on Two: Whatever we want is always in the direction opposite from where we began. For designer clothes, however, Saks has possibly the best choices in town. The children's floor has lots of young, hip styles and scads of Polo for boys. The store isn't as large as Bloomingdale's or Macy's, so you can't get overwhelmed. The men's floor is good, too. Generations of fathers and sons have been coming here. There are almost fifty Saks stores around the United States, but only a handful of them are tippy-top of the line. But get this: If you buy merchandise in New York State but return it to a Saks in another state, you are credited with the price of the merchandise but not the New York sales tax! You must mail your purchase back to the New York store to get a total credit. The store has full services for gift-buying, personal shopping, translators, etc. The ladies' room is large and clean, and possesses some chairs in case you need to get off your feet for a while.

Hours: Monday through Saturday, 10 A.M.–6 P.M. Thursday night until 8 P.M. No Sunday hours.

SAKS FIFTH AVENUE, 611 Fifth Avenue, at 50th Street

Shopping Centers

The big malls are in the metropolitan area—Stamford, White Plains, etc. In New York City, you get several floors of retail space in an office complex—such as "The Market" at Citicorp, which hosts Conran's and several other stores; "The Atrium" at Trump Tower; and Herald Center.

A&S PLAZA: If we saw the A&S Plaza outside of Manhattan we might yawn, stretch, and smile politely, explaining that we've seen this fancy Victorian Atlantic City glitz in other cities, and while we like it, it's not new. But in New York, where the concept of the vertical mall is totally new and this style of architecture is thrilling and exciting and invigorating, we aren't yawning at all—we're applauding. In fact, we like the architecture and the mall itself better than we like the A&S department store that takes up a huge hunk of the space.

A&S is a big-time department store on the same lines as Macy's; to compete with Macy's in a smaller framework they have made the focus of the store very narrow. It is therefore carefully bought for working women in the lower- and middle-income brackets. Those who never go anywhere in less than designer originals can shop elsewhere. This store, and the mall that surrounds it, are only slightly above blue-collar level.

That shouldn't stop you from browsing the mall, or A&S, and taking advantage of the convenience of the whole thing. Among the mall's tenants are **PLYMOUTH, BARNES & NOBLE, THE LIMITED, LECHTER'S, AU COTON,** and **SAM GOODY**. And don't forget, **THE GAP OUTLET** is across the street. Mall hours: Monday, Thursday, and Friday, 9:45 A.M. to 8:45 P.M.; Tuesday, Wednesday, and Saturday, 9:45 A.M. to 6:45 P.M.; and Sunday, 10 A.M. to 6 P.M.

A&S PLAZA, Sixth Avenue at 33rd Street

▼

THE TRUMP TOWER ATRIUM: The problem with the Trump Tower is that everybody wants to see it but nobody thinks they can afford anything there—so little actual shopping is going on while the mobs come and go. Donald Trump has gone on to other adventures, but still gets a lot of mileage out of his luxury tower where you can live or shop. The atrium space is Glitz City, with tiers of space (and lots of marble and brass) on five levels devoted to stores—many are branches of famous names, such as **MARTHA, CHARLES JOURDAN, KENNETH JAY LANE, ASPREY, CARTIER,** etc. An escalator connects the floors, but you can also come up to each level in an elevator. Every visitor to New York should see this place. And if you want to buy something, you can get earrings at Kenneth Jay Lane for $35. There are two places to eat lunch here. Trump Tower is also the ideal place to arrange to meet someone.

THE TRUMP TOWER ATRIUM, 725 Fifth Avenue, at 56th Street

▼

HERALD CENTER: Once upon a time Herald Center might have been a good idea. It's hard to remember that far back. As the years have passed and its time never came, the shopping center across the street from Macy's went from bad to worse. We've heard Toys "Я" Us will open in this space. But before Barbie moves in, the discounters are having their day: **REAL NEW YORK BARGAIN STORES** are taking over a lot of space with their discounted sportswear and bargains, advertising items in the $10 range. It's pretty sad in here, but if atmosphere doesn't bother you, you just might find a bargain. And several of the few good stores on the ground floor seem to be hanging on, at least for now. There's an **IL PAPIRO** and a **CASWELL-MASSEY**.

HERALD CENTER, Broadway at 34th Street

▼

575: The poor man's Trump Tower in the not-so-shabby neighborhood of Fifth Avenue and 47th Street. This shopping plaza is anchored by a **RODIER** and also has branches of some big-name boutiques, such as **ANN TAYLOR, LINEA GARBO,** and **JINDO,** and a fancy gourmet chocolate shop.

575, 575 Fifth Avenue, at 47th Street

▼

ROCKEFELLER CENTER ARCADE: On rainy days we've been able to make our way from Time, Inc., all the way to Saks through the elaborate underground system that links some very fancy shopping to the subway station to many of New York's major office buildings. Besides fast-food restaurants and a few nice ones (American Festival Cafe), there are food markets, party stores, demi department stores (**PLYMOUTH**), candy shops, and many service-related businesses—banks, a post office, Federal Express, and men who shine your shoes. Most of the stores are not anything you haven't seen before, but the system is nothing short of amazing.

Above ground is a tiny avenue of storefronts that leads to the Christmas tree (in season) and the ice-skating rink at Rockefeller Plaza. There's a **JAEGER** shop here, a **FIL À FIL,** a **BERNARD HILL,** and a few other nice shops ... including a chocolate shop.

ROCKEFELLER CENTER ARCADE, 30 Rockefeller Plaza, off Fifth Avenue, at 50th Street

▼

PIER 17 PAVILION: This is actually part of the South Street Seaport complex, and if you are just wandering around happily you will probably discover it for yourself. But if you aren't paying much attention, or the crowds are too dense, you might not realize that besides the Faneuil Hall–like South Street Seaport complex, and the short stretch of street-level shops on Fulton Street, there is an additional building along the water next to the lightship *Ambrose* that is really a mall on its own, complete with escalators and a branch store of many of the major chains in America. There's **BANANA REPUBLIC, THE SHARPER IMAGE, THE LIMITED, EXPRESS, FOOT LOCKER,** etc.

PIER 17 PAVILION, Pier 17, South Street Seaport

YAOHAN PLAZA: OK, we admit it—this is a ringer. But it's so much fun you must give it a little consideration. Yaohan Plaza is in New Jersey, home of the Manhattan shopping centers and where everyone who craves a mall should be going. But wait, this is no mall or ordinary shopping center. It's a small strip village that is totally Japanese! The largest store is a supermarket that includes eateries; there's a row of stores selling cosmetics and gift items as well as clothes. The supermarket has a cozy combination of Japanese goods that you can't get in too many other places, as well as American goods, and then a Japanese dry-goods selection (you know, rice steamers, teapots, etc.). The packaging alone will make you nuts with glee. This is a shopping and artistic adventure if ever there was one. You may drive from Manhattan (the complex is just about under the George Washington Bridge), you can take a ferry from 11th Avenue and 34th Street in Manhattan to the Port Imperial ferry terminal and get a taxi there, or you may take the Yaohan shuttle bus across the street from the north exit of the Port Authority Terminal on West 42nd Street. (One-way fare is $1. Shuttles go in both directions with departure on the hour.)

YAOHAN PLAZA, 595 River Road, Edgewater, New Jersey

The Fashion Chains

Note: Many of these chains have additional shops throughout the city. Check a phone book for a complete selection and for the store most convenient to you.

BANANA REPUBLIC: Banana Republic began as a mail-order firm selling the clothes the company's owners found on their travels around the world. When they decided to open stores, they did it the right way. Although each store is somewhat different, they all have a jungle feel to them, with grass-thatched roofs inside the store, animal heads (often wearing hats) on the wall, giant fake elephant tusks, and everything but tom-toms beating. The clothes are preppy fashion through the eyes of army surplus and the world's best bazaars. High style, lots of fun, good prices.

BANANA REPUBLIC
   130 East 59th Street
   2376 Broadway, at 87th Street
   South Street Seaport, Pier 17

▼

CASUAL CORNER: There are almost a thousand Casual Corner stores around the United States, but the Rockefeller Center (Simon & Schuster Building) store is the flagship, and offers a wonderful selection of leathers, suits, dresses, and petites. We think the separates are better than the dressy clothes; we also like the coat selection each fall. A good place to find Tahari, Max Studio, and Kikit. Prices are middle-of-the-road; the fashion accessories are very inexpensive.

CASUAL CORNER, 1220 Avenue of the Americas, at 48th Street

THE GAP: There are Gap stores all over the United States and all over New York—we'd bet there's one in every big mall in America. They have conquered Manhattan as well. Everyone dresses in The Gap clothes; our kids do too. We know where the outlet store is as well. Below, a selection of their many locations:

THE GAP
   1164 Madison Avenue, at 83rd Street
   527 Madison Avenue, at 54th Street
   89 South Street (South Street Seaport)
THE GAP OUTLET STORE, 60 West 34th Street

▼

HONEYBEE: Honeybee is a Midwestern chain with just a small store in New York and a huge catalogue business. They specialize in small sizes but have regular sizes as well. The line offers dressy clothes, knits, suits, and some accessories at moderate prices. They have an excellent return policy, even for mail order.

HONEYBEE, 7 East 53rd Street

▼

THE LIMITED: Sure, you know all about The Limited, since you've probably got one in your hometown. But you have never seen anything like the New York store in any American mall. Don't just walk in the door; stand back and take in the architecture. (The store allegedly cost $5 million to renovate.) Then walk in and don't miss any nooks or crannies, or you may miss Victoria's Secret, the lingerie resource that The Limited owns. (There's also a Victoria's Secret on East 57th Street.) Go up the staircase for more and more and more. While you're walking and gawking, don't forget to look up at the ceiling and then down at the spiral of the staircase. This is amazing stuff that just proves the fact that shopping really is theater. There are hundreds of other stores out there in America, but there is not another one of these.

THE LIMITED, 691 Madison Avenue, at 62nd Street

▼

ANN TAYLOR: Ann Taylor was the first of the new young stores to find East 57th Street, and helped to put a lot of energy back into that neighborhood. Although the store has changed a lot in the past ten years, it still remains a good Ann Taylor, with an excellent selection. This store is a little fancier than other Ann Taylors in Manhattan. Prices are moderate to high—there're good work clothes with the right fashion statement. The catalogue is a must-have if you love the look of stylish separates and the notion that you can find just about everything you need under one roof. This is specialized retailing at its finest, with private-label merchandise and a few big names, all coordinated into understated fashion chic. Don't miss the Joan & David shoes. Call (800) 228-5000 for catalogue or mail order.

ANN TAYLOR
3 East 57th Street
South Street Seaport
575 Fifth Avenue, at 47th Street

Less Expensive Chains

I f you're looking for the latest fashions but not the highest prices, you might want to wander into any of the several less expensive chain stores we recommend. These are big operations that make it their business to copy the latest looks and deliver them to the masses. If you shop carefully and have a good eye, you can mix your real designer clothes with some of these trusty look-alikes.

COMPAGNIE INTERNATIONALE EXPRESS:
To those of you in the know, this is simply The Express, a spin-off of The Limited. But the story is one of the most exciting in retail: The Express stores, cheapie versions of The Limited meant for teens and tweens, didn't make it into retail history. The Limited people tested several overhaul concepts and came up with a nearly perfect makeover: a fancy French name and inexpensive merchandise with panache and flair. There are now seven Express stores in Manhattan. Most are huge spaces; we warn you that the one on Madison Avenue in mainstream Euro-chic is somewhat hard to shop, since it's so cramped. Try the Upper West Side store (which offers men's clothing), or the Lexington Avenue or West 34th Street addresses. After all, space is paramount to the look and the feel of the store, where you can buy summer dresses for $29 and handknit sweaters for $69. The look combines a dash of preppy safety with a hint of London funk.

COMPAGNIE INTERNATIONALE EXPRESS, 7 West 34th Street

▼

PLYMOUTH: Believe it or not, Plymouth is one of our favorite stores. We're great believers in mixing couture with copies. Why pay $250 for a hat when you can get a copy at Plymouth for $28? Some things look tawdry; most look great. Use your discerning eye and you'll consider this a find. There are about three dozen Plymouths all over Manhattan; we offer a selection of convenient Midtown stores below.

PLYMOUTH
630 Fifth Avenue, at 50th Street
661 Fifth Avenue, at 52nd Street
417 Fifth Avenue, at 38th Street

Finds

ARTBAG: It's not that Artbag is the world's greatest handbag store. While yes, it is crammed with handbags and offers much selection, it is a drab sort of store without much romance to it. Better you should know their specialty: handbag accessories and repairs to fine bags, as well as custom-made work. Need a new Chanel-style chain? Want to lengthen the strap on your Hermès Kelly bag? Need last year's bag dyed? Step this way. Their services are expensive, but few other stores offer high-quality work of this kind for those expensive handbags we desperately try to maintain.

ARTBAG, 735 Madison Avenue, at 64th Street

▼

PARTY BAZAAR: Although it looks like a glorified Hallmark shop from the outside, Party Bazaar is the retail outlet for a wholesaler of paper and party goods. Remember when you were a kid, long before the current sticker rage, when your piano teacher put a lick-it sticker on your piece? Dennison made those stickers. They still are sold here. This is where you find the kindergarten diplomas you've been looking for, the special cake decorations, and all your party needs. Right before Halloween is the best time, we think, but every major holiday has a few rows of store space devoted to the selection of cupcake decorations, party plates, and streamers. Don't forget the far back portion of the store, where the holiday items and supplies are.

PARTY BAZAAR, 390 Fifth Avenue, at 36th Street

▼

TENDER BUTTONS: If it's buttons you need, or even cuff links, this small but wondrous shop can occupy you all day. Even if you don't need buttons, you'd need your marbles examined if you don't stop by. *Tip:* You can buy Chanel buttons here. Open Monday through Friday, 11 A.M. to 6 P.M., Saturday to 5:30 P.M.

TENDER BUTTONS
143 East 62nd Street
Barneys, 106 Seventh Avenue, at 17th Street

▼

MARTHA INTERNATIONAL: You are perhaps the jet-set daughter of a big-name tycoon and are tired of borrowing Mummy's clothes or are simply bored with the too-too serious stuff at your favorite shop, Martha, where trunk shows and crystal pleating are a way of life. Sleep better tonight, sweetie. Martha has opened Martha International, a tiny shop one door away from her landmark store. It sells some of the younger, less-established, and kickier designers. Jewelry and accessories begin at $150–$200. While created for the younger generation, the shop expects some crossover from the moms who are also wanting a youthful approach to high-fashion dressing.

MARTHA INTERNATIONAL, 473 Park Avenue, at 57th Street

▼

HOWARD KAPLAN: We consider this store a real find. Celebrities shop here; the owner, Howard Kaplan, has become famous as a country-look expert. He's closed on weekends—that's when he goes shopping for more finds. Even if you can't afford to buy big pieces of furniture, if you love country-home decor, please stop by. He even has his own wallpaper and faience.

HOWARD KAPLAN, 35 East 10th Street

JENNY B. GOODE: The cutest little gift shop you ever did see, Jenny B. Goode is well worth the trip Uptown. Buy birthday and house gifts that are witty and unusual. If you've ever dreamed of owning your own gift shop, this is the one you should pattern it after. Or this is the place you've been dreaming of. Jenny B. Goode is famous for its ceramic giftables.

JENNY B. GOODE
1194 Lexington Avenue, at 81st Street
11 East 10th Street

▼

TIMBERLAND: While it has always been our practice to send every visitor to Manhattan to the Polo shop on Madison and 72nd Street to experience retail theater in action, we are amending our report by suggesting you stop by Timberland first, or on the same shopping trip. This store gives new meaning to the phrase "theatrical environment" in terms of retailing. A kayak hangs from the ceiling and the merchandise is displayed in a warm and woodsy atmosphere that makes you think of a hunting and fishing cabin in Canada. What's more, the merchandise (meant to be worn in your cabin in Canada or in your preppy lifestyle) is—as it always has been—excellent: well made from the highest-quality materials. While shoes and boots are the primary fixtures, there are also outercoats and sweaters and ready-to-wear items for sale. Europeans gobble this stuff up as premier American goods to take home as status symbols.

TIMBERLAND, 709 Madison Avenue, at 63rd Street

▼

THE BERMUDA SHOP: For years we disdained this store for its name—thinking it sold only shorts or bathing suits. Then we fell in love with the clothes in the window and disdained the store because we thought it would be one of those overpriced Madison Avenue boutiques. Imagine our immense shock when we finally walked in and found the dress of our dreams for $90! All the clothes are special in a combination of unique yet traditional—everything is well designed yet inexpensive; unique yet wearable. One of our best secret sources.

THE BERMUDA SHOP, 605 Madison Avenue, at 58th Street

▼

PUTUMAYO: Putumayo is not a new store, and it has survived the hippie look of the early 1970s and the Annie Hall look of the late 1970s. Known for their ethnic clothes—sweaters, skirts, hats, and accessories mostly from Latin and South America. Princess Di wore one of their sweaters a few years ago and gave ethnic combos a shot in the arm—ever since, preppies have found a comfortable mix in wearing one great ethnic piece with rather ordinary regular clothes for a smart statement—and Putumayo has been able to supply just the right touch. There are stores all around the United States, with three locations in Manhattan.

PUTUMAYO
   147 Spring Street, SoHo
   339 Columbus Avenue, at 76th Street
   857 Lexington Avenue, at 65th Street

▼

COUNTRY FLOORS: Country Floors is an old and well-known resource for designers, but there are several new twists that will interest everyone. The store has moved to the Lower Fifth Avenue area and also stocks ceramics and giftables . . . all of the same nature as the floor tiles they are so famous for. Country Floors is best known as the place to buy ceramic tiles from all over the world. Now they have many accessories produced by the tilemakers and painters themselves, like plates and bowls and candlesticks. They also have an accessories catalogue for mail-order business. Unlike most showrooms, Country Floors keeps the kind of hours a retail store will keep. They are open until 8 P.M. on Thursday evening and on Saturday from 9 A.M. to 5 P.M. Weekday hours are 9 A.M. to 6 P.M.

COUNTRY FLOORS, 15 East 16th Street

▼

JADED: Awash in a sea of jewels, Manhattan also has an ocean of imitations out there. For the rare piece that is part *faux* and part art (an original creation that is not made with precious stones), stop by Jaded, where the designs are private-label and the action is Uptown. Prices range from $40 to $80 for earrings, but the workmanship is excellent and the pieces are unique. This is the "in" place for the Ladies Who Lunch who want to look fashionable and yet different.

JADED, 1048 Madison Avenue, at 80th Street

▼

J. McLAUGHLIN: Concept, concept, concept. J. McLaughlin stores are a blend of art and science: They are carefully bought for the rich prepster who wants to look different and elegant, almost a contradiction in terms. The stores are decorated in country comfort, and offer clothes for men and women; our best find is the handknit sweater secret. Handknit sweaters from the big-name English designers are sold here for about $300 each when they should normally cost $500 and more. Why? Because the store uses a supplier who gets the sweaters knitted in Uruguay. Bargain hunting for $500 sweaters takes talent, you know. This is a lifestyle store for men and women; if you love the look but can't afford it—try Talbots.

J. McLAUGHLIN
976 Second Avenue, at 51st Street
1343 Third Avenue, at 77th Street
1311 Madison Avenue, at 92nd Street
7 West 57th Street

Housewares Finds

t's not hard to find neighborhoody, cutesy-pie housewares and tabletop shops in New York. But there are three bazaars that have a tremendous amount of selection and that specialize in this area, which can make your shopping quick and easy. Mikasa has closed its spectacular Chelsea shop; Barneys has to-die-for things, but we find the prices are astronomical; Bergdorf's has a small but good selection at various prices. But the big bazaars will probably have it all. Conran's even has furniture and bed linen.

WILLIAMS SONOMA: Part of the large California-based chain, Williams Sonoma has a huge catalogue business and a great store in New York where you can buy cookbooks, cooking supplies, gifts, and all the tabletop accessories you ever wanted, needed, or dreamed of. They also have bridal registry.

WILLIAMS SONOMA, 20 East 60th Street

▼

POTTERY BARN: Pottery Barn is a huge chain with better stores outside of Manhattan than in. But wait: Whenever we need something for the house, or Christmas gifts, or a wedding present that's affordable—we're off to the Pottery Barn around the corner from Bloomingdale's. They also advertise giant warehouse sales every now and then—watch *The New York Times*. After checking out Williams Sonoma you're not far away from the store we've listed below.

POTTERY BARN
  117 East 59th Street
  250 West 57th Street
POTTERY BARN WAREHOUSE, 231 Tenth Avenue, at 23rd Street

▼

CONRAN'S HABITAT: Originally created by Terence Conran of London fame and fortune, Conran's is a home-furnishings, tabletop kind of store that has something for everyone. While their specialty may be the furniture, the smaller items (vases, glasses, picture frames, etc.) are well-designed, well-priced, and a ball to look at. Conran's credo seems to be value and high design for moderate price. An especially good resource for gifts under $50. If you're furnishing a first home, this should be your first stop.

CONRAN'S HABITAT
  The Market at Citicorp, 160 East 54th Street
  Broadway at 81st Street
  2–8 Astor Place

Menswear

Almost every man to live in, or even to visit, New York has probably been to Barneys and has an opinion about it. Barneys is surely the most famous men's store in New York. If you want more, stroll the area we call Men's Mad—Madison Avenue in the mid-40s where there is a cluster of men's shops (most of them famous names), or go for the gusto and get in some discounts. (See page 232 for more on men's discounters, and, for heaven's sake, don't miss Dollar Bill's!)

BARNEYS: The main store is a virtual department store of men's clothing, with everything in every price range. It's absolutely mindboggling. The annual Barneys Warehouse Sale is legendary. Word of mouth has it that you should have your own tailor do your alterations. Open every day of the week and until 9 P.M. except Sunday evening, when they close at 5 P.M. A small but extremely elegant shop is in the World Financial Center—this store has suits and everything the businessman who has to dash out of town for a few days needs.

BARNEYS
106 Seventh Avenue, at 17th Street
Two World Financial Center

▼

HARRY ROTHMAN: The old Harry Rothman store on Fifth Avenue is gone, but this new store, on Park Avenue South, is run by Harry's grandson. There's quite a little cache of discount stores in this block, flanking Harry. So the Mrs. can shop while men take in the glories of Harry's and the discounts on bigname designer clothes and suits. A wide variety of sizes, so that any man can be fit. Sunday hours, noon–5 P.M.

HARRY ROTHMAN, 200 Park Avenue South, at 17th Street

▼

BIJAN: Since Bijan is sort of closed to those without an appointment (the doorman may or may not let you in, depending on his mood), you probably want to know what's inside. So here goes: Very expensive, traditional clothes—

the sort worn by kings and sheikhs, who are the typical Bijan customers. High-quality merchandise is carried here, except with a Bijan label and a Bijan price tag. The service is really what makes Bijan special. After all, he will fly to your house in his private jet if you need a fitting.

BIJAN, 699 Fifth Avenue, at 55th Street

▼

PAUL STUART: One of our favorite stores in the world, Paul Stuart is a very traditional men's store that also sells women's clothing. Everything is of the highest quality, but what makes the store really special is the service. When you walk in, even before you've bought anything, you feel rich, privileged, and pampered. The store is also one of those "look" stores, where the salesmen can put you together with names and private labels and give you an entire wardrobe that will make you look rich, sophisticated, and just right for any occasion. Most Paul Stuart customers shop nowhere else.

PAUL STUART, Madison Avenue, at 45th Street

▼

BROOKS BROTHERS: You can tell a Brooks Brothers suit by the square boxy cut, which is why it's a uniform for a certain kind of businessman. Brooks Brothers does a steady business in ultraconservative, always correct uniforms. This is actually a better store for sportswear and casual clothes, and it does have women's and boys' departments. Sales are famous. We are not against traditional looks—but we think men deserve a better fit. But Brooks Brothers has been doing fine for a hundred years without our opinion. Now owned by Marks & Spencer in Great Britain; the main store was just remodeled, and new emphasis is being put on the women's collection. Boys' sizes begin at 4.

BROOKS BROTHERS
346 Madison Avenue, at 44th Street
1 Liberty Plaza, Financial District

▼

DIMITRI: Real couture for the man who wants perfect Italian tailoring comes from Peter Dimitri, whose real name is Pietro but whose friends call him Peter. Peter will see you only by appointment, but all the models we know and many of the celebrities swear by him. He has won the Coty Award for outstanding work. Call (212) 431-1090 for an appointment; closed the last two weeks in August. As far as we're concerned, Peter Dimitri makes the best suit in New York.

DIMITRI, 110 Greene Street, 6th Floor

▼

MANO À MANO: For the hipster who likes his clothes from the pages of a fashion magazine and wants leather, Italian shirts, movie-star clothes, and dark sunglasses.

MANO À MANO, 580 Broadway

▼

MOE GINSBURG: Moe Ginsburg is a one-stop discount department store. It is on several different floors, so ask for what you want when you get there. Suits retail from $110 to $170. Shoes are on the 4th floor; tuxedos are on the 3rd. This also is a Downtown location, so you can get to several other big discounters on the same day. Hours: 9:30 A.M. to 7 P.M. on weekdays; until 8 P.M. on Thursday; and until 6 P.M. on Saturday and Sunday.

MOE GINSBURG, 162 Fifth Avenue, at 21st Street

ASCOT CHANG: Ascot Chang is a famous institution in Hong Kong: He is one of the city's best-known and best-loved shirtmakers. Now he's come to New York (well, his son has) to open a more conveniently located shop for those who know how comfortable a custom shirt can be. Prices are higher than in Hong Kong, but not unreasonable—you'll pay about $50 for a custom shirt. (It's $30 in Hong Kong.) The shop has ready-made shirts, as well as made-to-measure; you can choose from about 2,000 fabrics. Women's shirts are not available ready-made as in Hong Kong, but can be custom-ordered. There are also suits, suspenders, and the usual needs of a well-dressed gent.

ASCOT CHANG, 7 West 57th Street, 2nd Floor

▼

LOUIS OF BOSTON: Louis has been as famous in Boston as the Cabots, the Lodges, and the beans and the cods. His menswear store is the fanciest shop in town. It's also one of the fanciest stores in New York. The prices match the decor. Both men and women can buy from the New York triplex (the women's shop is a fraction of the total store space), which is perfectly located for those who are shopping 57th Street and are on their way to Bloomingdale's—the shop is your last stop before you cut Uptown. Don't miss it, or your tour of New York's best won't be complete. Most of the merchandise comes from Italy—often made by designers you've never heard of. That's the point: Louis's offers such impeccable taste that just to have bought in this store means you will be perfectly groomed. And broke. What a way to go.

LOUIS OF BOSTON, 131 East 57th Street

▼

LONDON MAJESTY: For the big and tall man, there is a small chain of outfitters called London Majesty, which is from—you guessed it—Britain. They have shops all over Europe and also in Stamford, Connecticut, should you be more inclined toward a trip to Connecticut than a browse along Sixth Avenue (Avenue of the Americas). The shop is traditional and carries a full range of clothes from sport to active gear to suits and formal wear. These well-made clothes do solve problems for the hard-to-fit man. All styles are smart and refined. The location is right near Rockefeller Center, so don't let the address throw you. Ask about the sales.

LONDON MAJESTY, 1211 Avenue of the Americas, at 48th Street

▼

J. PRESS: Another of the old-fashioned, always steady resources, for those who fall in the crack between Brooks Brothers and Paul Stuart. You say you love button-down collars? You say you need another navy-and-cranberry-striped tie? You love navy blazers with charcoal slacks? Opens at 9:15 A.M. except on Sunday, when the store is closed. They've added two new floors in their new location, across the street from their old shop.

J. PRESS, 7 East 44th Street

▼

F. R. TRIPLER & CO.: Established right after the War Between the States as an outfitter for the traditional British look. The clothes are still from England and Scotland, as well as the United States. A trusted resource for Hickey-Freeman suits. A little more with-it than Brooks Brothers, and not as with-it as Paul Stuart.

F. R. TRIPLER & CO., 366 Madison Avenue, at 46th Street

CHIPP: Could it be that the store is named for Mr. Chips of book and movie fame? Surely the English prep–school look is the same. Sales can be downright amazing. The clothes are safe and traditional. The store opens at 9 A.M., as any sensible store should. No Sunday hours.

CHIPP, 342 Madison, at 43rd Street

▼

BEAU BRUMMEL: Begun in Queens and now branching out to dress chic men everywhere, Beau Brummel specializes in European clothes that look good on skinny men. Hugo Boss, the German line, is a big seller, but there's also Gianfranco Ferré and other big names. There are on-premises tailors for instant fixes; and best of all, businessmen can make a private appointment for a room upstairs where—should they care to—they may eat and shop at the same time. It's not cheap, but it is exclusive.

BEAU BRUMMEL
1113 Madison Avenue, at 83rd Street
410 Columbus, at 79th Street

▼

ALAN FLUSSER: The most secret and sophisticated shop in New York, for those gentlemen who think Polo is a cliché. The look is very traditional, expensive, and elegant in a European-American mixture, but the body is strictly American. Flusser himself is the leading authority on the subject of men's fashion in New York, and is expert on what goes with what. Pink socks are his trademark.

ALAN FLUSSER
16 East 52nd Street, Penthouse
50 Trinity Place, Upstairs

▼

ARTHUR RICHARDS: From our days at *Gentleman's Quarterly* we know that Arthur Richards makes a good suit, so we continue to follow his sales and retail practices with interest. The twice-a-year clearance sales are great events, and since the store is near Barneys, the two can often be put together in a one-stop shopping spree. Because this is a showroom, the business opens at 9 A.M., which we love. Choose from just about 10,000 units: traditional suits, silk sport coats, and summerweight suits. Arthur Richards is a manufacturer, so that's not really a private label you see there. These are good suits we have known for years; women's suits and blazers as well.

ARTHUR RICHARDS, 85 Fifth Avenue, 5th Floor, at 16th Street

▼

SAINT LAURIE: Well advertised and appealing to the masses, Saint Laurie is another department store of suits—well-stocked and ready to outfit you totally and make life a breeze. They manufacture their own suits and usually are jammed with visitors looking for quality at good prices. Step this way. They also sell women's suits and have a petite and tall department, as well as regular stock on sizes from 2 to 18. This is rather an extraordinary place. Open seven days a week; each day (except Sunday) they open at 9 A.M. sharp (Sunday, 11 A.M. to 4 P.M.). You can even get made-to-measure. Delivery takes four weeks. There is a swatch club for mail order.

SAINT LAURIE, 897 Broadway, at 20th Street

▼

SYMS: While you're Downtown, don't miss Syms (near the World Trade Center). Syms is part department store, part meeting ground for men who know, and part heaven. It also sells women's and children's clothes and some towels, luggage, and whatnots, but it has built its reputation primarily as the leading discount resource for men's ready-to-wear. If a day of shopping at department store prices has put a strain on you and your wallet, then get on over to Syms and see the suits, sportswear, shoes, shirts, bathing suits, sweaters, pajamas, tuxedos, ties, and socks. Syms is convenient for businessmen who are working in the Downtown area; it's also convenient for tourists who visit South Street Seaport (you can easily walk), and certainly is worth a special trip. Our friend Joanna, who moved to the East Coast after ten years in California, took her husband to Syms for two hours and bought him an entire East Coast fall wardrobe at 50% to 70% off regular prices. The size range is excellent; the selection is grand.

SYMS, 42 Trinity Place

Jewelry

J ewelry is more expensive in Paris and less expensive in Hong Kong, but in New York you have selection that will leave you breathless, drooling, and possibly broke. As with every other type of merchandise, many kinds of retail shops sell the sparkle plenty you crave, and there are many ways to show the world just how wealthy you are.

▼ Jewelry shopping in New York, as in any other place in the world—big city or small—is a matter of trust. The big, fancy jewelers exist not because their designs are so irresistible but because the house has provided years (maybe centuries) of trust. True, every now and then you hear about a trusted jeweler of fifty years going to the slammer for passing off bottoms of Coke bottles as emeralds. But it's rare. The big-name New York jewelers, whether they are American or European, have no such scandals attached to them. We're ready to stake our reputations on the big reputations. And that is why we recommend the big stores. Yes, you pay top-of-the-line prices, but you get something very worthwhile: reliability.

▼ Trust is also related to resale. You can always sell a piece of jewelry made by a status firm, such as Tiffany, Cartier, Harry Winston, etc. No matter how old it is, a genuinely fine piece of jewelry from a trusted house is a good investment. It may even appreciate over the years.

▼ As our friend Hans Stern, who is an internationally famous jeweler, explained to us: "Buying from a well-known jeweler is like buying a painting. You are paying for the quality of the art as well as the quality and the reputation of the signature." Some people buy paintings because they like the picture and don't care if it has value; other people have to go to the big dealers and buy signed works by renowned artists so they can trust their purchase. This is a personal choice.

▼ There is a Jewelry District, and you are welcome to shop there (see page 173). You may find many wonderful things. The prices will be better than at Van Cleef, for sure. It's unlikely that you will be totally "taken." On the other hand, you will never know if you could have done better. *Tip:* It pays to know something about what you are doing, but you can have a perfectly good time and walk away satisfied even if you don't know what you are doing. Remember that fun and big-time investments are two different things.

▼ Like all other businesses, the jewelry business is run by insiders. Strangers off the street can, and do, get taken. Industrial-grade diamonds may be sold to you; color-enhanced stones may be touted as the best money can buy; irradiated stones will not give you cancer, but they may not be what you had in mind. Dealers know what they are doing; we do not. Consider yourself warned. If you want fun, go to the District. If you want safe, go to a trusted jeweler.

▼ You can buy inexpensive pieces at the big, famous jewelers. You needn't be in the market for a $106,000 bracelet to be a customer at a fancy jeweler. You may find something for as little as $50; surely you will find many choices at $500. How you are treated is a function of how well dressed you are and how you demand to be treated. Some places pride themselves on having a fancy name but being accessible to regular people like us; Tiffany is one of those places.

▼ You can do very well at a sale at a big, famous jeweler's. Recently we observed a promotion at H. Stern where the snootiest names in watches (such as Piaget) were on sale for 40% off retail. That means you could have bought at the wholesale price; a better bargain you can't get anywhere. Even in Switzerland. Watch for ads in *The New York Times*.

▼ *Faux* jewelry is, of course, socially acceptable. It's always been worn, but fewer people talked about it, that's all. Almost all important jewels are copied in paste—to fool the burglar. Even Elizabeth Taylor has admitted that there are paste copies of her gem collection. With the Chanel look so popular now, big, glitzy fakes are even more common. Women who have real gems are still opting for phony.

▼ Cheap *faux* often looks blatantly fake—the gold is too brassy; the gems are lackluster; the fixings are not fine. If you are planning on passing off your collection as something related to the Crown Jewels, choose carefully and pay the extra money. A good fake necklace will probably cost $300; good earrings may be $50 to $100.

▼ If you want a bad copy of a good watch, they are currently sold on every street corner for about $25. A good eye can see that the watches are too thick to be real.

▼ Used and antique jewelry can be bought at auction, in certain jewelry shops, and in antiques shops and country shops. But even junk earrings from the 1950s are pricey these days, so have a good eye and know what you are buying. For old and used watches, check out **AARON FABER,** 666 Fifth Avenue.

▼ Sterling silver with semiprecious gemstones is a great look; it's also immensely affordable. While Tiffany does sell this look, many smaller boutiques have come to specialize in it. Most of the big jewelry shops do not have this style.

▼ A few wholesale resources also sell retail. The wholesale price is in code; you must show your business card and be legit to get wholesale, but at retail you still get a discount.

The Big Names

CARTIER: In a very nice town house, Cartier is cramped, crowded, and four floors of fun. Don't be put off by the fancy front; you can come in and browse. The gift department and stationery department are affordable. Crown jewels are available upon request. Note the royal warrants on the door as you enter from Fifth Avenue. The famous tank watch is well priced at the duty-free shop at JFK Airport.

CARTIER, 653 Fifth Avenue, at 52nd Street

▼

H. STERN: A folksy shop rather than a *haute* one; watch for deals on watches. Buy

Brazilian-mined stones in Brazil and save 30%; rubies and sapphires do not come from Brazil but still can be bought here ... thank God. Jewelry repair is downstairs. Amazing return policy: Anything you buy from them can be returned in one year if you decide you don't like it. There are absolutely glorious rings in the $300 to $400 price range that look like you spent thousands on them, and they are totally real. If you are looking to knock out your friends and family with just one purchase, consider one of these rings.

H. STERN, 645 Fifth Avenue, at 52nd Street

▼

TIFFANY & CO.: Jewelry on the first floor; more delights upstairs in this mini department store. The table settings are always worth a look, and this is the place to buy wedding gifts. Elsa Peretti and Paloma Picasso may be in your price range, so don't be afraid of the old reputation. Contrary to popular thought, Tiffany is not that expensive. Or, put more properly in perspective, Tiffany has many items you can afford. The private rooms on the left are for the fancy stuff. Don't miss the scarves and leathergoods on the 2nd floor.

TIFFANY & CO., 727 Fifth Avenue, at 57th Street

▼

VAN CLEEF & ARPELS: Tucked into the front corner of Bergdorf Goodman, this is for serious shoppers only. They do sell items for less than $15,000, but we haven't bought any of them lately. So sorry. There's also a boutique located inside Bergdorf's.

VAN CLEEF & ARPELS, 744 Fifth Avenue, at 57th Street

HARRY WINSTON: We were inside and even upstairs once, but it is an intimidating kind of place. Not for casual browsing, although there are some boutique items that are fitting for mortals rather than royals.

HARRY WINSTON, 718 Fifth Avenue, at 56th Street

The Fancy *Fauxs*

CIRO: A bread-and-butter resource for imitations that are so lovely they pass for real. Pins begin at $25; pearls with pavé clasps at $100, etc. The store does sell some nonimitation items, but they are famous for the *faux* pieces.

CIRO, 711 Fifth Avenue, at 55th Street

▼

JOLIE GABOR: Expensive but very good copies of important jewelry and gemstones, not so much costume jewelry as very serious imitations. These gems are so fancy they are called reproductions instead of fakes. Dahling, these are the ones the celebs wear on TV. And Eva told us her mom sold the shop, by the way.

JOLIE GABOR, 699 Madison Avenue, at 62nd Street

▼

GALE GRANT: Avoid this place at lunch hour, when every other chic woman in New York is trying to buy her fakes. Some of it sparkles a bit too much, but you can get great costume jewelry and some fabulous imitations here. Earrings begin at $25; $40 buys a much better pair. King Tut's tomb wasn't this much fun.

GALE GRANT, 485 Madison Avenue, at 52nd Street

KENNETH JAY LANE: He's a legend for his imitations of expensive jewels, and only Chanel does it better; now we can shop at the Trump Tower store. Also in London and Paris. All big-name designs (Bulgari-inspired, etc.) as interpreted by Mr. Lane are available for a fraction of the expensive designer cost. Prices average $25 to $250.

KENNETH JAY LANE, Trump Tower, 725 Fifth Avenue, at 56th Street

Discounters

FORTUNOFF: You name it, they've got it—from pearls to diamonds to gold to precious and semiprecious; sterling to wear and sterling to eat with; and even some modern high-fashion pieces. We love the catalogue, and we love to look in their glitzy neo-Deco Fifth Avenue showroom, but to be frank, there's something lacking in these styles that we just can't put our fingers on. Maybe the designs are just too ordinary. Lots of people shop here for a bargain and like it. This is not as sophisticated as we would like, but it is a good source for discounted basics such as pearls, mabe earrings, simple contemporary gold earrings, chains, silverware, etc. Don't forget to go upstairs. Open late Thursday and on Sunday afternoon, noon to 5 P.M.

FORTUNOFF, 681 Fifth Avenue, at 54th Street

▼

47TH STREET PHOTO: We hear the jewelry department is a Fortunoff lease, but many like to shop here thinking they are getting the best prices in town. We look but never buy.

47TH STREET PHOTO, 67 West 47th Street

Worth Noting

YLANG YLANG: Lots of *faux* Deco and glitz and costumey fun. These are fashion statements that finish off an outfit. You'll pay $50 to $100 in New York for earrings or whatnots.

YLANG YLANG
806 Madison Avenue, at 68th Street
324 Columbus Avenue, at 75th Street
4 West 57th Street

▼

ZOE COSTE: Glitz from Cannes. A slightly different look from Ylang Ylang, but similar enough still to be competition. Zoe has a more glamorous South of France attitude. Prices begin at $50, but the pieces are unusual. We also like the interior decor—any store with gold lamé throw pillows can't be bad.

ZOE COSTE, 1034 Third Avenue, at 61st Street

▼

MISHON MISHON: A glitzy store that isn't quite as sparkly as Zoe or Ylang Ylang but has plenty of contemporary works and is known to show works of leading designers such as Stephen Dweck, Wendy Gell, Eric Beamon, and Johnny Farah—all of whom do one-of-a-kind pieces for the store. Prices range from $100 to $500.

MISHON MISHON, 899 Madison, at 72nd Street

The Jewelry District

If you stroll along the west side of Fifth Avenue, when you get to 47th Street you'll notice

that the street sign says Diamond Way. This is
the diamond district, in the heart of the wholesale jewelry district. At 578 Fifth Avenue at
47th Street is the International Jewelry Mart;
behind it, at 4 West 47th Street and with its
entrance on 47th Street, is the National Jewelry Mart. All of 47th Street is dotted with
little jewelers, but these two buildings host a
variety of stalls of dealers who sell everything
from gold chains to antique estate pieces to
silver with cabochon amethyst and copies of
Tiffany's best-selling earrings. Of the two buildings, the International Jewelry Mart is decidedly fancier. The National Jewelry Mart is much
more folksy and unpretentious. As you walk
the aisles in either mart, salespeople will smile
brightly and ask if they can help you. They are
not offensively pushy, and most are young
enough to be your buddies. Occasionally a
group of men in suits huddle over some pack-
ets, but mostly men buy birthday gifts for
the women in their lives, and women compare
prices, trying to figure out if anyone has a
better deal than anyone else.

The answer is simple: Who knows? All of
these dealers will negotiate with you. There's
more room on antique and used pieces; paying
cash also helps. Beyond that, you have to go
with trust or just your own common sense.
What looks good, fits your pocketbook, and
makes you happy? Most of the dealers have
copies of the catalogues from the big-name
jewelers and will gladly copy anything for you.
You can have a "Paloma Picasso" for less than
at Tiffany, but it will not be signed. Do you
care? If you trust yourself, go with the dealers
in the Jewelry District. If you are making a
major purchase, go with a reliable firm.

International Jewelry Mart

Somewhat fancier than the National Jewelry Mart, the International Jewelry Mart is full of shops offering enough choices to make your head spin. We always check in on **BUCCIARI**. We were ready and willing to buy everything in this man's windows, although it all looks like copies of the big-name designs and we have no idea if the prices are fair or the quality of the stones is worthwhile. We just want it all. **MAURICE BADLER** has a rather steady business going, and we've seen many well-crafted sets of gold earrings, and some original designs, as well as some copies of famous works seen in big-name stores. Prices seem reasonable to us, and we continue to go back. We have seen similar styles in department stores for more money, and at big-name shops for a lot more money. You can get a catalogue for $3 and do some armchair shopping. Write: Badler Catalogue, 578 Fifth Avenue, Department F, New York NY 10036. **LAURENCE W. FORD** is an antiques dealer who has a little of everything. You can go just to stare.

Shoes and Leathergoods

The best thing about shopping in New York is that you will inevitably wear out your shoes and need new ones. Did we say *need*? Need is not why you buy shoes in New York. It's more like greed.

Because it's totally acceptable to wander around New York wearing a designer suit and a pair of tennis shoes with bobby socks, the one thing to remember about shoe shopping is to bring the essentials with you—you should have a pair of stockings or footies or something in your handbag (although most stores will loan these to you).

Some tips:

▼ If you wear a big size, a small size, a wide width, or a narrow width, rejoice: New York has shoes for you.

▼ Most of the large department stores usually have two or more shoe salons—one for expensive shoes and one for cheapie shoes—as well as different designer nooks for handbags and belts. Both Lord & Taylor and Bloomingdale's are known for their shoe departments.

▼ Madison Avenue is good for seeing it all, but don't miss Susan Bennis/Warren Edwards on Park Avenue.

▼ The Lower East Side is chock full of discount shoe stores, which may or may not have what you want, need, like, or care to contemplate. Some of these shoes are unsold orphans from previous seasons in *haute* stores; others are just current styles sold at discount.

▼ The first floor of most department stores sells handbags, belts, small leathergoods, and accessories, and many department stores have marvelous handbag departments. Check out Bergdorf's and Bendel's for pricey leathergoods.

▼ The big names all have incredible shoe sales. We know women who fly to New York just for the shoe sales. *One final word of advice:* If you have a hard-to-fit foot, buy at the beginning of the season and don't wait for the sale.

BELTRAMI: A European delight for high-fashion, slightly wild, and extravagant shoes as well as other leathergoods. Traditionally high prices, as you would expect for this kind of artwork, but sale prices are 30% to 80% off. Open until 7 P.M. on Thursday.

BELTRAMI, 711 Fifth Avenue, at 55th Street

SUSAN BENNIS/WARREN EDWARDS:
You have to believe in the toe fairy, or at least believe that shoes make the man (or woman), since these pieces of art can retail for $500 a pair. What's wrong with us that we think they are worth it? Get in line for the sale. The most extravagant shoes in New York.

SUSAN BENNIS/WARREN EDWARDS, 440 Park Avenue, at 56th Street

▼

CHARLES JOURDAN: The Trump Tower store, situated right there on Fifth Avenue and smiling at you, beckoning to come in, is an invitation to go nuts. The shoes have status, despite the fact that they are not as pricey as other big names. The woven leather bags are smart. There are less expensive shoes here, and you can do well at a sale. There are two shops; we think the Trump store is more fun.

CHARLES JOURDAN, 725 Fifth Avenue, at 57th Street

▼

FENDI: The Fendi sisters take Manhattan, and, wow, what a store. Look for shoes, handbags, luggage, clothes, and furs as this famous maker of leathergoods fills up over 20,000 square feet in regal Roman panache. A must to visit. Some affordable gifts in the accessories area.

FENDI, 720 Fifth Avenue, at 56th Street

▼

WALTER STEIGER: Expensive, well-crafted, high-fashion design. Costs less, but not that much less, in Paris. Wait for the sale, then buy, buy, buy. *Our personal note:* These shoes seem to run small. We don't know many people who have gotten good comfort for a long day's wear. Buy carefully; don't go for the risky shoes that you expect will get comfortable someday.

WALTER STEIGER, 739 Madison Avenue, at
   64th Street

▼

MARIO VALENTINO: You know how they all swoon for Valentino. This one is Mario, and isn't related to the Garavani part of the family, but his leathergoods are internationally famous. They're also cheaper in Italy, but men and women often find the price is worthwhile. Pricey but not as expensive as some others.

MARIO VALENTINO, 645 Fifth Avenue, at 51st
   Street

▼

GALO: The low heels and fashion flats you've wanted for under $100 are in abundance. All European merchandise.

GALO
   504 Madison Avenue, at 52nd Street
   692 Madison Avenue, at 62nd Street
   825 Lexington Avenue, at 63rd Street

▼

SOLE OF ITALY: Everyone raves about Fine & Klein, a store where you'll get a 20% to

30% discount on some pricey bags. They will order for you if it's the top of the season and you have a picture from an ad or a style number. It's a good resource for some people, but we just never find what appeals to us. What we love most is upstairs at Sole of Italy, their shoe counterpart. We've been buying our everyday shoes there for several years. Large sizes; good choice of low heels.

SOLE OF ITALY, 119 Orchard Street

▼

J. S. SAUREZ: So it came to pass that we were in need of a status handbag and were shocked that the average such animal now sells for $500 and up. We were further shocked to realize we hadn't stocked up at any sales and would be forced to buy regular retail. A daylong search of every handbag possibility in Manhattan ensued, and we are pleased to announce J. S. Saurez the winner: They have the large Kelly-style bag (Hermès look-alike) for $375 in a stressed leather that is just beautiful.

J. S. SAUREZ, 26 West 54th Street

▼

LOUIS VUITTON: Vuitton has gone beyond the monogram canvas with those very famous LV's and has introduced hot colors that are the rage. For those who think that just about everyone has the monogram and it's time to do something a little bit outré, bright green, navy blue, orange, or yellow luggage is just the thing. The commitment to quality is intense. Check out the different pieces of the line: The made-in-America line is less expensive than the European imports.

LOUIS VUITTON, 51 East 57th Street

▼

LOEWE: It's Lo-eh-vay, not Loew's, and it's superb, if pricey. Shoes, leathergoods, and clothes (suede coats to die for) from a famous Spanish house. Prices are exactly the same as in Madrid; sales are the time to score.

LOEWE, 711 Madison Avenue, at 62nd Street

▼

JOAN & DAVID: Joan and David are indeed a couple, and they have branched out from making shoes to making clothes and having their own shops. They even have a shop in Paris, right on the Faubourg! They continue their arrangement with Ann Taylor, but have expanded into retail as well. The Madison Avenue shop has more than an Ann Taylor store— the complete range of shoes, boots, belts, bags, and clothes that happen to be very moderately priced and quite hip. Hurray.

JOAN & DAVID, 816 Madison Avenue, at 68th Street

▼

IL BISONETE: You want status symbols? Then trot downtown to Il Bisonete, where the Italian leathergoods firm is selling their trademark bags to those who like a casual (almost funky) handbag with the hand-stamped seal that elevates it from simple to "in." The store is a franchise and it is very, very small, but it has what you need.

IL BISONETE, 72 Thompson Street

COACH: Sort of the ultimate preppy resource for an old-fashioned, sensible handbag, Coach has long been a manufacturer of a certain look. Now they have a new store, which replaces their previous one on Madison Avenue. A Coach bag has a distinctive look—all good leather and fine stitching. . . . It says "I will last for ten years" in an invisible message that practical people can read. The bags are not inexpensive (prices start around $75 and can go as high as $250), but they are superbly made and will go with anything and everything.

COACH
    710 Madison Avenue, at 63rd Street
    South Street Seaport

▼

TIFFANY & CO.: Yes, this is the same Tiffany & Co. you've come to count on for diamonds by the yard. But perhaps you don't know that Tiffany has changed dramatically in the last few years. They now sell leathergoods (and scarves) and all sorts of high-quality knickknacks that you can possibly afford and that have nothing to do with registry for your wedding. The really ritzy evening bags do cost thousands of dollars, but you can buy a bag for $200–$400.

TIFFANY & CO., 727 Fifth Avenue, at 57th Street

▼

MARK CROSS: For fine leathergoods of the traditional school, walk into the wood-paneled Mark Cross showroom and open your wallet. In fact, empty your wallet and buy a new one while you are there. Mark Cross offers a status gift for the man who has everything—their belts, wallets, passport cases, desk sets, key chains, briefcases, etc., have been making Father's Day a special occasion for many a man. You can find a $25 gift here if you look hard enough.

MARK CROSS
645 Fifth Avenue, at 51st Street
Building Two, World Financial Center

Children

If you buy Valentino for your little girl, you'll find a nice selection in New York. We prefer J. C. Penney's, but will spring for Esprit (bought at the outlet) and some other names when we can get them at discount. We like outlet shopping in Flemington and Secaucus for one-stop, preseason big hauls, but you can find everything you need and much, much more in New York. All of the department stores are well stocked; Macy's has a huge Esprit department; Saks has lots of just-like-Mommy and/or Madonna clothes; Lord & Taylor still has navy-blue jumpers and plaid kilts. The Benettons and 012 shops all over the city dress most of the area's kids, but you may want to poke in on some of these shops. Also, count on the Lower East Side for some of the basics.

LAURA ASHLEY: Laura Ashley freaks, unite: Now you can dress your daughters in the same clothes you love. As more stores open, there will be more with children's departments, but you can stock up on gift items for babies and little-girl clothes in the New York shop now.

LAURA ASHLEY, 21 East 57th Street

BENETTON 012: As many Benettons as there are in New York, few of them have children's clothes. But despair not: New 012s are beginning to pop up and sprinkle the sidewalks with their smiling faces and nattily cute clothes. Or you can go to the flagship 012 Uptown to get The Look in tyke size—hoping you luck into a sale. Not to be outdone by big-size Benetton, 012 is designed with kids in mind. Prices were not—$32 for a lamb's-wool sweater; $42 for corduroy cotton trousers. The good news: There are some 600 pieces in the line, and all the colors coordinate with each other.

BENETTON 012, 1162 Madison Avenue, at 85th Street

▼

CERUTTI: Not to be confused with that hunk Nino Cerutti, the Italian tailor and mentor to Mr. Armani, Cerutti is a famous children's store for people who pay $10,000 a year in tuition at private school for each child and think nothing of it.

CERUTTI, 807 Madison Avenue, at 68th Street

▼

THE CHOCOLATE SOUP: Formerly a no-name neighborhood cute store, now professionally cute on Madison Avenue. This is where we bought the T-shirt for $25, and we're proud of it. You can probably make a lot of this stuff yourself if you have some talent and a good eye. Pricey but wonderful. Open Sunday, 1 to 6 P.M.

THE CHOCOLATE SOUP, 946 Madison Avenue, at 74th Street

▼

JUDY CORMAN: Corman's place is one of the tiniest of the cute kiddie stores in New York, but its selection of the clothes you love is jam-packed. Tartine et Chocolat, Boston Trader, and Oshkosh are just some of the labels in the infants-to-size-7 boutique. Handmade quilts hang from walls, and glitter sparkles off an occasional T-shirt. A lot of the merchandise has the handmade chic touch, and paper dolls display much of the clothing. Many of the items in the store are one-of-a-kind. Prices can be high, but the store oozes West Side charm.

JUDY CORMAN, 198 Columbus Avenue, at 69th Street

▼

ENCHANTED FOREST: A SoHo spot for the kids, filled with trolls and make-believe and magic in an honest-to-goodness forest that is populated by many handcrafted and one-of-a-kind items. Prices range from 10¢ to $2,000. No clothes.

ENCHANTED FOREST, 85 Mercer Street

▼

ESPRIT KIDS: There are a few freestanding Esprit Kids stores. But Macy's New York has the largest Esprit collection inside a department store in the United States, and an Esprit Kids shop is being discussed for New York as a specific site becomes available. The line for kids is inspired by the grown-up look but has its own designs, fabrics, colorways, and even shoes. Very tight control is kept on the product: The boys' line was scratched right before its debut because management felt they were spreading themselves too thin.

ESPRIT KIDS, Macy's Herald Square, 5th Floor

GREENSTONES ET CIE: One of the most famous, and longtime, residents of the reborn Upper West Side, Greenstones et Cie thankfully is not one of those cute kiddie stores that's as big as a closet. It strings along several row houses with beautiful woodwork on the outside and everything simply displayed on the inside. There are almost a hundred different European lines sold here, as well as American standard faves such as Oshkosh and Wibbies. Greenstones' owners happen to be longtime garmentos, by the way, with impeccable fashion sense, and they will help you coordinate an entire wardrobe for your kids. They prefer to work with parents as a major source rather than kids. Everything we like always costs $50, but socks are $5.

GREENSTONES ET CIE, 442 Columbus Avenue, at 81st Street

▼

KIDS' TOWN: Now you're talking real. This is a discount outlet that's up one flight in the Wall Street (corner of Fulton and Nassau streets, to be exact) area but worth the trip to stock up on camp clothes or back-to-school needs. If you can't make it to an outlet city, do your one-stop shopping here. All big names such as Carter's, Billy the Kid, Jordache, Mighty-Mac, Health-Tex, etc. From layettes to size 18, boys' and girls'. Piggyback this trip to a visit to South Street Seaport so you can reward the kids for trying on all the clothes you'll want to buy.

KIDS' TOWN, 93 Nassau Street

▼

MOTHERCARE: Yuppies secretly bemoan the fact that New York has very few reasonably priced children's outlets. Sears and Penney's, which out-of-city moms know about, are not in Manhattan. Cutesy-pie stores, even 012, can be very pricey on a regular basis. Enter Mothercare, with coordinated clothes, fashion looks, everything for Mom (even maternity), layette, infant, and kids. What's more, the prices are moderate. For people who are used to paying $38 for a pair of boy's jeans, the prices are actually pretty reasonable.

MOTHERCARE, 2305 Broadway, at 84th Street

▼

PENNY WHISTLE: A nice selection of European and American toys. Britain's toy knights are $1 and $3 each. Halloween items are well stocked. The store is high on some items, then surprises you by being reasonable on others. There are many run-in-and-buy-a-silly-something kinds of gifts and child-pleasers if you are out with your tots and need a sudden bribe.

PENNY WHISTLE
448 Columbus Avenue, at 82nd Street
132 Spring Street
1283 Madison Avenue, at 91st Street

▼

F.A.O. SCHWARZ: F.A.O. Schwarz is in the General Motors Building, in what used to be a car showroom. If you walk in from the Fifth Avenue side, you enter next to an elaborately built clock that has all sorts of wooden moving parts that sing and dance. Go up the escalator to see the life-size stuffed animals and the remote-control Ferraris that cost as much as the monthly payment on a Mercedes-Benz. We give the store a lot of credit for being fun, inventive, colorful, and warm—especially when the prices are as high as they are. Every item in the store can be found cheaper somewhere else—but if you don't like to hunt, or if you want to be wild and crazy, you may actually enjoy buying here. At Christmastime it is a zoo. Gift wrapping is free; restrooms are clean; the store now is selling clothing—which it did not do at its old location. No trip to New York is complete without a visit here. *Oh, yes, a final tip:* We know of one mother who told her child this was a museum—you could look but couldn't buy!

Hours: Monday through Saturday, 10 A.M. until 6 P.M.; Thursday evening until 8 P.M.; Sunday from noon to 5 P.M.

F.A.O. SCHWARZ, 767 Fifth Avenue, at 58th Street

▼

TYKE-OONS: This is a specialty kids' shop that has a fabulous gimmick for locals. One may join the Executive Mom (or Dad) program and pay a fee that authorizes the store to automatically send a "care" package of clothing to your child. The clothes come twice a year and cost about $600 for the top-of-the-line package.

TYKE-OONS, 858 Lexington Avenue, at 64th Street

▼

GAP KIDS: We hate to be part of the rah-rah team that endorses fashion for the masses, but heck, Gap Kids is one of our favorite

stores in the world. We like it even better than
The Gap or The Gap Outlet. The quality is
high; should something shrink (it does happen), they will make an exchange or refund
your money. There are as many locations as
there are for the regular Gap stores. We only
list a few convenient locations, often the kids'
line will be in part of a large Gap store but
you're likely to stumble across a Gap Kids in
almost any neighborhood. Our only regret is
that sizes stop at 14, which one of our boys
has now passed. Prices are a tad high, but
there are frequent sales. Mothers of large-size
boys: Return to the Gap for men's size S
(small); it will fit size 14s and up.

GAP KIDS

527 Madison Avenue, at 57th Street
250 West 57th Street, at Broadway
2373 Broadway, at 86th Street
215 Columbus Avenue, at 70th Street

▼

BABYGAP: You got it. First there was The
Gap, then Gap Kids. Now we've got Baby-
Gap in selected Gap and Gap Kids stores. If
you haven't got one in your local mall—not to
worry—we've got a few of the infant and toddler ready-to-wear shops right here in the Big
Apple. Freestanding stores do not exist (yet),
but we are expectant.

BABYGAP

250 West 57th Street
354 Avenue of the Americas, at Washington
Place
527 Madison Avenue, at 54th Street

▼

BONPOINT: If you're rich or well traveled
you already know about Bonpoint, the *grand-*

mère's delight of expensive and to die for children's clothes. Barneys has a Bonpoint department on its 1st floor, but the Paris firm has opened its own freestanding store way uptown so that Mom can buy some ready-to-wear for herself, her daughter, and then throw in some furnishings. All at less than modest sums. The workmanship is so divine that you won't care about the prices.

BONPOINT, 1269 Madison Avenue, at 91st Street

▼

JACADI: OK, so you care about the prices after all. Well, someone got smart and put two and two together and got more than four: They got Jacadi, another French line that looks a lot like Bonpoint but isn't nearly as expensive. Not that we're talking K mart, folks, but for the prissy preppy BCBG French-dandy look, you can come away quite satisfied. Serena, age ten, likes to shop here because she can get the dress, the headband, the handbags and the ballet slippers to match all in the exact same fabric.

JACADI, 1281 Madison Avenue, at 91st Street

Special Sizes

New York is one of the best cities in the world for specialty sizes. Many designers, retailers, and boutiques are willing to help you look as elegant as possible, no matter how big or how small you may be.

If you can get in over a weekend, or can buy wholesale, try 498 Seventh Avenue for its large-size showrooms. Many established names also have petite or plus sizes, such as Anne Klein,

Liz Claiborne (petites), or Jane Schaffhausen for Belle France (plus). Don't forget that Bill Blass cuts up to size 16 (he's the only big name that does) and that any couture garment can be made to measure. Macy's and Bloomingdale's take pride in their departments for petites.

ASHANTI: Ashanti began as a counterculture fashion store and now considers itself a type of couture house for large-size women. Although they do have a good selection, the best thing about the store is that it's in the same block as Forgotten Woman, so you can go to both shops at one time and get some idea of what's available.

ASHANTI, 872 Lexington Avenue, at 65th Street

▼

FORGOTTEN WOMAN: This is a chain or a franchise or something, but we love it. The Lexington Avenue store feels very California; there's even a coffee bar (but no salad bar) so you can relax; the place feels peppy and upbeat. The Rockefeller Center store is larger and more convenient for visitors from out of town who may not be on upper Lexington Avenue otherwise. Lots of casual fashions as well as better dresses; many special items are made up by designers just for this chain. Sizes begin at 14.

FORGOTTEN WOMAN
888 Lexington Avenue, at 66th Street
60 West 49th Street

▼

FORMAN'S: Forman's of Lower East Side fame has two separate shops for specialty sizes—one for petites and one for plus sizes. Expect a

20% discount on first-rate fashion. If you need a special size, run here immediately after hotel check-in.

FORMAN'S COATS/PLUS SIZES, 78 Orchard Street
FORMAN'S PETITES
94 Orchard Street
59 John Street

▼

PERSIS: Another petite specialty shop for those under 5'4", where you can not only buy the latest from the petite lines but have custom-design services as well.

PERSIS, 989 Madison Avenue, at 77th Street

▼

SMART SIZE: Another discount source, and a large chain. Their motto: "Smart women do not pay full price." We read that to mean full sizes but not full price tags. Discounts are touted at 20% to 70%, with new merchandise arriving every week. Also half sizes.

This is a good-sized shop with a large selection of mostly sportswear and casual looks but also bathing suits and dressy dresses. It's also in the Garment Center, so you can do a good bit of specialty shopping in the area. Write to Director of Consumer Affairs, 2 Emerson Lane, Secaucus NJ 07094 for outlets near you.

SMART SIZE, 20 West 39th Street

▼

LANE BRYANT: Lane Bryant has remade itself in the new image of the large woman—elegant and voluptuous. The main store, on Fifth Avenue, is a place for anyone to enjoy—no matter what size she is. It's just a pleasure to be in the store. To shop there is a little

more difficult, simply because the store is
sprawled across several levels and you go up
and down stairs and around the floor looking
at everything—all of which is beautifully displayed. This is all fun, but you can feel a tad
lost. Prices are as sensational as the decor;
selection is huge. Sizes begin at 14; there are
clothes, coats, and accessories—as well as things
like panty hose. You can also buy an excellent
book of tips that Lane Bryant publishes for
the large-size woman for about $3. Most of the
merchandise, by the way, is made expressly for
Lane Bryant, and will not be seen elsewhere.
Prices are inexpensive to moderate. A Chanel-
style suit costs under $150!

LANE BRYANT, 452 Fifth Avenue, at 39th
Street

▾

JEANNE RAFAL: Just across the street from
Lane Bryant, Rafal is a million miles away in
style. Just as the Bryant store is big and glitzy
and made for everyone, Rafal is small and
quiet and more like the specialty store where
you know everyone and what they have. Rafal
has more high-fashion items, many from France,
and much higher prices than Bryant. They also
have a fur department. Shop them both and
compare for yourself.

JEANNE RAFAL, 435 Fifth Avenue, at 39th
Street

Active Sportswear

HERMAN'S: Herman's is a large chain with
stores all over the country, but we think the
selection at the 42nd Street store is mindboggling—although they do have much more

for Mr. Sport than for Ms. Sport or the kids. Also, sometimes we have found New York sold out on kids' boots and had to go to a suburban store to get the size we needed. No matter; for equipment, clothes, gear, and gifts, Herman's is a well-priced, one-stop source— it's not the fanciest place in town and, for shoes, probably isn't the cheapest. They do have all the sport team merchandise for all sports. The West 34th Street store is open on Sunday afternoon; the others are not.

HERMAN'S
845 Third Avenue, at 51st Street
110 Nassau Street
135 West 42nd Street
39 West 34th Street
1185 Avenue of the Americas, at 47th Street

HUDSON'S: This is a family hangout. We've never met anyone who wasn't amazed with Hudson's, and that includes our kids when they are in one of their I-hate-to-shop moods. If you combine a trip to Hudson's with a trip to Paragon you will never need to go shopping for sporting goods again, and you will have saved enough money to pay for a camping trip. Hudson's is a surplus store. We buy long underwear here, camping supplies, and even party favors. Don't forget the mail-order catalogue. Who needs L. L. Bean?

HUDSON'S, 97 Third Avenue, at 12th Street

HUNTING WORLD: If you think shooting and hunting are sports, then you probably already know about Hunting World. We like the store because we think their handbags, totes, and safari jackets are first-rate fashion at reasonable prices. Not bargain prices, mind you, but a safari jacket costs less here than at

Yves Saint Laurent. You can also get a similar look from Banana Republic, of course.

HUNTING WORLD, 16 East 53rd Street

▼

H. KAUFFMAN & SONS: Anyone who knows anything about horses in New York knows about Kauffman's. If you're just visiting but are the consummate horseperson who is missing her horse as much as she misses her children, a visit to Kauffman's will thrill and delight you. And if Kauffman doesn't have what you want, don't forget to try Miller's, which is almost next door.

H. KAUFFMAN & SONS, 139 East 24th Street

▼

M. J. KNOUD: If you want to know where Jackie O buys her saddle, or where the well-to-do horsey set does business, you'll go to Knoud's, which is quietly buried among the high-roller European designer boutiques on upper Madison Avenue. Even if you don't have a horse, you may want to step in here to smell the saddle soap and recall days gone by when all retailing was done through specialty stores such as this one.

M. J. KNOUD, 716 Madison Avenue, at 63rd Street

▼

MILLER'S HARNESS CO.: A dazzling new store for the Mr. Ed crowd. Everything from Hermès saddles to boots.

MILLER'S HARNESS CO., 117 East 24th Street

▼

PARAGON: One night a madcap friend kidnapped us to take us to his favorite store in New York. Was it Barneys? No way. Macy's? Guess again. It was Paragon, a sporting-goods supermarket not far from Gramercy Park. This is the kind of store you whirl through with a shopping basket—they truly have everything you can imagine. The prices are the best in town.

PARAGON, 867 Broadway, at 18th Street

▼

PECK & CHASE SHOES: Peck & Chase also owns All Star Shoes. Both of them discount sneakers, running shoes, the infamous Reeboks, and all the big-name sports shoes. Expect to pay 20% to 25% less than at an Uptown shoe store. Many shoe shops on Orchard Street discount running shoes; prices seem to be the same from place to place.

PECK & CHASE SHOES, 163 Orchard Street
ALL STAR SHOES, 135 Orchard Street

▼

ORVIS: If L. L. Bean came to Manhattan, he would probably check into Orvis, a small store in Midtown not far from Grand Central Station. You can get your fishing supplies here, and that's what Orvis is famous for, but you can also get gifts for fishermen (ties and pillows) and clothes rather suitable for weekending in the country or for visiting Balmoral. This store offers fisherman chic with a name that is famous to those in the know.

ORVIS, 355 Madison Avenue, at 45th Street

▼

EASTERN MOUNTAIN SPORTS: Part of a larger chain of active outfitters, E.M.S. has one of its largest stores on the edge of NoHo and the cutting edge of fashion—this is the place to go for both price and selection. They bill themselves as "The Outdoor Specialists." You can get your skiwear, camping gear, or fishing or hiking supplies at this well-stocked, one-stop sporting-goods mart.

EASTERN MOUNTAIN SPORTS
611 Broadway, at Houston Street
20 West 61st Street

Furs

One of the best things about coming to New York to shop is that the selection of specialty items is immense. If you've been dreaming of a fur coat (who hasn't?), then we think you'd be nuts to buy it anyplace else in the United States than New York. And you'd be nuts to pay retail. In fact, we think you can pay for your trip to New York with the savings on a fur coat. And we're not just talking about an exotic fur. New York happens to be the home of the $3,000 mink coat!

The fur business has changed tremendously in recent years; now coats are being made in the Orient, where labor costs are lower, and the world of fur has been more than turned upside down. Yet the coat made in the Orient is vastly different from a coat made in Europe or the United States. As Mother always said, you generally get what you pay for.

And Mother believed in fur coats. These days, not every woman does. Which brings us to a new wrinkle in the fur business. Antifur campaigns have taken their toll.

What you're looking at therefore is a business that has been hit with two problems at the same time: the availability of cheapie coats from the Orient, of which every young woman who was going to buy a cheapie coat from the Orient has already bought one, and the fact that in some strata of society, there is peer pressure not to wear fur.

The results? Many furriers have closed; more will do so. Those who are still in business need your business, so their prices (especially at wholesale) are negotiable.

The fur industry as a whole is looking within to cure its ills. With the understanding that there will always be a high-end fur business, breeders are taking a look at the 1990–91 auctions with a plan to kill off breeding stock if things don't get better. Once the breeding stock is dead, you guessed it. Prices will go sky-high.

So, if you ever wanted to buy a fur coat, now is the time to do so. Avoid the mass producers; avoid the warehouse sales held in giant coliseums and stadiums (if you want quality, anyway), and go for a well-known furrier in the district.

We have always bought top-of-the-line fur coats from top-of-the-line makers, and although we have shopped the fur supermarkets around the world, we admit that we rarely like what they have to offer. We are fur snobs and we have learned this much:

▼ Coats made in the Orient are usually not as good technically as coats made in the United States. Collars are usually not turned as well; sleeves may be set in very tightly.

▼ European skins are not as fine as U.S. skins. By European we do not mean Russian (Soviet sable is the best). There are only a certain number of minks being ranched in the United States; the rest have to come from somewhere else.

▼ The fur union went to hell in a basket a few years ago, and ever since there has been such deregulation—much like for the airlines—that anything goes. You must be on your toes.

▼ The markup in the fur business is in less expensive coats. So you can get a $3,000 fur coat in the Orient for $1,500. You cannot get a $6,000 coat in the fur district for $3,000. The markup on fine skins from a superior wholesale furrier is less than 10%. The real savings in a New York fur-buying spree comes in buying a top-of-the-line department-store $10,000-to-$12,000 coat for $7,500 to $8,000 at wholesale. See Leonard Kahn or Leslie Goldin.

▼ Mink is the most practical fur—it goes everywhere in style and wears the longest. Long-hair furs do not wear nearly so well and certainly are not meant for rugged, everyday wear over a prolonged number of years. You'll be lucky to get five years from a good raccoon coat. Fox is just for dress.

▼ Color is not as important as the quality of the skins; black fur really means nothing (this is in mink, of course). Color will change over a period of years, but only slightly. Do not confuse the names of black colors with Blackglama, which is a trade name. Some people will try to tell you that a similar name means the same thing. Wrong. The Japanese have driven up the price on black and gray mink. Fall in love with brown!

▼ Silkiness counts in mink; if the hairs are spiky, long, or coarse, they will wear out. Look at the underfur, which should be dense and thick.

▼ A good coat should be practically indestructible. Roll it in a ball and watch the hairs jump back. If the coat doesn't perform, jump away from the sale.

▼ Do not ask a furrier to send an empty box to the home of an out-of-state relative so you can avoid paying New York State sales tax. Tacky, tacky.

Superior Furs

Cheap fur looks great until you put it next to
quality fur; then you get the idea that quality
pays. If you can afford a quality fur, you never
will be sorry. A superior mink coat will give
you ten to twenty years of superior wear, looking just about as good as new for the first ten
years. A quality mink coat should be female
skins, which are lighter than male skins and
wear better. Most mass-produced coats are
made of male skins. A quality fur should be
ranched in the United States and made in the
United States—and by someone you trust. Although there are a half-dozen famous furriers
in the fur district, most of whom take customers with references, we are only going to give
you the names of the two we have used. Both
these makers are top of the line. They have
private showrooms and are not open for brows-
ers; you go to buy, not to waste their time. If
you want a $3,000 mink coat, they are not for
you. If you want a $10,000 mink coat for
$6,000 to $7,000, these are your new best
friends.

GOLDIN-FELDMAN: A solid source for
fashion furs. Goldin-Feldman makes coats for
many big-name designers. You can get on the
mailing list if you are a sale customer, or go in
for an appointment. Leslie Goldin is so knowledgeable about furs that she wrote a book on
the subject. You may buy off the rack or
have a custom order made. You don't have to
buy, but only serious shoppers should venture
forth.

GOLDIN-FELDMAN, 345 Seventh Avenue, 12th
Floor, at 29th Street

▼

KAHN & PINTO: If the name sounds slightly familiar, it could be because Ben Kahn is one of the world's most famous furriers. Leonard Kahn, of Kahn & Pinto, is his nephew. You can buy an already made-up coat, design your own coat, or work with Leonard's designers to get a custom coat that fits and hangs like a cloud. We have bought mink and raccoon from Leonard and had the coats appraised for twice the paying price. A custom mink coat will be about $7,000; raccoon, $3,000. We don't want to rave and rave and embarrass ourselves, because we obviously haven't bought a lot of mink coats in our lives, but Leonard reminds us that when you buy an important fur coat you really are buying a furrier; that means trust. And we'd go to the wire with Leonard. We trust him perfectly and send you there knowing you will get the best deal in New York. Call for an appointment; serious shoppers only. Telephone: (212) 564-1735.

KAHN & PINTO, 130 West 30th Street, 7th Floor

Used Furs

We have thought about used furs but always chicken out for the simple reason that you never know what you are buying. Age is everything in a mink coat, and after three years the coat isn't worth what it once was. The skins begin to lose moisture. But if you're game for a used coat, here goes:

NEW YORKER FUR THRIFT SHOP: There are tons of coats in seemingly perfect condition here. They buy, sell, and trade. What's not to like? Prices start at a few hundred dollars.

NEW YORKER FUR THRIFT SHOP, 822 Third Avenue, at 50th Street

RITZ THRIFT SHOP: For years the most famous furrier for used furs in New York, Ritz has a reputation as big as the Ritz. They buy, sell, and trade and are a wonderful resource for getting the feel of fur. You may do well on a first fur coat here also. The good location makes it probable that you'll be in the neighborhood, anyway. Full-length fur coats, $1,000 and up.

RITZ THRIFT SHOP, 105 West 57th Street

Linens

The Big Names

DESCAMPS: It's pronounced "De-cam," and if you can't afford the Porthault or Pratesi lines but crave a fancy bed that is more sophisticated than what you get at K mart, you'll find Descamps a nice upper-price but still moderate choice. The baby linen is very special.

DESCAMPS, 723 Madison Avenue, at 63rd Street

▼

FRETTE: Frette has changed its marketing approach, redone its shop, and introduced a lingerie line, so you have something to wear between their fancy sheets.

FRETTE, 799 Madison Avenue, at 67th Street

▼

PORTHAULT: The most expensive beds in America probably are dressed in Porthault prints from France—a set of king-size sheets with standard cases is well over $1,200. If you have lots of pillows (who doesn't?) and like the shams with scalloped and handcut ruffles, figure another $300 a pillowcase. There are Porthault made-in-America designs for Wamsutta, but the really fancy stuff from France is here. Every January the store still has a half-price markdown spree. There are less expensive knickknacks, by the way, and we know some women who treat themselves to one pillowcase a year. As time goes by, they have a delightful mélange of Porthault prints, which they mix with white sheets (always a style classic) and American quilts, and the look is stunning.

PORTHAULT, 18 East 69th Street

▼

PRATESI: As much as we admire Porthault, we don't know how they stay in business when people can choose Pratesi. Pratesi offers more designwise—you don't have to have flowers if you don't want them—the quality is excellent, and the prices are less than half. You can get a set of sheets at Pratesi for $450, which is a bargain compared to $1,200. Pratesi also has numerous styles that are suitable for the man who doesn't want to be in a bed of roses or a scattering of hearts. The Pope sleeps on Pratesi (white sheets with a yellow-gold border), and Pratesi advertising states that most of the royalty of Europe were conceived between Pratesi sheets. The best testimony we can give is our own: We got a set of sheets from Athos as a baby gift in 1980, have washed them twice a month for ten years, and find them still in perfect condition. You can't beat that kind of quality. There are twice-a-year sales.

PRATESI, 829 Madison Avenue, at 69th Street

▼

SHERIDAN: From Down Under to up top—Sheridan is an Australian company that is tops with us! We like this store because it's bright and pretty and nice to be in (don't miss the downstairs); because the prices are moderate to low for designer sheets and things; because they sell the sheeting by the yard so we can properly decorate a room without having to buy extra sheets; and (but not finally) because we love the work of artist Ken Done, who does wild and colorful prints, and we buy not only his sheets but his plasticized tote bags and wallets. There are three designer lines (Done, Jill FitzSimmons, and the house line) with an assortment of styles; some twenty-three other shops around the world.

SHERIDAN, 595 Madison Avenue, at 57th Street

▼

SCHWEITZER'S LINENS: This shop has no discount sheets, nor do they have average sheets—everything is either the special high-end line of a major sheet company (like the Royal Collection or the Versailles Collection) or a European sheet made to look like an even more expensive European sheet—the only Porthault look-alikes we've ever seen come from this shop. Their small stores feel European and cater to a well-off local crowd that wants top-of-the-line quality. There is a catalogue; they do custom work. A few designer prints are available (like Kenzo), but the mainstream here is the subtle print (stripes, dots, bows, flowers) and the European look.

SCHWEITZER'S LINENS
   1132 Madison Avenue, at 84th Street
   457 Columbus Avenue, at 81st Street

▼

ABC LINENS: Actually, this is just part of the entire ABC complex, which includes carpets and antiques, but their linen department is so upscale and so with-it that it deserves special attention. Do not be fooled into thinking that prices here are better than in other parts of town (unless you get a sale or a promotion); we're talking convenience and selection and sometimes a good buy. ABC carries the Sheridan line (see page 203), our favorite new sheet company, as well as the Descamps line and the Kenzo line, which is not easy to find. There are also giftables and home-decorating items on the 3rd floor—what is billed as the bed, bath, and linen floor. Open Sunday, 11 A.M.–6 P.M. For credit card orders call (800) 888-RUGS.

ABC LINENS, 880 Broadway, at 19th Street

Discount Linens

ELDRIDGE JOBBING HOUSE CORP.: Not to be confused with Eldridge Textile Co., another Lower East Side discounter that is around the corner, Eldridge Jobbing House Corp. is in a tiny space that is crammed, like the stacks in the library, with sheets. Many of the high-style lines that are not carried elsewhere are available here. The store does stock Gear Kids and even has the crib sheets, which are very hard to find at a discount source. Prices may be only 15% to 20% off, but it is a good saving on high-fashion items.

ELDRIDGE JOBBING HOUSE CORP., 90 Eldridge Street

▼

ELDRIDGE TEXTILE CO.: This large store looks and feels like the typical Lower East Side home and dry goods general store. Current styles are their prime business; discounts are small and compete with department-store "white sale" prices. This is a good source only at the beginning of a season. They will custom-make (and send) a dust ruffle to match your sheets. Their workmanship is excellent; prices for custom work are fabulous.

ELDRIDGE TEXTILE CO., 277 Grand Street

▼

HOMEWORKS: Homeworks is one of the new-style Lower East Side shops that looks just as nice as anything on Lower Fifth Avenue. It's really a bath-and-table boutique, not a sheet house. But you can get towels, napkins, and fancy stuff here—at a flat 20% discount. This is top-of-the-line department-store merchandise, with napkin rings, at the price it will be during the January department-store sale. Why wait?

HOMEWORKS, 281 Grand Street

Museum Shopping

While we feel appreciative toward whoever invented museums, we really want to thank whoever invented museum gift shops. New York has, possibly, the best museum gift shops in the world. If you feel a big shopping spree coming on, ask about member discounts. Membership in a museum can be as little as $25 a year and you will get a 10% to 25% discount on items you buy in the gift shop.

Almost any museum you go into has a shop, but here are some of the best:

AMERICAN MUSEUM OF NATURAL HIS-TORY: This one is tricky, folks: There are *several* shops, on two different floors. And they have different merchandise. If you are looking for dinosaur favors for a birthday party, try them all. Open seven days a week for your shopping pleasure.

AMERICAN MUSEUM OF NATURAL HISTORY, Central Park West, at 79th Street

▼

COOPER-HEWITT MUSEUM: The Smithsonian Institution of Washington, D.C., runs this little mansion-turned-design-museum. The collection is fabulous. The gift shop also is excellent. Closed Monday.

COOPER-HEWITT MUSEUM, 2 East 91st Street

▼

METROPOLITAN MUSEUM OF ART: Shopping, shopping, shopping. Just as the collection never ends, neither does the gift shop. Have you ever seen such books in your life? It's even better than Rizzoli. The reproductions aren't bad, but aren't our cup of copy. Fabulous Christmas cards. Closed Monday.

METROPOLITAN MUSEUM OF ART, Fifth Avenue at 82nd Street

▼

MUSEUM OF MODERN ART: A vast shop on the main lobby floor, with more downstairs. This location now features a huge range of art publications, posters, calendars, and unusual cards. You'll want to check them out at Christmas. Don't miss the new Design Store listing.

MUSEUM OF MODERN ART, 11 West 53rd Street

THE MOMA DESIGN STORE: A new store for fans of the Museum of Modern Art and the crazy giftables and artsy-craftsy fun stuff they sell. An excellent resource for gifts for the hard-to-please people on your list. We found pewter perfume bottles at $45 each that were wonderful and unusual. Prices can be quite moderate for merchandise that is so exclusive and expensive-looking. To order, or to get the catalogue, call (800) 447-6662.

THE MOMA DESIGN STORE, 44 West 53rd Street

▼

MUSEUM OF FOLK ART: A perfect gift shop for T-shirts, scarves, books, toys, and home items, all with an American folk motif. We think all the cow merchandise is a hoot. This is a freestanding store that is not attached to a museum, by the way. Also please note that when interesting American antiques shows are held in New York, this museum runs a bus service.

MUSEUM OF FOLK ART
  62 West 50th Street
  2 Lincoln Square (Columbus Avenue at 66th Street)

▼

CHILDREN'S MUSEUM OF MANHATTAN: The city gets a new museum and a new museum gift shop in one fell swoop. Many of the toys and playthings for sale are the size and price appropriate for stocking stuffers, although there is also a book and science section as well as a crafts section. A very exciting addition to the kiddie shopping scene. . . . A must before Christmas or at birthday time.

CHILDREN'S MUSEUM OF MANHATTAN, 212 West 83rd Street

WHITNEY MUSEUM OF AMERICAN ART:
The Whitney has a shop inside the museum
and then one next door in a separate building
on Madison Avenue. The gift items in the
separate shop are fun and different from what
you'll see anywhere else—contemporary and
imaginative and perfect for people who have
everything . . . if they also have a sense of
humor.

WHITNEY MUSEUM OF AMERICAN ART, 945
  Madison Avenue, at 75th Street
THE STORE NEXT DOOR, 943 Madison Avenue,
  at 75th Street

Flea Markets, Crafts Fairs, and Swap Meets

New York's flea markets, crafts fairs, and
swap meets have a reputation of their
own, and you may want to check out
one or two of them—especially if collectibles and knickknacks are your kind of
thing. Crafts fairs are particularly big in the
summer on weekends, and are perfect outings
for a day in the country. You can rent a car or
even take a bus to the big, well-organized
events.

**THE ANNEX ANTIQUES FAIR & FLEA
MARKET,** Sixth Avenue from 24th to 26th
streets: Over 200 vendors with the largest selection of furniture and paintings of any of the
city's markets. There's an on-site office to arrange for delivery. If you've got a good eye
you can find some excellent pieces here. Hours:
Saturday and Sunday, 9 A.M.–5 P.M.

CANAL WEST FLEA MARKET, 370 Canal
Street: Good buys on some new merchandise,

bargains on discounted panty hose, blue jeans, etc. Not worth a special trip, but if you're in the area anyway, stop by. SoHo itself is far more wonderful than this market; other street merchants set up in neighborhood lots, weather permitting. The real fun to this flea market is observing the other shoppers. Hours: Saturday and Sunday, 7 A.M.–6 P.M.

ANTIQUE FLEA & FARMERS MARKET AT P.S. 183, East 67th Street between First and York avenues: Its location in this upscale neighborhood means it attracts a lot of celebrities. There are some great vintage jewelry booths, and outside in the schoolyard farmers spread out their tempting wares. Hours: Saturday, 6 A.M.–6 P.M.

GREENWICH VILLAGE FLEA MARKET, P.S. 41, Greenwich Avenue at Charles Street: Outdoor booths featuring bargains in antiques, jewelry, and vintage and modern collectibles. Hours: Saturday, noon–7 P.M.

I.S. 44 FLEA MARKET, Columbus Avenue between 76th and 77th streets: Over 300 indoor and outdoor vendors offering an amazing array of new and vintage clothing and jewelry, antiques, quilts, even furniture. This is another good market for celebrity spotting. Hours: Sunday, 10 A.M.–6 P.M.

TOWER MARKET, Broadway between West 4th and Great Jones streets: This youth-oriented outdoor market is a must for any teen after a stop at nearby Tower Records. Much of the merchandise is new, including T-shirts, jewelry, fun watches, and some vintage clothing. Hours: Saturday and Sunday, 10 A.M.–7 P.M.

COLUMBIA UNIVERSITY CRAFTS FAIR: Sponsored by American Arts & Crafts Alliance, Inc., this has become a major crafts fair that even hosts a wholesale day. This is an annual fund-raiser. Call (212) 866-2239 for exact dates.

ACC CRAFTFAIR: The old Rhinebeck Crafts Fair became such a big event that it was transferred to Massachusetts. Don't let that faze you. You can take a bus or join a tour for a fabulous one-day shopping spree. This is an annual event usually held in late May; call (914) 255-0039 or (413) 787-0140 for details. There are all-inclusive bus tours from Manhattan. Don't miss it!

YONKERS RACEWAY FLEA MARKET: This is almost as good as the flea market at the Rose Bowl in Pasadena, California. Collectibles shows are also held here, so one weekend we took in baseball cards, jewels, and minerals, and still the swap meet. This is how a Sunday should be spent!

ROOSEVELT RACEWAY FLEA MARKET: We were heartbroken to give up California and the Rose Bowl Swap Meet. But life has come back to us now that we have discovered the Roosevelt Raceway Flea Market, in Westbury, New York. To tell you just how devoted we are, we drive a total of three hours to get there. (It's just not that close to Connecticut; it's easier from Long Island or Manhattan.)

The Roosevelt Raceway Flea Market is a full-day trip. Ideally, plan to go with some friends and rent a truck. You can go on the train (from Penn Station: Take the train to Westbury.) You can take a city bus or a taxi or even walk to the raceway from the train station. But you'll need to call a cab for getting back to the train—you will be so loaded with packages.

Although the market is held rain or shine and there is indoor space, the event just isn't as much fun in the rain. On sunny days, about 1,500 vendors set up in the parking lot to sell an assortment of everything. Most of it is new—there are no antiques here—and much of it is designer quality. This is where we buy T-shirts ($5 each); this is where we buy luggage, socks, underwear, clothes for the kids for camp, stationery, wrapping paper, plastic bins, and sweats. We've bought Kenneth Jay Lane jewelry here; Ultra Pink clothes; Champion brand sweats; and even framed Disney posters ($5!).

A few announcements: You can buy foodstuffs like fresh pickles, chopped garlic, incredibly creamy cheesecakes, and some fresh fruits. Many dealers will not take checks or credit cards; be loaded with cash or traveler's checks. The Sunday event feels entirely different from the Wednesday event—there are about 25% more vendors on Sunday, and they are different; it's a more commercial fair those days . . . not quite so warm and neighborly as on Wednesday. Remember sunscreen or a hat in summer—it can be brutally hot out there. The bathrooms are clean; there are several snack bars for hot dogs, etc. Hours: 9 A.M.–3 P.M., Wednesday and Sunday; closed for the winter season. Admission fee is by carload: 50¢ on Wednesday, $1 on Sunday.

BRIMFIELD: We have done this as a day trip because we are nuts, because it's not quite as long a schlepp from Connecticut, and because it is such a zoo that if you aren't organized, you won't be able to find a hotel room anyway. But here goes: The country's wildest flea market is held three times a year in a small Massachusetts community (near Sturbridge Village) called Brimfield. About 50,000 people show for each of the three events, which last a week each. The May fair is the most popular, but all three are worthwhile for dealers and pros. If you aren't quick-witted, you'll be trampled to death!

Pros are there when the gates open at 7 A.M., and run around like maniacs papering the place with money. We realize that it's impossible to compete, so we go more slowly—arriving after the main rush at the door and merely to look, bargain, and maybe find a great deal.

Please note that there are several areas where the flea markets are held, and that it really does take most of the week to do this properly, the way a dealer should. Thousands of dealers from all over the country will be in Brimfield for the do; this is truly the largest flea market in the world. For the dates of the market (it's in May, July, and September) call the Brimfield market office at (413) 245-3436 or (508) 597-8155. The 1991 dates are May 10 (all week), July 12 (all week), and September 13 (all week). Remember, the event lasts six days, but most fields are only open three of the six days.

Antiques Markets

THE MANHATTAN ART AND ANTIQUES CENTER: This conglomeration of shops is the brainstorm of a real-estate development company that saw what was happening to the antiques shops in the area. Instead of forcing more shops out of business, they created a home for over sixty-five shops. Within this complex you can find every price range and variety of antique. The emphasis is mostly on small items, as the spaces are not, for the most part, enormous. Each dealer operates independently. You have to go frequently; the luck of the draw reigns supreme. Some people have done very well here; others come up empty-shopping-bagged.

THE MANHATTAN ART AND ANTIQUES CENTER, 1050 Second Avenue, at 55th Street

▼

PLACE DES ANTIQUAIRES: The fanciest antiques market in America is doing a lot to get people to stop by and shop. Only the Aga Khan can afford the prices. But don't let that stop you. Many dealers here are Europeans who do not exhibit elsewhere; a few are Americans who can afford the rent. Most of the furniture is formal period stuff, but some *objets* can be found here and there. You can get coffee and croissants downstairs. There are often room sets. Shows and lectures for the public. A true treat.

PLACE DES ANTIQUAIRES, 125 East 57th Street

Antiques and Collectibles

The New York market in antiques and collectibles is multinational and enormous, and someday we plan to write a book about it. Until then, this is just a little spoonful of information to point you in several interesting directions.

There aren't too many bargains in New York, but there is selection—and a wide selection at many price points. You'll find value in country Swedish looks, on the lesser-quality country style pieces, and on good reproductions in various periods. In these areas you still can make some wonderful purchases that will appreciate in value over the years. As the finer pieces become more rare, the secondary pieces gain importance and value. Art Deco furniture used to be easy to find and inexpensive. Now you have to sell the family jewels to buy the better pieces. Who would have thought that 1950s furniture would ever be worth more than the junkman would charge to haul it away?

The antiques business seems to have segmented itself into areas according to price range, due mostly to the high cost of rent. If you are selling fine high-ticket items, you can afford to pay more rent. The lesser-quality and lower-price-range goods are in the lower-rent neighborhoods.

Since what you call an antique may differ from another person's definition, or because you may not enjoy looking at $10,000 *bombés*, we have arbitrarily divided the market by price and district and interest fields to help you get a better grip on it. Antiques and collectibles become specialized by price and by category. Those who collect rare sheet music are just as serious as those who collect Picasso, but each has little in common with the person who wants a Louis XV *escritoire*. The best, and worst, thing about serious collectibles shopping in New York is selection. You could easily furnish a museum, let alone a house. At a certain point, making the rounds just becomes ridiculous. If you are looking for a good day's fun, stick to country antiques shops (Connecticut!) or try our section called University Place (see page 219). You just may want to go to Newel Galleries or ABC Antiques and call it a day. If you are in the market for something more serious, the world of yesterday's wonders awaits you. But be warned: The bill may be just as amazing as the selection.

Hoity-Toity Antiques/ The Upper East Side

The Upper East Side is home to the best of the best. If you are looking for a Ming vase, Empire chairs, a Federal hutch, or a Louis sofa and have a well-endowed checkbook, go no farther. These shops are superb in both quality and selection. The owners are knowledgeable and willing to help you find what you are in search of. They will authenticate and help you ship. We have listed some of the best shops by address to make searching easier. This is the one area of town where it is possible to go from shop to shop without much hassle. Please note that we have not listed every shop and that this listing is by neighborhood. It's just to get you going—these are some of our favorites; these are places where we have done business. There are lots more that are probably just as good. *A tip:* Some shops are on the ground level, some are upstairs.

East 56th and 57th Streets

All these shops are top-quality and not to be missed, whether you are browsing for a serious look or collecting something special. Most are specialists; some are known as specialists (you would think A La Vieille Russie just had tsarist antiques . . . wrong, they have all sorts) but have other related items. Seek and ye shall find; shop and ye shall spend:

RALPH M. CHAIT, 12 East 56th Street: One of the city's most important collections of Oriental porcelain; scads of blue and white; exhibits at the important shows.

DORIS LESLIE BLAU, 15 East 57th Street: By appointment only; carpets—the kind you are afraid to have your kids walk on.

JAMES ROBINSON, 15 East 57th Street: Silver, silver, silver, silver, and more and even better silver. Also some jewelry like Grandma never wore.

JAMES II GALLERIES, 15 East 57th Street: Above James Robinson, this is a less formal shop of Art Deco, Victorian silver, accessories, dishes, and even some jewelry. When we're rich . . .

ISRAEL SACK, 15 East 57th Street: Fine, old, traditional firm specializing in important furniture; 3rd floor.

FRANK CARO, 41 East 57th Street: Very interesting and unusual Oriental furniture and accessories; for the true specialist.

DALVA BROS., 44 East 57th Street: Let them eat cake—on tables that Dalva Bros. brought over from France, of course.

ARTHUR ACKERMAN & SON, 50 East 57th Street: Old, good, and grand English traditional furniture. God save our gracious Queen.

S. J. SHRUBSOLE, 104 East 57th Street: Similar to James Robinson; if you didn't buy it in London, now's your chance.

NESLE, 151 East 57th Street: Chandeliers for the palace.

A LA VIEILLE RUSSIE, 781 Fifth Avenue: Fabergé and such. If you're big on the double eagle and imperial dreams, you'll even love the ambience. And you may get an Easter egg . . . not the chocolate type.

Not to Be Missed

This one is in a category by itself and is one of those "Gee, Toto" kinds of places. They do not have one of these in your hometown, and we don't care where you come from. It's a little farther east than you may normally travel, but we think it's worth the walk—or taxi fare.

NEWEL GALLERIES: Shocking and wonderful and weird and fabulous and incredible and not to be believed and, well, you just have to go see this for yourself. Newel is an antiques resource of extraordinary proportions. Many pieces are for rent; all are one of a kind. Every variety of antique can be found somewhere in the vast recesses of the six floors of warehouse space. You have to experience Newel to appreciate its unusual nature. If you think this is a pass, you get us wrong. This is theater. This is what you came to New York for.

NEWEL GALLERIES, 425 East 53rd Street

Madison Avenue—Sixties to Eighties

The largest concentration of fancy antiques shops is on Madison Avenue in the 70s; however, they start at 61st Street with G. Malina (680 Madison Avenue), and go as high as Gallery Madison 90 (1248 Madison Avenue). We thought about writing a separate book about them ... here're a *few* of our favorites. The rest are wonderful and easy to find if you look upstairs as well as on the ground floor.

AMERICA HURRAH, 766 Madison Avenue: All our quilts came from here; America Hurrah is one of the acknowledged leaders in Americana—quilts, samplers, and hooked rugs are their specialty.

DIDIER AARON, 32 East 67th Street: You can also catch them in Paris. Important European furniture, mostly French. The New York showroom doesn't look like much from outside, but never judge a book by its cover.

LINDA HORN, 1015 Madison Avenue: It's not as hoity or as toity as some of the others; you absolutely *have* to walk in just to see the walls and the decor. The selection is affordable in the lower expensive range; the store wins top awards for ambience and charm. You came all the way to New York just to see this place and tell your children about it.

JUAN PORTELA, 783 Madison Avenue: How many times can we say incredible? Whatever piece is in the window probably will bring tears to your eyes.

MINNA ROSENBLATT, 844 Madison Avenue: Art Deco and Art Nouveau lamps et al; Tiffany and such.

DE LORENZO, 958 Madison Avenue: They call it "Twentieth-Century Decorative Arts"; we call it fabulous. Art Deco, Art Nouveau, Giacometti chairs. Ah, the things money can buy.

FLORIAN PAPP, INC., 962 Madison Avenue: Did you hear a pin drop? Maybe it was our teeth. Formal and fabulous.

Not-So-Fancy Antiques

You don't have to grow up in Versailles to want to buy antiques. Even if your budget is limited, you still can find enough selection and specialty items to make the trip worthwhile. Recent college grads and young professionals take note: You can have your cake and eat it, too. Enjoy Madison Avenue, but take your checkbook when you travel to 12th Street or to Brooklyn—these are the areas where designers go to nose through lots of stuff, hoping to find hidden jewels. The shoppers wear blue jeans or are properly dressed professionals, although Brooklyn on a weekend is decidedly laid-back.

Atlantic Avenue

Many of the antiques shops that could no longer pay the rents in Manhattan moved to Atlantic Avenue, Brooklyn. The street is incredibly long, and houses many, many antiques stores of varying quality and price range. If you're coming from Manhattan, we think the safest subway is the "F" train to the Bergen Street stop. Walk (quickly) back along Smith Street and turn right onto Atlantic after only three blocks.

The greatest concentration of antiques shops starts at Hoyt Street and continues along Atlantic Avenue for about ten blocks. Shops to stop and visit include: **TIME TRADERS** (No. 368), **CIRCA** (No. 374), **CITY BARN** (No. 362), **THE ANTIQUE ROOM** (Nos. 412, 414, and 416), **ATLANTIC ANTIQUE CENTER** (No. 367), **DAN'S ANTIQUE SHOP** (No. 363), **HORSEMAN ANTIQUES, INC.** (No. 351), **IN DAYS OF OLD, LTD.** (No. 357), and **REPEAT PERFORMANCE ANTIQUES** (No. 377A). Best days to visit are Saturday and Sunday. Many of the shops are closed midweek while their owners comb the countryside for more treasures. If you want to be part of the rebirth of Brooklyn, now's your chance.

University Place

University is a street on the East Side of Manhattan, just below 14th Street; along with Broadway, which at this point in its life is now on the East Side, it creates a very little neighborhood that is crammed with antiques shops and warehouses. We're talking one resource that may have six floors of great stuff. This is not the home of the $35 bed frame. But this is where affordable furniture can be yours. You should know your market if you are spending a lot of money or think you have a serious piece; otherwise, just enjoy. The area is so well combed by dealers that the diamonds get ferreted out very quickly. You may be forced to make do with rhinestones.

If this sounds like we've just told you about the funkiest little yet-to-be-discovered part of town ever created, think again. Some very sharp dealers have already moved down here and are slowly creating a gentrified zone connected to the renewal of the entire Fifth Avenue area between 23rd and 14th streets and of the Gramercy Park area.

While prowling, check out:

KENTSHIRE, 37 East 12th Street: Six floors of furniture and accessories of good quality with high prices. It's mostly European and Oriental; there's not much French. It's neither dusty nor dirty nor warehousey, but it's not Madison Avenue, either.

ABC ANTIQUES, 880 Broadway, at 19th Street: Chances are excellent that you'll find everything you need at ABC and never get to another store. ABC is in an old, huge, New York kind of building; they began as a discount carpet source. Now it's virtually a discount department store ... although a lot of the antiques are reproductions. Who cares?

GEORGE SUBKOFF ANTIQUES, 835 Broadway: One of New York's most famous names for American, English, and European goodies. High-end stuff. There's also a store in Connecticut.

6 ▾ BARGAIN BASEMENTS AND TRADE SECRETS

Bargain Basements

Ｎew York is filled with bargain basements: Some are readily identifiable as such; others are secrets. We've been to very few that really were basements, but whether they are at street level or at skyscraper level, New York's bargain basements are phenomenal. The most important thing to remember, however, is that many places that look like bargain basements merely offer inexpensive merchandise. We want expensive merchandise at low, low prices. Don't you?

We do most of our shopping in bargain basements. We go to them regularly; we work some of them as if they were political allies. We keep in touch; we check in to check out the stock. It's often a hands-on, eyes-out business. It helps to work in packs; local women always have a few other friends who keep their eyes out for hot bargains and then send out the word. If we spot a special markdown on a favorite designer, we buy first and then run for a pay phone to alert the troops. We receive as many phone calls as we initiate. It pays to have spies. (Our friend Laurie even has a friend who works at Loehmann's and who calls her the day of the shipments.) When you're visiting a city and don't have a regular network, it's harder to know which bargains are the really incredible ones. That's why we're here.

When shopping the bargain basements, remember:

▼ Bargain basements may or may not have new merchandise. Some get their goods at the beginning of the season; others don't get new merchandise until stores have dumped their unsold merchandise. Old merchandise always is less expensive than new merchandise.

▼ Look for damages.

▼ Know the return policy before you buy.

▼ Try everything on; actual sizes may be different from the marked sizes.

▼ If you are shopping in a chain, understand that another branch of that chain will have some of the same merchandise and some different merchandise.

▼ Expect communal dressing rooms and sometimes primitive conditions.

▼ Be prepared to check your handbag and/or your shopping bags. Security can be offensively tight at a bargain basement.

▼ Few bargain basements mail packages for you.

▼ Prices can vary from one bargain to another. Learn your stuff; shop a department store before you get to a bargain basement. At various well-known (and listed in this book) bargain basements, we saw the same designer blouse on the same day for several different prices, with a range of over $100. The Saks Fifth Avenue price was $230. We saw it at different outlets for $180, $163, $142, $109, and $93. It is impossible to know which bargain is the best bargain when you are shopping, but try to do a little homework first.

▼ Some bargain basements offer only 20% savings.

▼ Don't be surprised if you see totally different merchandise from the same designer at various bargain basements. It may have been made especially for that bargain basement; it may come from another country or another distributor. Particularly with the Calvin Klein label, you won't believe all the fabulous merchandise you'll see on a one-time basis in a plethora of different outlets. Nipon, too.

AARON'S: "If your husband isn't in the business," says the sign near Aaron's, a Brooklyn bargain basement that is worth the trip a thousand times over. Indeed, while our husbands aren't in the business, we are pretty well connected with garmentos, and we still think Aaron's is one of the best deals in New York. The fact that it's in Brooklyn does not deter us when it comes to stalking the wild, big-name bargain. Aaron's does take some organization to get to, but if we were on a three-day visit to New York, we would schedule it for the top of the morning rather early in the trip. It might even be more worthwhile than the Lower East Side.

Let's put it this way: If you like designer merchandise, you will find more designer names in one easy-to-shop location inside Aaron's than you will by spending hours on the Lower East Side. You might save more on the Lower East Side, if you get lucky—that's impossible to say for sure—but for one-stop, one-haul, God-this-is-fun shopping, you cannot beat Aaron's. Don't mind that it's twenty to thirty minutes away on the subway; it's worth the trip. The Brooklyn subway station is clean and nonthreatening; the one-block walk from station to store is safe and simple.

Aaron's has about 10,000 square feet of clean, well-lighted space with neat racks and handwritten cardboard signs that say things such as "Carole Little" and "Adrienne Vittadini." You'll see all the big names you love, and many names that you might not know. There's no Bill Blass, but there is Escada, which is hard to find in a discount source. Stock is kept in the back, so if you don't see your size, ask. It can be brought forward. The sales help is nice; no one is too pushy. The tags are marked down

20%, which might not be the bargain of the century. However, there usually is a sticker on the tag that has another percent number (say, 20%, meaning a 40% discount).

If you make only one bargain trip out of New York, this just might be it. It's easier than a day in Secaucus; you can be in and out in two hours (one hour to shop; one hour for transportation back and forth to the city), and you'll have enough fun to pass the tale on to your other shopaholic friends at your next meeting. Aaron's opens at 9:30 A.M., which makes it a good first morning stop. Leave your hotel at 9 A.M., and avoid rush-hour traffic.

Directions: Take the BMT "R" train, and go to Prospect Avenue in Brooklyn (you must get a train going in the Brooklyn, or Downtown, direction!). You'll get off at Fourth Avenue and 17th Street. Walk one block to Fifth Avenue. It's easy, you can't miss it. Aaron's charges $5 to send a large package out of state. Their refund policy is posted.

AARON'S, 627 Fifth Avenue (17th to 18th streets), Brooklyn

▼

ALTMAN'S: Not to be confused with the late department store, this is a discounter on Fifth Avenue in Manhattan with a branch on the Lower East Side. The discount usually is a rather straight 20% to 25% unless you hit a sale, but these are straightforward, good-for-working clothes, suits, silk dresses, etc. Start here and then swing west toward Seventh Avenue to get in a whole bunch of discounters (See our Seventh Avenue Stretch tour, page 260).

ALTMAN'S, 206 Fifth Avenue, at 26th Street

▼

BOLTON'S: Bolton's is a chain. This is where you get very serviceable fashion items for a lot less money—we've bought business suits and bathing suits. You can luck into designer merchandise at sensational prices, although the average item is a moderately priced copy of a hot style. Check your bags at the front desk. A convenient alternative to Loehmann's. We like the West 57th Street store, since we are most often in that neighborhood, but Bolton's shops seemingly are everywhere. The addresses below represent a few conveniently located stores. Check the phone book for more options.

BOLTON'S
27 West 57th Street
1180 Madison Avenue, at 86th Street
225 East 57th Street
4 East 34th Street

▼

CENTURY 21: Century 21 is actually a discount department store, located in Downtown Manhattan, almost across the street from the World Trade Center. If you work in that area and can come regularly (who needs to eat lunch?), you will probably love the bargains and the funky atmosphere. If you make a special trip down here (by subway or the Fifth Avenue bus marked South Ferry), you may be disappointed. Century 21 is the kind of place where you have to hit it just right to feel triumphant. Otherwise it can seem like floors and floors of junk. There's a children's department, as well as housewares, handbags, cosmetics, and several floors of women's items on split mezzanines—so you are always walking up or down five or six stairs. The lingerie, sleepwear, and underwear is the best department (to us, anyway), but we know people who have bought name-brand sportswear here. Perfumes are discounted and you can sometimes buy Nintendo games that no one else has. Fun to prowl if you have no expectations.

CENTURY 21, 12 Cortlandt Street

▼

CONWAY: If we were smart, we would be embarrassed to admit to our love affair with Conway's. Conway is not what you would call swank. It's real Turkish bazaar time in an air-conditioned haven of tables piled high with merchandise—out-of-season, discontinued, unloved styles and designer overruns. It's the souk of your dreams, but you have to like the jumble. There are actually over five different branches in the same neighborhood, and you have to be strong for this kind of shopping, but if you like cheap clothes for your kids, inexpensive towels for summer camp, or discounted household goods, you just might have a good time here. It's close enough to Macy's that you won't have made a trip in vain. We've sent some people here who said to us, "How could you send us there?" So we are warning you right out front. This is not Bendel's. This is a bargain basement in the truest sense of the word; all it lacks is basement space. Saturday can be very crowded. Excuse our enthusiasm, and take our warning to heart: We can't help ourselves, we still love this place.

CONWAY
   everything: 1335–1345 Broadway, at 35th
      Street
   ladies: 11 and 245 West 34th Street
   large sizes: 251 and 253 West 34th Street
   kids: 243 West 34th Street
   mens: 147 West 34th Street
   bed 'n' bath: 49 West 34th Street

▼

DAFFY'S: It was Dale, who knows everyone's secrets, who told us about Daffy Dan's in New Jersey. This is their New York outlet for men's, women's, and kids' discounts. Right in the heart of the trendy SoFi district. Who said Fifth Avenue was expensive? Major, major bargains of the Loehmann's kind can be found. We think that perhaps the combination of Daffy's and Barneys in the same shopping spree is the ultimate in having it all. The store on Madison is packed with Euro-designer fashions. Take the escalator down to the large selection of women's clothing.

DAFFY'S
111 Fifth Avenue, at 18th Street
335 Madison Avenue, at 44th Street

▼

FORMAN'S: There are three Forman's outlets, so don't get confused; get happy. Get joyous, in fact, because out of three shops, at least one of them—maybe two—will be for you. There is a main store, a shop for large sizes, and a shop for small sizes. Special "sale" racks in the main store may offer dirt-cheap markdowns.

The three Forman's shops are as fancy and sophisticated as any Uptown or mall boutique. *Warning:* The run-of-the-mill discount in all shops is only 20%. This is a nice discount, but unless you are buying tons (as you should be), it may not be worth the cab fare to the Lower East Side. We are such penny pinchers that we're not impressed with a 20% discount unless we're doing a big haul. Forman's does have impressive sales, when the discounts are more.

FORMAN'S MISSY, 82 Orchard Street
FORMAN'S COATS/PLUS SIZES, 78 Orchard Street
FORMAN'S PETITES
94 Orchard Street
59 John Street

LABELS FOR LESS: Imagine our shock the day we went to visit Mom on Park Avenue and discovered she lives right next to a major New York discounter. All these years we thought Mom's neighborhood could boast only the likes of Martha—the fanciest store in New York—and now, right across the street from Martha, is a Labels for Less. Labels for Less is a chain that you will like or hate according to luck. The day we walked into a pile of Gloria Vanderbilt sweaters and only a little Diane von Furstenburg thrown in, we were almost in tears of disappointment. This is moderate-to-lower-end big-name and medium-name designer merchandise, with some no-name, commonsense clothes thrown in for good measure. There are scads of these shops in New York. Check the phone book for the one nearest you.

LABELS FOR LESS, 470 Park Avenue, at 58th Street

▼

LOEHMANN'S: Naturally, you've heard of Loehmann's and probably shopped in one of their many stores. Ah, Loehmann's, you are a part of the very fiber of our social life. Every dress-up occasion we've been to in the past twenty years has called for a trip to Loehmann's—in one city or another. Every book tour has prompted another trip to Loehmann's. And every birthday check that Dad sends our way. Ah, Loehmann's.

Loehmann's is America's leading off-price resource. Fortunately, Loehmann's recently abandoned its store in the dicier part of the Bronx and opened a new store in a former ice-skating rink in a lovely section of the Bronx called Riverdale-Kingsbridge. You can't miss the structure: Its domed roof is easily spied from afar. The store itself is clean and spiffy, although lacking the selection the Fordham Bronx store was famous for. But there is a

Back Room—all carpeted and pretty and swank, with the usual big-name bargains. While this Loehmann's is nice, it's no different from the Loehmann's in your own neighborhood, and might not be worth the trip if you are visiting from out of town. *Note:* There is a long bench in the front lobby for husbands.

Hours: Monday through Saturday, 10 A.M.–9 P.M.; Sunday, noon to 5 P.M. By train: Take the IRT No. 1 to West 238th Street. By bus: Take the regular Bx 9 to West 236th Street, or express bus BMX No. 1 at Third Avenue and 34th Street in Manhattan to West 239th Street, or BMX No. 2 (express bus) at Sixth Avenue and 34th Street in Manhattan to the same stop in the Bronx. By car: Drive north on the Henry Hudson (toll); exit at West 239th Street. For more specific directions, call (212) 543-6420.

LOEHMANN'S, 5740 Broadway, at 236th Street, Riverdale, the Bronx

▼

LAST CALL: Last Call is the name of the outlet stores operated by Neiman Marcus, the one and only. They have one such store in Austin, Texas, and another not too far from Manhattan. You'll need a car to get there, but if you can make it to Wayne Towne Center in Wayne, New Jersey, it's not the Penney's store you're looking for. Clothes here are those that did not sell on the floor, and are priced 50% to 80% below regular retail.

LAST CALL, Wayne Towne Center, Wayne, New Jersey

▼

KLEINFELD'S: If you ever thought that Brooklyn was too far to go for a shopping expedition, consider that we found a Zandra Rhodes dress at Bendel's for $5,000 and the exact same dress at Kleinfeld's for $3,500.

Kleinfeld's is famous for dressy-dressy clothes, and provides many a wedding gown. All sorts (and all lengths) of dresses are available, at prices from 30% to 70% off regular retail. One store sells wedding dresses, the other store (across the street) sells bridesmaid's dresses. If you have a big do to attend, you can't afford not to come to Brooklyn! The store is closed on Sunday and Monday. They open at 11 A.M. other days, and stay open until 9 P.M. on Tuesday and Thursday. On Wednesday, Friday, and Saturday, they close at 6 P.M. Directions: Take the "N" train to 59th Street in Brooklyn, change to the "R" local, and get off at 86th Street and Fourth Avenue. *Please note:* We know a bride who wished she had paid full retail rather than dealt with Kleinfeld's. Service may not be their best thing.

KLEINFELD'S, 82nd Street at Fifth Avenue, Brooklyn

▼

REMIN'S: Remin's and Loehmann's are the two big-name off-pricers known to New York shoppers who want the best in bargains. Remin's is out of town a bit and offers much higher-end merchandise than any other off-pricer, possibly in the world. We bought our trousseau at Remin's and have been steady customers despite the out-of-the-city schlepp. (It's a half-hour drive to Remin's, and you really need a car.)

Remin's specialty is European and big-name American designer merchandise. We love the end-of-season sale that's held for six weeks in June and July, when the store prepares to close for its summer holiday. They reopen in the fall, totally stocked with the biggest and best names. There are few pikers at Remin's. If you've never seen discounted Giorgio Armani, this is your chance. Jimmy Galanos sells his samples here. Most of the merchandise is European;

some does not have labels; some is from makers whose names we do not recognize. The quality is excellent, although prices are steep. You can call collect for directions. These people accepted our anonymous, collect call immediately and were filled with warmth, although they only give directions—not a critique of what's in the store. Why, oh, why did we ever pass up that Elie Wachs coat?

Directions: Take I-95 north to Exit 16 in New Rochelle. Without traffic this takes thirty minutes from Manhattan.

REMIN'S, 665 North Avenue, New Rochelle, New York

▼

S&W: Some days we love S&W, other days are a little disappointing. The good news: S&W has lots of designer clothes and tons of Calvin Klein; the coat store (at a separate address) is downright wonderful. The part we hate: The discounts are only 20%. But that's not the end of the story. S&W has incredible sales and also offers discount coupons at certain times of the year—the kind of thing where you bring in an ad from *New York* magazine and get an additional 20% off. You have to be on your toes to take full advantage of this store and to find these ads. Several S&W shops are clustered around the corner of Seventh Avenue and 26th Street—a coat shop, a shoe and leathergoods shop, a lingerie shop, and then the regular store for ready-to-wear. Don't miss any of them. This is part of the Seventh Avenue Stretch, by the way. All stores are closed on Saturday but are open on Sunday. Open Thursday evening until 8 P.M.

S&W NO. 1, 165 West 26th Street (suits and sportswear)
S&W NO. 2, 169 West 26th Street (furs)
S&W NO. 3, 173 West 26th Street (outlet store)

S&W NO. 4, 283 Seventh Avenue, at 26th Street
(shoes and handbags)
S&W NO. 5, 287 Seventh Avenue, at 26th Street
(coats)

Men's Specialty Discounters
(That Also Sell Women's Wear)

BFO: This is a discount chain that is popular
in the Northeast. They do a large out-of-state
business (UPS) and will do alterations on the
premises. BFO charges about $150 for a $300
suit; $200 for a $400 suit. We call that half
price. It's another resource in the Lower Fifth
Avenue area, so get to this one when you do
the others. We buy many a man's pullover to
wear ourselves.

BFO, 149 Fifth Avenue, 2nd and 6th Floors, at
21st Street

▼

DOLLAR BILL'S: We're not sure what you
would call Dollar Bill's—sort of a mini general
store jobber and discounter. He sells everything and anything. He's also located in Grand
Central Station, so he's conveniently placed.
But best of all, he sells major, major designer
clothes at low prices. The merchandise varies
from week to week, and Bill's loudly pro-
claims that they can't advertise the names of
the designers whose goods they are unloading.
We've heard tales of Armani suits for zip.
Big-name ties (Chanel, Armani, Fendi, etc.)
as well as sweaters and some women's wear.

DOLLAR BILL'S, 99 East 42nd Street

▼

SYMS: Yes, they also sell women's clothes and shoes and undies. Like all good businesses, Syms opens at 9 A.M. Did we tell you about the Perry Ellis heels for $30? Oh, we didn't? Well, why talk when you could be out shopping at Syms? Near Century 21, so visit both and let us know how you make out.

SYMS, 42 Trinity Place

Garment Center Outlets

TERRE GRAFF: By appointment only for the last remaining big-name designer discount deals in Manhattan since 22 Steps closed. Call (212) 206-4014 to see the deals in sizes 4–12 from your biggest of big names. The clothes are what's left after the sales and markdowns in the designer boutiques, and you can find anything or nothing. Cash and local checks (Tri-state area) only.

TERRE GRAFF, Michel Kazan Townhouse, 16 East 55th Street

▼

STANROSE: This is one of our favorite Seventh Avenue sources. Although the discount may be only 20% to 25%, the merchandise is sublime. While it's very hard to find discounts on Donna Karan, you can do so here. There's a room filled with Donna Karan panty hose. The clothing stock is not huge, but what's there is excellent. This is a very fashionable, chic crowd of fashion mavens. Ask to get on the mailing list; ask for special orders on current merchandise.

STANROSE, 141 West 36th Street

ELLEN TRACY OF LYNDHURST: Yep, it's our beloved Ellen Tracy by Linda Allard, also known as Ellen Tracy of the department stores, the one that we love but can't afford until the markdowns. Now we find discounts. There are many Ellen Tracy factory outlets in various outlet malls and outlet cities around the United States—the closest one to New York is probably at Woodbury Common.

But wait, you can go to the true outlet store in the honest-to-goodness factory in New Jersey where it actually says "Ellen Tracy Factory" on the building. *First, the warning:* This store is identical to every other Tracy outlet in the malls. That doesn't mean it isn't great (it is great), but simply that prices here are no different from those in Woodbury Common and elsewhere. So if you're going to drive for hours to get here, you might as well drive for hours and get to Woodbury Common and have hundreds of outlets. (But there's no tax in New Jersey.) Also note that the gorgeous merchandise in this gorgeous store may not be identical to what's on sale in the department stores—we think that Ellen Tracy cuts the same patterns in different colors just for the outlet stores. But no matter, this stuff is indeed gorgeous and well-priced in the $99-and-up range, although you will find a few things for less. They take credit cards.

You just might want to call for directions (201-935-3425)—this place is in an industrial area sort of in the middle of nowhere. If you've done this before, please note that this is a new address—the other nearby New Jersey factory outlet is now an insurance office. We drove around with a New Jersey pro or would have been hopelessly lost hunting down both addresses.

ELLEN TRACY OF LYNDHURST, 165 Polito Avenue, Lyndhurst, New Jersey

Other Bargain Basements (Nonfashion)

Bargain hunters of the world, here we are. We are not just pretty faces. We are not just after clothes and jewels and Judith Leiber handbags. We have bargain basement resources for everything. Or just about everything. Mostly non–ready-to-wear resources, and some not so fancy, these are jobbers and secret sources from our files that are either fun for the real shopaholic or will solve gift problems. Many of these places are not pretty. But if you need silver or an answering machine, step this way.

MICHAEL C. FINA: All major china, crystal, and silver lines are discounted here—Lenox, Val St. Lambert, Wedgwood, Spode, Noritake, Royal Doulton, etc. The jewelry counter is boring, but the gift shopping is tremendous fun. On a price-by-price basis, Fina may not offer you the best prices in the world. The Wedgwood china pattern we always check (Runnymede) is $96 at Fina, $67 in London. But for $15 to $25 wedding gifts, and for $13 teachers' Christmas presents—look no further. Use (800) 223-6589 to reorder by phone.

MICHAEL C. FINA, 3 West 47th Street

▼

HOME SALES: It doesn't pay to truck appliances any great distance, but Home Sales is one of the best and cheapest sources for locals. You can call in with a catalogue number or get a price quote on the phone. They specialize in telephone business, which is just how we like to buy our appliances. Discounts are about 40%. Phone orders only: (718) 241-3272.

HOME SALES, no showroom

▼

ODDLOT JOB TRADING: When we get to visit friends at Time, Inc., we always laugh at the number of preppy types scurrying around the main floor with the Oddlot shopping bags. Located only two blocks from the Time-Life Building, this dime-store sort of place sells closeouts and discontinued items at pretty low prices. Sometimes amazing prices. You end up buying items you don't want or need because it's all so much fun, but if you like this sort of fancy junk store, you'll have a great time here. And it's virtually in Rockefeller Center, so the location couldn't be better.

ODDLOT JOB TRADING, 66 West 48th Street

▼

ROBIN IMPORTERS: We've given Robin most of our gift and wedding business because they are conveniently located in Midtown Manhattan. Why go to some screwy place when this one is convenient? And wonderful? They even register brides. A bride who picks a discounter is our kind of bride. And they have a toll-free number. To make it even better—if possible—they have everything, from big-name crystal, silver, and china to picture frames that look like the expensive ones at Cartier. Windows you can look in, street-level access as opposed to going into an office building. They will even gift-wrap. Their toll-free number is (800) 223-3373. An excellent source for whimsical teapots.

ROBIN IMPORTERS, 510 Madison Avenue, at 52nd Street

NAT SCHWARTZ: Any store with an 800 number is our kind of store. Nat Schwartz's is (800) 526-1440, and it is the kind of store you shop by phone and by catalogue; you tell them what you want and they send it to you—all major names in silver, crystal, china, the works. Did we say major, major names? You get the idea. One hitch: They're closed on Wednesday.

NAT SCHWARTZ, 549 Broadway, Bayonne, New Jersey

7 ▾ FACTORY OUTLETS AND DAY TRIPS

Factory Outlet Villages

There are four factory outlet villages in the greater New York area that offer a different type of shopping center to the eager public. All are different, although Woodbury Common and Liberty Village are owned by the same company and have some similarities. We feel very strongly that no trip to New York could be called a proper shopping excursion without a visit to at least one of these versions of the new American shopping dream. *Note:* New York shopping mavens are very opinionated (about everything) and invariably will think that one of these sources is better than the others. We find them so extremely different that we beg you to ignore other opinions (can you compare apples, oranges, and grapefruit, we ask you?) and see for yourself.

Secaucus Warehouses

The Secaucus Warehouses are exactly what they sound like—but better. They are a series of showrooms, 20,000 to 50,000 square feet, new, clean, and well lit, in a development of one-story warehouses in an industrial complex created on landfill in the Meadowlands area of New Jersey—near the industrial capital of the United States, good old Secaucus. They are on a strip of a street that looks like Dallas. In the same complex, you'll find a sports arena, a Hilton hotel (with a good coffee shop for a postshopping break), and a total industrial-business complex of the highest order. The outlets are in three different areas: Harmon Cove, Industrial Park, and Castle Road.

We have considered contacting the owners of the warehouses to beg them to let us write a book about the area, as that's what it would take to explain the whole thing to you. There is a guidebook that has a big section on Secaucus (*Factory Store Guide to All New York, Pennsylvania, and New Jersey*—The Globe Pequot Press), but there is also a free newspaper listing all the outlets, so you can get there and then figure it all out. *A few tips:*

▼ Never, never attempt to go to Secaucus and Flemington in the same day, unless you are a masochist.

▼ Avoid bringing young children with you, if possible.

▼ Wear comfortable shoes—you'll do a lot of walking.

▼ Carry high heels in a tote bag if you need them to get the right look for clothes you may try on.

▼ Drive if you can; it's worth the price of a rental car. The distances among the various warehouses are not lots of miles, but we are talking a walk this way, a walk that way, and an area that is bigger than Disneyland (and much more fun). Be prepared to move your car constantly—at least three different times, even if you walk to three times as many outlets from one parking space.

▼ Try to eat at off-peak hours—there are not enough restaurants around. It's worth it to get in your car and drive over to the Hilton's coffee shop, where there's free self-parking.

▼ Consider spending a night at the Hilton to pace yourself.

▼ Regular hours usually are 10 A.M. to 5 P.M.; most stores are open until 8 or 8:30 P.M. on Thursday.

▼ Remember that Sunday hours are noon to 5 P.M., so you don't get as much shopping in.

▼ Weekends are very crowded; a weekday is to be preferred if possible.

▼ You can overdose here. This is far more serious than Tokyo. You may begin to hyperventilate when you see what's available. To help you put it in perspective, we consider ourselves world-class shoppers, and we limit ourselves to six warehouses in a day. (Three in the morning; three after lunch.) You can be reduced to stuttering in no time at all if you don't watch out.

▼ Read the newspaper that is free at your first stop. Our first stop is always Calvin Klein (50 Enterprise Avenue), and we think yours will be, too. They have a stack of papers there. In the newspaper you'll see a lot of coupons and will get sale information and news about special promotions.

▼ There is some give and take with outlets—they do open and close. The giveaway newspaper will help you better than any guidebook.

▼ Most stores take checks; no hassle for out-of-state checks. You must have a driver's license and two IDs. Traveler's checks are accepted; some credit cards are taken.

▼ Return policies are carefully posted; read the signs before you buy. The rules vary from store to store, but most warehouses allow returns in a seven-day period.

▼ Each warehouse has a mailing list. Out-of-state addresses will be honored; addresses out of the United States may not.

▼ Don't judge a book by its cover. While all the outlets are attractive in that they are clean, some of them bear decidedly uncute names. Who wants to go browsing in a store called United Status Apparel of America? Don't be a snob. Some of the best places we visited had these kinds of names. The Perry Ellis clothes are sold in the Manhattan Industries outlet.

▼ If someone is carrying an interesting bag, ask questions. Discount shoppers love to help others.

▼ Do not go in your grubbies. We've never seen a better-dressed bunch of shoppers in our lives.

▼ Go with a friend; share driving if you've come a long way. You will be exhausted at the end of the day. Pace yourself for a long drive or traffic on the way home. This kind of shopping is more fun with a friend, anyway.

▼ There are kids' clothing outlets but no toy outlets. If you are bribing your kids into good behavior, be prepared with your own bribes.

Welcome to Secaucus

Secaucus is different from almost any other outlet area because the outlets are pretty much spread out, and because, in many cases, these are real outlets—for better or for worse. There is a small mall, but there is nothing fancy here; there isn't anything cute like Liberty Village in Flemington or developed like Woodbury Common. Secaucus is difficult to shop, so we're here to take you by the hand and put you through the exact same tour we use when we come to visit.

Although this trip is best done by car (or bus), you can walk to all of the outlets we will mention from one central parking stop—but you're going to need sensible shoes and maybe

your own shopping cart. This tour is easiest by
car, and we will tell you when to walk and
when to move the car, but do look at a map so
that if you get bored by our choices you can
decide where to jump ship.

Secaucus in a Day

1. Begin at Calvin Klein, which has its own
   parking lot and will serve as a base parking
   spot if you want to walk. The Calvin Klein
   shop is located behind a few others, so you
   have to look for it. The address is 50 Enterprise Avenue; it is directly behind the
   Andrew Marc outlet, but you may not see
   the Klein sign until you are in their driveway.

2. Waste no more time. Rush right into Calvin
   Klein, which is a four-room salon selling all
   kinds of Calvin Klein clothes, from the cheapest to the most expensive. We mourn the
   passing of the Classifications line, but you
   can still find the mortal remains. Merchandise arrives shortly after it ships to the stores,
   so the best selection is in late July or early
   August for fall, and in February for spring.
   But there are sales as well, so come in the
   middle of July, before the fall clothes arrive,
   and you'll find summer clothes marked down
   to very reasonable prices. The farthest room
   to your left (if your back is to the front
   door) is a real markdown paradise, where
   sizes are not even categorized—it's just merchandise on racks. These items have been
   marked down several times, and may be
   several seasons old. The rest of the selection
   in the other parts of the store is arranged
   nicely by color or type of clothing. The
   price on each piece is more or less half the
   regular retail price—which on top-of-the-

line Calvin Klein still means over $100 for a silk blouse. But if you want designer clothes at the beginning of the season, this is the place for you.

3. Now move the car, or leave your packages in the trunk and walk on to Enterprise Avenue. Cross the street and walk one block to your left, right to the Gucci outlet at 45 Enterprise Avenue North. This is one of the fancier outlets in town: It looks and feels like a shop, and is crammed with merchandise. Most people don't know it, but the Gucci sold in America is made in the United States by a company called Gucci USA, which is a different company from the ones that supply Europe or the Far East. Hence different styles and different prices than in Europe or Hong Kong, etc. GG merchandise is not outrageously expensive to begin with, and becomes downright moderate at the outlet—a large satchel-style handbag costs about $100. The expensive items are the leather clothes and knits, but they can be on sale (if you're lucky) and quite reasonable— like $99 for a pair of leather pants! The best thing to buy in this outlet is gift items. Your friends (and boss) will never know how little you spent when you present each with a status symbol bought here.

4. Now hop back in the car, pull out of the Gucci driveway as if you are going away from Calvin Klein, and hit Secaucus Road on the left, then turn right onto Enterprise Avenue South. This road has many outlets which you can stop in at if so inclined, but we have not been sufficiently impressed with anything here to beg you to stop. Head on to Metro Way, where you will have to turn right (no left turn) on County Avenue, which becomes New Castle Road. Turn right at Castle Road and pass a dozen outlets, stopping briefly at the L'Eggs outlet to stock up on panty hose and socks. If you have your

man with you, stop off for Church's English shoes; if your children are with you, get the bribes at Toy Liquidators. Otherwise head back the way you came and down American Way to Enterprise, where this time turn left on Enterprise Avenue North and stop at the Harmon Cove Outlet Center. If it's lunchtime now, grab some fast food upstairs in the food court. You'll also enjoy the fifty-plus outlet stores in this one mall. Among our favorites: Tahari, Bally shoes, Barbizon nightgowns and Cambridge Dry Good.

5. Leave the car here, and walk next door to Syms. *Warning:* This isn't a very good Syms, but a quick look never hurts. Syms has men's, women's, and some children's items at 20% to 25% off retail. It has always been better for men's clothing than anything else, but truly, this isn't one of Syms's better branches.

6. Cross the street to Liz Claiborne's outlet (4 Emerson Lane), which takes cash or local checks (from the Tri-state area) only. The store stocks mostly women's wear but there are some men's fashions and some accessories.

7. Now walk back to the car and drive around Emerson Lane to Secaucus Road, where you will immediately see Building 600. In the back half of this building is the Natori outlet. Natori is not inexpensive, even at the outlet—but it becomes possible to own some if you've been saving for the fanciest underwear you've ever seen. Underwear, nightgowns, towels, and gift items are beautiful. A silk teddy costs about $35, but it's the most beautiful silk teddy you have ever seen.

8. Refreshed from seeing those gorgeous undergarments, drive up Secaucus Road until you hit Enterprise Avenue North again, turn right, and then turn into the parking lot at United Status Apparel, which fronts on Amer-

ican Way. You are now across the street from Calvin Klein, where you started out. United Status Apparel is a warehouse the size of a soundstage, with various makes, models, and sizes of moderately priced sportswear from the likes of Carole Little and Adrienne Vittadini. You can go mad here.

9. After you have bought out the store, walk next door to Mikasa. Mikasa is very large and thoroughly stocked, but we have one word of warning: We have seen some of this merchandise for less money during sale or promotion times in the Mikasa store in Manhattan. You must know your prices to know if you're getting a bargain or not! Mikasa should be your last stop, since what you buy here may be heavy. If you aren't strong enough to drive home after all this, don't worry. You can roll into the nearby Hilton hotel for the night. But first, look to the newest outlets right there across from the Hilton: Outlets at the Cove, truly across the street from the Hilton and in walking distance from lunch to a stunning dessert—this new high-tech mall with gray tile and aubergine trim has two stories of fun and many a high-end outlet, making it one of the better stops in Secaucus. Check out Fenn Wright & Mason, Calvin Klein Sport, Bass, Van Heusen, Harvé Benard, and Bugle Boy, as well as other choice choices.

10. Back in the car, after either a sleepover at the Hilton or a refreshment and freshen-up stop, drive the car to the strip center that says "Designer Outlet Gallery" in big letters on the front and has the big words "New York New York" hanging off the front of low-slung, modren beige stores right there next to the freestanding (and not that exciting) Wilroy outlet. Among the winners in this small strip are Carole Hochman (who makes the Christian Dior lingerie),

Argenti, Joan & David, Andrea Carrano, Jindo, and Puma. Whew, now you can rest and head home. What a haul!

Welcome to Woodbury Common

Visually speaking, Woodbury Common is the most attractive of the outlet villages. It's a fake colonial village. Each shop is a different pastel shade; you may want to move in.

Woodbury Common is extremely similar to Liberty Village (same developer), so you must really decide if you want to go north to Up-state New York or south into New Jersey for your day trip. The drive to Woodbury Common is easy (on a gorgeous highway) and beautiful almost any time of the year, and especially in the autumn. It takes approximately an hour and a half from Manhattan to either village, although Flemington is probably a bit closer to New York than Harriman. Also please note that there is some crossover of outlets with Secaucus ... although Secaucus is certainly not as charming as either of these.

If you are choosing only one outlet village to visit, Woodbury Common is probably the one to pick. It's easy to get to (if you drive, anyway) and it's easy to shop. Also, there are no distractions. If you go to Flemingon, you have not only Liberty Village but the entire town of Flemington to contend with, and it can be overwhelming. Flemington really is a weekend trip, or at least an overnight, if you want to do it properly.

So welcome to Woodbury Common, a wise choice for a beginner—a sound choice for a day of stocking up on everything ... or better yet, for holiday shopping. Bring your station wagon, bring your van, bring your pals. And for heaven's sake, bring your credit cards.

Details and Directions

Shops in Woodbury Common are open seven days a week, so merely hop on the New York State Thruway (Interstate 87) and get off at Exit 16, almost immediately after going through the tollbooth. You will see the mall to your right. There's plenty of free parking.

You can take a regular Shortline bus from the Port Authority, but you will take it to the town (Harriman, New York) and then take a taxi out to the mall. Get the phone number of your taxi company, as you'll need to call for a pickup. Buses run every day from Manhattan to Harriman; call the Port Authority for details. Some days of the week there is additional service to Spring Valley, New York, a community slightly closer to Woodbury Common.

There are about seventy-five outlets in the village, including many big-name shops like **GUCCI, CALVIN KLEIN, ADRIENNE VITTADINI, RODIER, CARLOS FALCHI, CAROLE LITTLE, HARVÉ BENARD, CHARLES JOURDAN, CAROLE HOCHMAN LINGERIE** (that's Christian Dior, friends), and **ELLEN TRACY**. There is also an information center, a free map and newspaper, and a clean restroom station.

Hours: Monday through Saturday, 10 A.M.–6 P.M.; Sunday, 11 A.M.–5 P.M. Open until 9 P.M. on Thursday and Friday evenings from May 1 to December 31. Closed from 3 P.M. on July 4, Christmas Eve, and New Year's Eve. Closed all day on Easter, Thanksgiving, Christmas, and New Year's Day. Phone: (914) 928-6840.

Woodbury Common, Our Way

1. Enter the parking lot from the New York State Thruway and drive toward the restroom and information center, which looks like an old-fashioned town center, complete with clock tower. Our tour begins at the clock tower. Park as nearby as possible.

2. Walking into the village from the lot, with the information center to your back, you will pass through the center of the village, past McDonald's (on your left in the area called the Food Court) and on to the end of the strip called E-49 on your little map. You're going to be tempted to stray from this path, but don't worry, we're going to get you into all of the good shops.

3. Walk to the farthest end of the strip of stores in the center plot and into the Adrienne Vittadini Factory Outlet Shop. This is a large, spacious, modern shop that looks as nice as any retail store. Unfortunately, it's not always full of the clothes we love—but if you get lucky, you can come away a winner.

4. Slowly work your way back to the center of the village, visiting those outlets that attract you (they should be on your right-hand side as you return toward the village from Vittadini) and being certain not to miss Ellen Tracy, Anne Klein, Joan & David, and Charles Jourdan. These have "E" addresses, but look across the courtyard to the "W" numbers and stores like Boston Traders (W50), Carole Hochman (W41), where the Christian Dior nightgowns are 30% to 40% off retail, and Rodier (W45).

5. By now it should be lunchtime, and you should be right at the Food Court, anyway.

We eat lunch at 11:30 A.M. in order to miss the crowds; however, during the week this mall may not be too mobbed.

6. Coming out of the Food Court, walk straight across the plaza and into another wing of the village, walking toward Calvin Klein (W26).

7. Finish up in the area around Klein and you'll be back on the main drag near the entry to the Food Court and ready to shop Skyr (say "skier"), an unusual shop filled with preppy togs that are practical and well-priced. Although we had never heard of this brand previously, we find it often in factory-outlet malls. We buy our husbands their ski turtlenecks here, and stock up on cotton sweaters and everyday clothes, which go on sale for $10 a garment at the end of the season.

8. Coming out of Skyr, we walk toward the information center as if we were going to leave (fat chance), then hang a right at the corner and explore the entire strip around the fountain. There's a Gucci shop back in here, and lots of other good resources that you might otherwise miss, like Carlos Falchi and Carole Little.

9. When you finish this strip, work the stores on the left-hand side of the main entry, including First Choice (W5), which sells Escada clothes at discount.

10. Hop in the car and onto the freeway to head for home. You can stop at the Ramapo exit for coffee and a snack before heading into Manhattan.

Flemington Outlets

No offense to religious types, but when we die, we hope to go to Flemington. Not everyone we know likes Flemington because it is so cute. It is, indeed, professionally cute. But we are not offended when you can have two Calvin Klein outlets, an Anne Klein outlet, and Villeroy & Boch all next door to each other. Flemington is everything Hong Kong should be. Flemington is clean, it's well organized, it's easy to shop, it's friendly—it's got everything.

The actual town of Flemington has been taken over by retail fever, and even residences have been renovated and rezoned so that businesses can be opened. Note particularly:

▼ Flemington publishes its own maps, guidebooks, and newspapers, which are free; get one at your first stop. There is an association of all the factory outlets: FFOA. Look for its logo.

▼ Not every shop is named clearly. The Anne Klein outlet is not called Anne Klein; the Esprit outlet is called Good Looks; Escada is at First Choice.

▼ The majority of the outlets are in two areas—Turntable Junction and Liberty Village, which are close together. But Main Street has a lot of shops, too. The area became famous because of the Flemington Fur vaults, but we prefer Manhattan for furs (see page 196). There also are places that have addresses based on the whereabouts of a traffic circle. It makes perfect sense when you get there; don't worry.

▼ There are almost 200 outlets, but they are not giant warehouses, as in Secaucus.

Some are small boutiques. A tram takes you to any or all of them for the all-inclusive price of $1.

▼ There are goods for everyone in the family, for the house, and in all price ranges.

▼ Flemington is a lot more like Disneyland than the other outlet villages—families come for the fun of it. Strollers and youngsters are welcome. Weekends are jammed. There is a much looser atmosphere here than in Secaucus; people wander around eating ice-cream cones. The shoppers here are not sharks, and do not have that gleam in the eye you catch more than occasionally in Secaucus.

Welcome to Liberty Village

L iberty Village offers a mere fraction of what is available in Flemington in terms of outlets. Many of the stores are free-standing structures—such as Mikasa—and you need to know where they are in order to get there. Liberty Village is just the heart of Flemington, but it's not all there is to the town. If you go to Liberty Village first, you'll get in a good dose of shopping, and you'll be able to pick up a free booklet that contains a map of all the other outlets in the town of Flemington. Locals will give you directions to a certain spot.

Details and Directions

F lemington is 55 miles from New York and 45 miles from Philadelphia. It's very close to New Hope, Pennsylvania (14 miles!), for those who want to make a Bucks County weekend out of it. In fact, there's so much to do in Flemington proper that a weekend here is appropriate. If you are just doing a day trip, Liberty Village and Turntable Junction will probably take up most of your time.

Bus tours originate from Philadelphia, New York, and Atlantic City. For bus service from the Port Authority in Manhattan to Flemington, call West Hunterdon Bus Service at (201) 782-6313. They leave every day; tell the driver you want to get off at Liberty Village. There's an 8:15 A.M. departure that returns from Liberty Village at 5 P.M. and arrives back in New York at 6:45 P.M.. If that sounds like too long of a day, don't panic; there are several arrivals and departures. Just make sure you're on a bus that will stop at Liberty Village, since not all of them do. It's about $15 round-trip; buy tickets at the Port Authority.

Shops are open seven days a week from 10 A.M. to 5:30 P.M., and until 6 P.M. Thursday through Saturday from May 1 to December 30. All stores close at 3 P.M. on July 4, Christmas Eve, and New Year's Eve, and are closed all day on Easter, Thanksgiving, Christmas, and New Year's Day. There may be special Christmas holiday hours; please call for details. Phone: (201) 782-8550.

Liberty Village Tour

When we go to Flemington, we have our shopping route down to a science. We usually do this as a day trip from Connecticut, and we want maximum shopping for our day. We can't go into every single store in Flemington if we don't spend the night or a few days. Our usual pattern is to shop mainly at Liberty Village and Turntable Junction.

1. Leave New York headed for Newark Airport (you are going against rush-hour traffic, so early morning is great), and connect to Route 3, a new highway that goes right to Flemington. Follow signs to Main Street and then Church Street, and park at Liberty Village. Free parking, of course.

2. Liberty Village is a freestanding village, with one end far more interesting than the other. This may be grossly unfair, but we always gravitate to what we call the Calvin Klein end. There are two Klein shops. One is for men's sportswear and the other carries all the women's clothes; both are in the same "end" of the village, although on different sides of a strip of stores. There used to be two different women's shops, but that has been changed.

3. Start at Anne Klein (No. 60) where you can sometimes luck into a Donna Karan bodysuit. The Karan merchandise is usually hidden toward the back, so ask. Now go shop to shop, stopping at Joan & David (No. 65) for shoes. We got a pair of Joan & David shoes for $20 and another pair for $44. The most expensive pair of shoes is $65, while boots are higher ... but not as high as in the Ann Taylor stores.

4. Finish this strip of shops without being disappointed that the Calvin Klein shop is small and geared toward jeans and men's clothing. You'll be in another Klein shop in just one second. As you round the crest of this line of stores and come to the information center and the junction between the two outlet villages, you'll see a big board with a map on it. Use this map to help you find Cambridge Dry Goods, which is only two shops away, but hard to find because of its position facing Church Street. Cambridge Dry Goods sells preppy-looking Ralph Lauren–look country clothes. They have their own shop in Bloomingdale's, as well as many freestanding boutiques around the country. The best thing about their outlet stores is that they are one of the few sellers with the exact same merchandise in their outlet stores as in their retail stores. You can see a sweater at Bloomingdale's for $76 one day and buy it the next day at the outlet store for $52. (There is a Cambridge Dry Goods outlet store in Secaucus, too.)

5. Now swing back down the main corridor of the village. You'll soon pass Calvin Klein (No. 43) on your right. Head down toward the pond in the center of the village and to the area where you started. Now it's time for lunch! We always go to the same place for lunch because we like it so much, although there are other choices. It's called the Bucks County Cafe (No. 74), and it is upstairs from a vineyard. Old stone walls greet you; the food is cafeteria-style.

6. Finished with lunch (bathrooms are downstairs in the vineyard), leave the restaurant and turn right to take in the stores adjacent to the café, including the huge Coat World. Turn right and visit a small niche of shops that you know is there only if you came by West Hunterdon Bus Service, since this is where the bus drops you off. The Fashion

Direct Outlet (No. 83) is a bit hard to find but will be worth it if you like Fenn Wright & Mason clothes. Corning has a large space on the end corner of this little shopping street. When you finish down one side, come back up the other side, which brings you back to the pond and the courtyard area.

7. Now walk with the stores to your right. Don't miss Villeroy & Boch (No. 37) for china or Carter's Little Gallery (No. 32) if you have kids.

8. You'll finish up at the top of the village by the Royal Doulton Shoppe (No. 31B), which is right next door to Cambridge Dry Goods, so you can go back for those items you held back on. Now you're ready to cross the street and tackle Turntable Junction. If you cross the street at Royal Doulton you can work your way around in an L-shaped pattern ending up at Good Looks Fashion (No. 24). Don't let that nondescript name fool you. This is the Esprit outlet! And they have kids' and adults' sizes. As you finish there, you can stop for tea (try Canterbury Corner Cafe, next door at No. 25) and then trudge back to the parking lot with all your bundles. What a day!

Norwalk Factory Outlets

The Norwalk Factory Outlets are in an old factory, which makes them a bit more romantic. Certainly this building has seen better days. You can take the train directly from Grand Central Station in Manhattan to the Norwalk Factory Outlets, or you can take a bus from the Port Authority terminal. The train ride is exactly one hour long.

Neither new nor sparkling nor cute, Norwalk is serviceable. We think it's worth doing, but not at the expense of a day in Flemington or Secaucus. Norwalk has nowhere near the number of stores or the big-name merchandise that the other two villages have. But there are some forty to fifty shops open, and you can still get a discounted pair of Nikes for your little boy for $20.

In the last year or two, the Norwalk Factory Outlets have changed a good bit. They'll never be hotsy-totsy like Woodbury Common, but they are far more upscale than ever before. There're a few new outlets; other outlets have jazzed up their appearance. This is not big-time outlet shopping by any means, but you can get some deals at The Company Store (Dooney & Burke leathergoods outlet), Harvé Benard Outlet Store, Royal Doulton Outlet, and American Tourister Luggage Outlet.

If you come by train, you want East Norwalk—the platform shares a parking lot with the outlets. All other Norwalk stops (South Norwalk, for example) are not within walking distance of the outlets.

Store hours are Monday, Tuesday, and Wednesday, 10 A.M. to 6 P.M.; Thursday and Friday, 10 A.M. to 9 P.M.; Saturday, 10 A.M. to 6 P.M.; Sunday, noon to 5 P.M. From Thanksgiving through Christmas all stores are open weekdays from 10 A.M. to 9 P.M., with regular weekend hours.

To schedule a tour bus for a group, call (203) 226-8731.

8▾MANHATTAN TOURS

Shoot for the Stars and See It All

1. Fasten down those Reeboks, because you are in for a lot of walking. Please wear nice clothes, no blue jeans. Running shoes are totally acceptable with designer suits. If you think you will be buying (of course you will be buying!), put your regular-height heels into a shopping bag or tote bag.

2. Leave your hotel (do eat a good breakfast— this is going to be a killer day) by 8:30 A.M. Take the "F" train. The "F" train has a strange route (it crosses from the east side of town to the west and then heads east again), so ask your concierge or check the subway map for the best place to get it.

3. Take the "F" train to the Lower East Side, which is in the Downtown or Brooklyn direction; get off at Delancey Street. Walk west along Delancey Street to Orchard Street.

4. Spend two hours on Orchard Street. Granted, this is not enough time, but you can make this a half-day tour or a whole-day tour on your own—this tour is going to take you all over town. While on Orchard Street, if you only get to a few places (make sure Forman's is one of them), you'll still be ahead of the game.

5. Return to the Delancey Street IND station and get back on the trusty "F" train, now going Uptown or in the Queens direction. Get off at the Fifth Avenue stop. As you come out of the train, you'll find a great

cosmetics discount source, where the prices aren't as cheap as in Europe but certainly are less expensive than in the department stores. Cosmetics Plus is a chain, and there are several of them dotted around Manhattan. Following today's tour, you will not pass another one.

6. Walk one half block east to Fifth Avenue and turn right without crossing the street. Now you are walking downtown. Continue down Fifth Avenue, looking in windows and taking it all in until 49th Street. Cross the street here and go into Saks Fifth Avenue.

7. Leaving Saks, stay on the Saks side of the street (the East Side side) and walk uptown, toward Trump Tower. This is only seven blocks. Look in windows or shop until your charge cards wither and die. *Good tip:* Pass Trump Tower to dash into Tiffany, where you owe it to yourself to see the table settings and upstairs floors even if gemstones bore you. Then go next door to Trump. If you go to Trump first, you will be too wrung out to go to Tiffany & Co. and you will miss one of the best stores in New York.

8. Be careful as you enter Trump Tower, especially if it is or has been raining. The marble floor is very, very slick. We've come close to thinking the atrium was the last thing we'd ever see. (What a way to go!) You may eat lunch downstairs at either the cafeteria or the restaurant, the Bistro. This is a fancyish restaurant—reservations are a good idea.

9. There are about fifty shops in the atrium, but don't stay more than an hour. Exit and turn right; go east on 57th Street.

10. Walk east three blocks to Lexington Avenue, cross, and walk uptown to Bloomingdale's. You can eat lunch at Bloomie's if

you have not yet eaten—there are several eateries. Spend one hour in Bloomingdale's.

11. Exit Bloomingdale's on the Lexington Avenue side at 59th Street and walk across the street to Zara, and then west to Madison Avenue. Turn right and walk uptown on Madison to 72nd Street. Mostly you only have time to look in windows and soak up atmosphere, but shop and adjust your schedule accordingly.

12. After the Polo shop, on the corner of Madison Avenue and 72nd Street, cross Madison and walk downtown.

13. Turn right at 57th Street and walk west until you come back to Fifth Avenue. Go to Bergdorf's, where you can get coffee and be dazzled by the best and the brightest.

14. If you have children with you (masochist), turn right at Fifth Avenue and walk to 59th Street, where you can go to F.A.O. Schwarz. If you have no children, go to the 7 West 57th Street branch of J. McLaughlin.

15. Continue downtown on Fifth Avenue on that side of the street, now seeing the new Fifth Avenue, including Bulgari, Fendi, and Henri Bendel. Then fall into a taxi and head back to your hotel for a hot bath and a foot massage.

New York Neighborhoods Tour

According to your personal interests, choose two or three neighborhoods from Chapter 4 and create your own tour. Buses and subways will help you make connections. New Yorkers prefer to walk twenty blocks or less; they take transportation only if a location is more than twenty blocks away. (Rumor has it that twenty blocks equal one mile.)

The Seventh Avenue Stretch

1. *Travelers' advisory:* This can be a two-hour or a two-day tour.

2. If you need a fur coat, begin the tour in the fur district, which is essentially 30th Street and Seventh Avenue.

3. If you don't need a fur coat and aren't even looking for one, begin the tour at Seventh Avenue and 25th Street. We get there on our old faithful, the "F" train, which will let you off at 23rd Street. If you take the "E" train, you also get off at 23rd Street, but you will be at Eighth Avenue and will have an extra block to walk over. (Look for the Empire State Building and head toward it; this is east.) This neighborhood is not Beverly Hills, but in daylight you should be safe.

4. Our tour unofficially starts at FIT, the Fashion Institute of Technology, which is one of three technical schools in Manhattan teaching design and retailing. It is in a modern building with many facilities and a great library. You need not go inside, but we just want you to know FIT is there and we're proud of it.

5. Across the street from FIT, on the east side of Seventh Avenue, is a stretch of discounters that will zig east on 26th Street and parade down on Seventh Avenue almost to Barneys. We call this area the Seventh Avenue Stretch. It was created by two different forces in real estate and gentrification and the one force that unites them: style. FIT built that gorgeous building, and Barneys expanded and became more of a department store and less of a discount source. These two points serve as the anchors. Wonderful stores are springing up between them.

6. Start wherever you like. S&W has two of its stores (coats and shoes) on Seventh Avenue in the block between 25th and 26th streets (the shoes are at 283 Seventh Avenue). S&W, like many of these discount stores owned by religious people, is closed on Saturday but open on Sunday. We don't suggest you do the Seventh Avenue Stretch on a weekend, by the way. But Sunday is better than Saturday if you can't go on a weekday.

7. Turn left at 26th Street and work both sides of the block toward Sixth Avenue. Most of the discounters here take a straight 20% discount off new merchandise. Sales are at the end of the season.

8. Return to the corner of 26th Street and Seventh Avenue.

9. Continue downtown on Seventh Avenue on the east side of the street, stopping at whatever stores interest you. There's another Cosmetics Plus at 26th Street, if you missed one of their five other Manhattan locations; and a Janovic Plaza, Inc., which is a wallpaper and paint store that has great press-on tiles and all sorts of home design things, at 215 Seventh Avenue.

10. You will know Barneys when you see it, and you can't miss it. Barneys carries big-name designer men's and women's clothes and accessories, gifts, and their own private label (Basco), which is excellent. Hard-to-fit men must remember that Barneys can and will fit them. Men's prices are somewhat discounted because the store does such a volume of business. You can eat at Barneys, by the way.

11. Continue down Seventh Avenue just a little farther because you don't want to miss Jensen-Lewis, which has more furniture and less in terms of glassware and giftware.

12. You can walk to 14th Street to get a subway.

Yupper West Side Tour

1. Take the bus from Sixth Avenue, going uptown (Sixth Avenue goes one way only). Make sure the bus goes to 66th Street and Broadway (ask), or take the No. 1 subway to the West 66th Street station (at Lincoln Center).

2. You are now standing at the corner of Broadway and West 66th Street, on the east side of the street.

3. Now head uptown on Broadway, on the east side of the street. At West 72nd Street, the avenue will fork apart. Stick to the left-hand fork, which is Broadway. Head up Broadway until you reach 86th Street, stopping at all the stores that interest you.

4. At West 86th Street, turn right and walk toward Amsterdam Avenue. As you walk downtown on Amsterdam be sure not to miss Allan & Suzi, if only to stare at the creations in the window. After checking out Amsterdam's other boutiques, turn left on 79th Street and walk one block east to Columbus Avenue.

5. Once on Columbus turn left and walk uptown on the west side until 85th Street (Frank Stella, Vittorio Ricci, Maxilla & Mandible, etc.), then cross to the east side and begin to walk downtown. Don't miss the Charivari on the corner of 81st Street, or Mythology at 78th Street.

6. Continue downtown on Columbus. Sorry, but even though you'll pass the Museum of Natural History, you have no time for museums. Unless you consider Shu Uemura (No. 241) a museum of makeup.

7. At West 72nd Street, you have a choice. You can turn left and see the Dakota, the apartment house you've heard so much about, or turn right and shop West 72nd Street down to the subway station on Broadway.

SoHo So Nice Tour

1. There are several different subways you can take to SoHo; we just happened to be on one train and it worked great, so we've always done the same thing. But this is where it pays to be adventurous, since whatever stop you use, you'll just get to explore more of glorious SoHo. We take the No. 6 train and exit at Spring Street.

2. Get out on Spring Street. You will have no idea what to do, but don't panic. This part of SoHo has not yet been developed, so you will not be stepping out of a hole in the ground and into a wonderland of delight. It's no more scenic aboveground here than it was in the station.

3. Walk left, crossing Crosby Street and then Broadway. If you don't cross these streets, something went wrong.

4. The street after Broadway is Mercer; this is where it begins. There are a few shops you can explore on Mercer, or you can stay on Spring Street.

5. Whatever you do, don't miss Rue des Reves, on Spring Street, just after Mercer. If you hate SoHo, you can leave now—you've seen plenty to tell your friends about. But give it a chance; there are more great places coming up fast.

6. Of course you didn't quit. So stay on Spring Street until you get to West Broadway, which is not the same street as the Broadway you recently passed. West Broadway is the main drag of SoHo. Work both sides of West Broadway (OK, you can skip the Benetton

shop) until you get to West Houston (House-ton) Street; turn left on West Houston.

7. Walk one block and turn left on Thompson. Follow Thompson and check out all the hot boutiques. Turn left onto Broome Street. Walk two blocks to Wooster Street and turn left.

8. Shop Wooster for two blocks, then turn right on Prince Street.

9. At Greene Street, turn left and walk to West Houston again. Turn right on West Houston, right on Mercer, and then left on Prince, which will get you to the Prince Street subway station. Or you can stay on Mercer until Spring Street, turn left, and go back to the same subway station that you arrived in.

10. Congratulations! You will have seen well over 100 of the best shops in the country.

Holiday Delight Tour

Every year we take our kids into Manhattan for a one-day spree that mostly includes looking at Christmas decorations and doing special preholiday things. We do very little serious shopping. But it's a great tour for hitting the highlights and for taking in the wonders of the New York holiday retail scene. We do this tour the day before Thanksgiving, but you can do it any day of the year—Christmas decorations or no—if you want to see a lot in a short time, or impress your kids with all that is Manhattan. The tour is geared for children, but you can modify it into the perfect tourist's day trip.

1. Arrive at Grand Central Station at about 9:30 A.M. or begin this tour at Lord & Taylor, Fifth Avenue and 38th Street. If you come in at the train station, walk to Fifth

Avenue and take the bus downtown. Children under age six are free. Get off at Lord & Taylor to stare in the windows and begin the spree. If your children are younger and you want to simplify things a bit, get the bus that goes to Penn Station. This bus will turn west on 34th Street and can let you off right at Kiddie City, which is stop number two on the tour.

2. If it's after Thanksgiving, pause to admire the mechanical windows at Lord & Taylor (always one of the best window sets in the city). Then go down to 34th Street, turn west, and head toward Broadway. Before you get to the corner of Sixth Avenue (Avenue of the Americas) or to Macy's, you'll see Kiddie City. Since this is a Toys "Я" Us–type warehouse, we don't want to put in a lot of big shopping effort here—we just let the kids run wild with good tidings of the season. There are four video-game displays here (Nintendo and Sega), so the kids can play for quite a while and try out many games. We give our kids $10 and let them buy something here, so they can say they have bought something in New York and won't nag us for the rest of the day.

3. After Kiddie City, cross the street (you're still walking west) and enter Macy's, which takes up a whole city block. Although you may personally want to go downstairs to the Cellar, remember this is the kids' day out, so go upstairs to their floor. Santa also has headquarters upstairs.

4. If your kids must have lunch and you're falling apart on the tour, backtrack east on 34th Street. There's a McDonald's here for a pit stop; it's conveniently located across the street from the Empire State Building. If your kids are older and are not failing you now, continue west—take the bus uptown

on Sixth Avenue and get off at 57th Street, where you'll find another McDonald's between Sixth Avenue and Fifth Avenue, closer to Sixth on the north side of the street. Once you've all eaten, you're ready for some big-time excitement.

5. Look at the first-floor decorations at Bergdorf Goodman (Fifth Avenue and 57th Street) before heading north on Fifth Avenue for one more block to F.A.O. Schwarz, the world-famous toy store. Should your child still have money left over, you'll be pleased to know that there are a few items in this store that are affordable—we guide little boys to the paper airplanes, which sell for $5. Kids can play the free Nintendo here, but there is only one machine, so the line gets long. Our policy here is a simple one: The kids have twenty minutes in the store; they can do whatever they want. We sit down and pray they don't wreck anything. The bathrooms here are clean; this is a good pit stop. Then it's back out to Fifth Avenue.

6. Walk downtown (south) on Fifth Avenue, taking in as many stores or windows as you please. Boys get bored with window decorations faster than girls, we've found. Saks always has good windows, and is the last store on the tour. Now head for the skating rink at Rockefeller Plaza (50th Street). Watch or join in; have tea and dessert downstairs at the Festival Cafe. If everyone has had it with shopping, take a chance at the Guild Theatre, right there at 50th Street, which usually shows Disney films. Or head to Radio City Music Hall for the Christmas show, if you have tickets.

7. Collapse at your room at the Hilton hotel, right there one block from Radio City Music Hall, on Sixth Avenue and 54th Street. Hilton is our choice because it's one of the headquarters for the Macy's Thanksgiving

Parade. . . . The hotel has special weekend and holiday rates, kids are free with their parents, and the Towers floors have tea and breakfast as part of the price of the room. During the holidays, this hotel will be jammed with kids, so you'll feel very comfortable here.

8. After spending the night at the Hilton, wake up early for the Thanskgiving Day parade. Walk the few blocks from the hotel to Columbus Circle, where all the action is. Don't forget your money. It may be Thanksgiving Day and normal stores may be closed, but this is a big day for this part of New York, so many stores are open! Street vendors sell plastic turkeys and Santas on a stick; all the electronics stores around Columbus Circle are open; many small shops on West 57th Street are open. Vendors selling scarves, sweaters, and all sorts of Christmas giftables line the streets. . . . The secondary parade is the assortment of goods for sale on a non-shopping day. The official parade will pass Columbus Circle by 10:30 A.M.—so you'll have time to go back to the hotel, check out, and hop on a train to get home for Thanksgiving dinner and a good night's sleep. After all, the day after Thanksgiving is the busiest shopping day in America, and we've got to be ready.

Size Conversion Chart

WOMEN'S DRESSES, COATS, AND SKIRTS

American	3	5	7	9	11	12	13	14	15	16	18
Continental	36	38	38	40	40	42	42	44	44	46	48
British	8	10	11	12	13	14	15	16	17	18	20

WOMEN'S BLOUSES AND SWEATERS

American	10	12	14	16	18	20
Continental	38	40	42	44	46	48
British	32	34	36	38	40	42

WOMEN'S SHOES

American	5	6	7	8	9	10
Continental	36	37	38	39	40	41
British	3½	4½	5½	6½	7½	8½

CHILDREN'S CLOTHING

American	3	4	5	6	6X
Continental	98	104	110	116	122
British	18	20	22	24	26

CHILDREN'S SHOES

American	8	9	10	11	12	13	1	2	3
Continental	24	25	27	28	29	30	32	33	34
British	7	8	9	10	11	12	13	1	2

MEN'S SUITS

American	34	36	38	40	42	44	46	48
Continental	44	46	48	50	52	54	56	58
British	34	36	38	40	42	44	46	48

MEN'S SHIRTS

American	14½	15	15½	16	16½	17	17½	18
Continental	37	38	39	41	42	43	44	45
British	14½	15	15½	16	16½	17	17½	18

MEN'S SHOES

American	7	8	9	10	11	12	13
Continental	39½	41	42	43	44½	46	47
British	6	7	8	9	10	11	12

INDEX

About the Authors

SUZY GERSHMAN is an author and journalist who also writes under her maiden name, Suzy Kalter. She has worked in the fiber and fashion industry since 1969 in both New York and Los Angeles and has held editorial positions at *California Apparel News, Mademoiselle, Gentleman's Quarterly*, and *People* magazine, where she was West Coast Style editor. She writes regularly for *Travel and Leisure;* her essays on retailing are text at the Harvard Business School. Mrs. Gershman lives in Connecticut with her husband, author Michael Gershman, and their son. Michael Gershman also contributes to the *Born to Shop* pages.

JUDITH THOMAS is a designer who began her career working in the creative and advertising departments of Estée Lauder and Helena Rubinstein in New York. Previously she was an actress in television commercials as well as on and off Broadway. In 1973 she moved to Los Angeles where she was an art director for various studios while studying for her ASID at UCLA. She later formed Panache and Associates, a commercial design firm. She is currently involved in developing and marketing new trends in building design for MPS Systems. Mrs. Thomas lives in Pennsylvania with her husband and two children.

DON'T LEAVE HOME WITHOUT BANTAM'S BESTSELLING BORN TO SHOP SERIES!

"As necessary as a passport when tackling boutiques, stores, flea markets, customs and shipping procedures, insurance and tax regulations"

—*The New York Daily News*

Bantam's bestselling and ever-growing Born to Shop *series is the final word on international—and American—shopping. With loads of up-to-date information and invaluable advice, each volume provides a grand tour of where to find the best bargains on the very best goods.*

Don't miss these *Born to Shop* volumes by Suzy Gershman and Judith Thomas:

☐ CANADA	#34687-3 $8.95/$9.95 in Canada
☐ FRANCE (3rd Ed.)	#34602-4 $8.95/$10.95 in Canada
☐ HONG KONG (3rd Ed.)	#34803-5 $8.95/$11.95 in Canada
☐ ITALY (3rd Ed.)	#34603-2 $8.95/$10.95 in Canada
☐ LONDON (4th Ed.)	#35205-9 $8.95/$11.95 in Canada
☐ LOS ANGELES (2nd Ed.)	#34804-3 $8.95/$11.95 in Canada
☐ NEW YORK (3rd Ed.)	#34945-7 $8.95/$11.95 in Canada
☐ MEXICO	#34767-5 $8.95/$11.95 in Canada

THE ONLY GUIDES YOU'LL EVER NEED—WHEREVER YOU'RE GOING!

Savvy, refreshing, modern and insightful, BANTAM TRAVEL GUIDES are an exciting new way to travel. Literate and lively, and focusing on the things that make a destination special, BANTAM TRAVEL GUIDES are available in two easy-to-use formats: trade size to plan a trip and gain in-depth understanding of what your destination has to offer, and pocket size—perfect to carry along!

Here's what BANTAM TRAVEL GUIDES offer:

- Full-color atlases—plus black and white maps
- Respected travel writers—and food critics
- In-depth hotel and restaurant reviews
- Indexed listings, invaluable advice, weather charts, mileage tables, and much, much more!

Don't miss these BANTAM TRAVEL GUIDES: